COMPUTERS AND SOCIALISM

Computers and Socialism

by Stephen Bodington

BLACK ROSE BOOKS, Montreal

SPOKESMAN BOOKS 1973

Printed by The Russell Press Limited
Set in 10pt.Press Roman

Published by The Bertrand Russell Peace Foundation Limited,
Bertrand Russell House, 45 Gamble Street, Forest Road West,
Nottingham NG7 4ET for *The Spokesman*.

CONTENTS

Preface

This book is about technology and new knowledge in relation to popular understanding and its socio-economic appreciation. It deals with social change – an issue whose outcome itself will be largely determined by popular understanding. It is written for adult students who may be studying intramurally, extramurally or within the new conditions of the Open University; for people concerned with issues rather than qualifications; but before all else for people who may or may not have formal association with institutes of learning but are simply concerned to get to grips with new issues in a changing society. It shares the view expressed in the 1970 Reith Lectures by Dr. Schon that 'the loss of the stable state' in institutions of advanced industrial society must be seen as linked to the rate of development of scientific and technical inventions impinging on social and economic life.

But I do not accept that social and cultural instability is necessarily associated with advancing scientific knowledge. The instability is in no sense absolute; on the contrary it signals the necessity of social change. This book is about what I regard as the most fundamental aspect of the new technical revolution, namely, the computer revolution. It looks also at the essential features of what we may call the socio-economic system, for we cannot meaningfully consider possibilities of change without some model in our minds of the working of the system as it is.

There is a field of education whose object is the lucid explanation of solved problems – the craftsman transmitting his craft to his apprentices. This is not that kind of book. Its aim is to pose problems and start a discussion. If this discussion sharpens vision so that more facets of the relationship between science and society, between technology and social activity, can be seen, then it will have achieved as much as could be hoped for. It deals with problems that remain to be solved. It has built on classical thought from the past, that of Karl Marx in particular, and has attempted to assimilate the work of leading academic thinkers of our time, such as Norbert Wiener, Noam Chomsky, T.S. Kuhn, Claude

Levi-Strauss, Georg Lukacs, J.Z. Young, Herbert Marcuse, Piero Sraffa and others, who are re-examining accepted disciplines and social theories. The aim is to help the reader to enter and make his contribution to an urgent and vital discussion.

The book contains a certain amount of mathematics which to some may seem elementary and to others may create an obstacle to understanding. Those without, or with insufficient, experience of mathematics I would urge not to be discouraged. The mathematical arguments used are probably easier when one gets into them than they may appear at first flush and in most cases the non-mathematical reader will see the general tendency of the argument without necessarily following the detail. Those who like ideas expressed mathematically may be helped to a more simple and clear understanding of the issues and for them some brief mathematical appendices are included.

It would be impossible to thank all who have directly or indirectly helped me form and put together my ideas. I must, however, explicitly mention Grace Moore, Sigurd Zienau, H.J. Fyrth and Michael Barratt Brown. Grace Moore typed, arranged and re-arranged the manuscript several times. Dr. Zienau criticised it at an early stage and gave welcome encouragement. Mr. Fyrth made many valuable suggestions and advised on ways and means of reducing the manuscript to a more suitable length. Michael Barratt Brown has devoted so much of his over-taxed time to the manuscript on two different occasions that I hardly know how to thank him. Invariably his comments strengthened and developed what at first writing were often mere embryos of ideas.

Add up the reckoning.
It's you who must pay it.
Put your finger on each item,
ask: how did this get here?

Bertolt Brecht

The question whether objective truth can be attributed to human thinking is not a question of theory but is a practical question. In practice man must prove the truth, i.e. the reality and power, the 'this-sidedness' of his thinking . . .

The standpoint of the old materialism is 'civil society': the standpoint of the new is *human* society or socialised humanity.

The philosophers have only *interpreted* the world in various ways; the point however is to *change* it.

Marx: Theses on Feuerbach

Direct labour . . . is reduced both quantitatively, to a smaller proportion, and qualitatively as an, of course, indispensable but subordinate moment, compared to scientific labour, technological application of natural sciences, on one side, and to the general productive force arising from social combination in total production on the other side – a combination which appears as a natural fruit of social labour (although it is a historic product). Capital thus works towards its own dissolution as the form dominating production.

* * *

The development of fixed capital indicates to what degree general social knowledge has become a *direct force of production,* and to what degree, hence, the conditions of the process of social life itself have come under the control of the general intellect and been transformed in accordance with it. To what degree the powers of social production have been produced, not only in the form of knowledge, but also as immediate organs of social practice, of the real life process.

Marx: Grundrisse

This new development has unbounded possibilities for good and for evil. For one thing it makes the metaphorical dominance of the machines, as imagined by Samuel Butler, a most immediate and non-metaphorical problem. It gives the human race a new and most effective collection of mechanical slaves to perform its labour . . . However any labour that accepts the conditions of competition with slave labour accepts the conditions of slave labour, and is essentially slave labour . . . It cannot be good for these new potentialities to be assessed in the terms of the market, of the money they save; and it is precisely the terms of the open market, the 'fifth freedom', that have become the shibboleth of the sector of American opinion represented by the National Association of Manufacturers and the Saturday Evening Post. I say American opinion, for as an American, I know it best, but the hucksters recognise no national boundary.

Norbert Wiener: Cybernetics

When Liberty goes out of a place it is not the first to go,
nor the second or third to go,
It waits for all the rest to go, it is the last.
. . . Then courage European revolter, revoltress!
For till all ceases neither must you cease.

Walt Whitman

Chapter I

Socio-Economic Relations: The Basic Models

Main Theme

There is one single problem that reflects the deepest contradictions of our times and is linked to and underlies almost all other problems – man's rapidly growing power to control and harness the forces of nature in contrast with loss of control over the socio-economic system and over application of the new knowledge of science. How many in 'wealthy' Britain or Europe have a sense of plenty or are without anxieties about money or work? How many in North America? Yet our national product a head in Western Europe is said to be twenty times and in North America fifty times that of India.

The means of controlling production processes and natural forces continue to evolve. Such means, in the shape of new technologies, arrive – or so it appears – before the ends they are to serve have been defined; and we, the people, breathlessly hustled by their exigencies, cannot find pause to study the nature of our own needs or fix the purposes we want our lives to serve. This book is about this problem. It is – to speak of its content in the broadest terms – about science, technology, man's understanding of his natural environment on the one hand and how, on the other hand, such knowledge enters into economic processes and acts upon, and is acted upon by, socio-economic relations.

The central argument of the book runs somewhat as follows: Discussion of technology in the abstract is not meaningful, technology is application of 'know-how' and scientific knowledge under specific, historically determined, social conditions. Therefore, before asking questions about the impact of technology in general or computer technology in particular, the first indispensable step is to present some 'models', that is, representations of the essential features and relationships, of the socio-economic structures, of the types of economic systems on to which the new productive knowledge impinges. So the first step in the argument – and this is the objective of Chapter I – is to present some basic models of socio-economic relations.

Next it is necessary to pinpoint the essential characteristics of the new technology, namely 'computers', that has been selected for special scrutiny. This done (in Chapter II), the next step is to see how technology and economic structure interact in the historically concrete circumstances under which our society has developed and is now developing. Analysis of this question shows that the key to it lies in the dynamics of productivity in a market economy (and this is the main theme of Chapter III).

A basis having thus far been laid for seeing how technical knowledge and economic structure interact, the next step in the argument (in Chapter IV) is to examine computer technology in relation to the contemporary socio-economic context, i.e. what impact, to be specific, knowledge in the field of electronics applied to information processing has on the existing socio-economic structures and what processes of interaction between technology and economic structure are being generated within society as it is at present. This phase of the argument points to the conclusion that the social and economic impact of 'the computer revolution' will be very far-reaching and also that the economic structure as it stands appears likely to become less and less compatible with the many-sided consequences of technological change and the emergence of new productive potentials in the field of science.

So, finally (Chapter V) the basic questions must be asked: "Is change in social structure desirable? Possible? Necessary? What constraints does technology impose on the possibilities for social change? How would socio-economic change in its turn change the technologies we use and the manner in which we develop scientific knowledge to serve social needs? What are the political constraints on change and how do these relate to the economic and technological constraints?" No pretence at answering these questions is made. The argument of the book is that the precondition to coherent and meaningful discussion of these questions is understanding founded on study of the underlying relationships between economic structure and the development of the production techniques through which accumulated experience and scientific knowledge act upon the socio-economic scene. The argument developed in the book does not therefore conclude, but aims rather to reach a stage in which its continuation is undertaken by those who read it and, hopefully, carry it into the arena of social practice where alone the final conclusion of theoretical arguments of this kind can be established.

The Market Economy

Man is a producer. He has long since given up gathering his food as it grows wild and instead he makes it grow by the art of agriculture. He builds his houses. He weaves his clothes. Also the day is long past when typically an individual, a family or even a village supplied, by its own effort, the main part of its needs. Production and distribution are social. Where industry has developed it is within the market framework that it has been nurtured. So right in the centre of enquiry must come an attempt to understand the relationship of techniques of production to the market system. Can the market contain the explosion of new technology? If not what happens, how and why?

Man produces and buys commodities, i.e. goods that exchange in a market. In this way men and women going their own ways in their own communities independent of others are linked by an external force – the force of the market through commodity exchange.

> "As a general rule, articles of utility become commodities only because they are products of the labour of private individuals or groups of individuals who carry on their work independently of each other . . . since the producers do not come into social contact with each other until they exchange their products, the specific social character of each producer's labour does not show itself except in the act of exchange." (Marx, *Capital,* Vol. 1, pp 43/44. Allen & Unwin, 1948).

Labour is private and independent; man works for himself. Yet he is not making things for himself, he does not produce for himself. His production is for the market and in this respect not under the control of the producer. It is under the control of the market and it is through the market that it becomes social, though private.

To understand these issues we need a socio-economic model, one that shows where and how the impact of technology will fall and what might be or could be the economic, social and political responses. We must extract from the shifting, complex scene of history certain essentials, certain more or less constant features or relationships round which revolve all socio-economic transformations. We are selecting one aspect, the economic/technological, in a complex whole in which the social and political structures interact with the economic and both are given shape by the system of ideas (the ideologies) in terms of which men define to themselves and others their respective functions in the social totality. Since we must refer to this whole to resolve many actual problems, we should not forget the limitations we are imposing on ourselves in an attempt to give a better focus to our enquiries.

I shall argue that, as the machine stood at the heart of the industrial revolution, so the computer (using the word computer as shorthand for a much wider sweep of electronic technology) stands – from the economic point of view – at the centre of the changes that are now overtaking us.

The *elements* of an economic *system* are people; the system consists of specific relations between people. But in talking of systems we are dealing with abstractions, with simplifications drawn from the complexities of actual history. Drastic abstraction is necessary to make the subject matter manageable, but we must not lose a sense of actuality, a feeling for the underlying historical reality.

A technological revolution may be provisionally defined as a change in production techniques that fundamentally disturbs the pre-existing economic and social relations. The coming of agriculture, rather more than ten thousand years ago, was such a technological revolution. The industrial revolution of two centuries ago was another. They represented dramatic turning points in the socio-economic history of mankind. New methods of production became established, leading to conspicuous changes in economic relations and vastly different forms of social life.

As a starting point, and in order to suggest some aspects of the reality from which we are abstracting, consider some of the economic relations implied in a common product, such as might be purchased at any time during the last thirty or forty years in an industrially advanced country such as Britain. An electric light bulb will serve as an example.

Some of its main components are a bulb, a cap, an exhaust tube, a glass support rod, leading wires, filament supports and a filament. The cap is made of brass, an alloy basically of copper and zinc. Copper wire is used for the lead-in wires. Molybdenum wire is used to make the filament supports, tungsten wire to make the filament, glass rod to make the support which carries the filament supports, and so forth. Materials from all over the world and a variety of techniques and manufacturing processes combined to make a product selling in 1948 at about 13d, of which roughly 8d went to the manufacturer, 1½d to the wholesaler and 3½d to the retailer. Of the 8d going to the manufacturer about 1d was for labour, 3d for materials and the rest for factory overheads and selling and administrative costs. In 1949/50 about 250,000,000 filament lamps were produced in Britain and 17,500 persons employed on their production and distribution. To be economic production must be on a very large scale involving heavy installations and plant, furnace equipment, bulb blowing machines, and much else besides. (The output of just two bulb-blowing machines being installed in 1950 was sufficient to meet all UK requirements.) There is the manufacture of tungsten and molybdenum wire, the precision operation of filament coiling, and many other processes involved at various stages. The individual worker will scarcely know, let alone control, all the processes involved in producing the electric bulb. But what he does, and the payment he receives, as a worker, establishes in fact a very concrete nexus of socio-economic relations with other people throughout the world. Each worker has a specific position in a production team, such as minding machines, packing products, writing invoices, managing the sales force, determining production schedules, and so forth. This production team has, in turn, specific relations with those who produce molybdenum, tungsten, etc. with the various manufacturers of machines that they use and with the producers of other means of production. Market links are indissolubly intertwined with relations to other groups of people through the money system that mediates sales and is the source of money capital. Capital itself hides a host of relationships between people as owners and employees, as those who pay and those who receive interest, and other forms of distributing incomes; capital structure and its control determine the distribution of resources as receipts flow in from sales and as payments out are made for means of production, for wages and salaries, for materials and much else. Thus behind the commodity exchanges and the associated monetary transactions lies a complex structure of social relations, relationships between people and classes of people established by these transactions and the patterns of behaviour through which they are implemented.

The worldwide economic system is a network of individual consumers and producers – of people and groups of people engaged in the production, distribution and exchange of innumerable different goods and services of which the electric light bulb – complex as its production is – is one minute sample.

Adam Smith's Model

With Britain's industrial revolution economic and social relations changed dramatically and the worldwide market system continued to change as it developed. The economic philosophies which guided the aims of the subsequently emerging industrial societies have been challenged, but the system the philosophies generated is still there. A matter for later consideration will be what economic philosophies, what models of new economic relations and systems, what new technologies, will emerge from the present complex of interacting technological and socio-economic processes. Indeed, the economic and social models around which political forces for change muster, will in themselves be important factors in determining the nature and purport of that change. We are looking for a model to guide new directions of change as models in the past have guided the emergence of new systems. Understanding both of the future and the present will be sharpened if we look at the model that guided the architects of the industrial revolution. Essentially this is to be found in the theories of Adam Smith, which are much more deeply rooted in socio-economic practice than their evaluation by contemporary economists might suggest.

The aim of Adam Smith's enquiry, as the title of his great treatise implies, was to discover what system of economic relations would be most likely to increase the 'wealth of nations'. This wealth he saw as derived from labour. The *Wealth of Nations* begins: "The annual labour of every nation is the fund which originally supplies it with all the necessaries and conveniences of life." This fund could be enlarged "by the skill, dexterity, judgment with which its labour is generally applied" and "by the proportion between the number of those who are employed in useful labour, and that of those who are not so employed". The great key to the freeing of this potential was the market, and everything possible should be done to remove constraints upon its operation, either within a country or internationally between countries.

Despite all the changes and all the interventions of governments, the market remains the basic organising force of our economy. One may see this, for example, in every statement of the Rome Treaty setting up the Common Market, in the constant pleas to free trade and free enterprise and free the movement of labour and capital.

The second model that we shall need to consider is that of the centrally planned economy. We shall need also to consider to what extent central planning can co-exist with or be superimposed upon a market structure. With those who regard Adam Smith's model as a thing of the past I would disagree and also add that important features of the market system have tended to reappear in centrally planned systems whose aim is to escape control by the market. Certainly the antithesis of commodity production for the market is production consciously regulated by a plan, but despite the fundamental character of the antithesis between plan and market one needs to note that the market in fact establishes certain definite forms of social relation between men and to ask whether these relations may or do assist when the paramount position of the market, as in the Adam Smith model, has been done away with or substantially modified.

All economies today have market and non-market sectors. Even the most individualistic market economist recognises some role for governments in the economy. Even the most totalitarian central planner includes plans for the sale and purchase of goods on the market.

The most explicit contemporary advocates for the market system (cf. Enoch Powell, *A Nation Not Afraid,* 1965, pp 10 and 27) argue that buying on the market is like casting a vote in an economic ballot box. Such advocates apply to today almost the same words as Adam Smith used in relation to the country's economy 200 years ago. Economic activity, Adam Smith argued, should be left to the free regulation of the market.

> "Every man, as long as he does not violate the laws of justice, is left perfectly free to pursue his own interests in his own way, and to bring both his industry and capital into competition with those of any other man, or order of men. The Sovereign is completely dis-

charged from a duty, in the attempting to perform which he must always be exposed to innumerable delusions, and for the proper performance of which no human wisdom or knowledge could ever be sufficient; the duty of superintending the industry of private people, and of directing it towards the employments most suitable to the interest of the society." *(The Wealth of Nations, Book IV, Chapter 9.)*

Adam Smith saw competition in the market and the freedom of each to pursue his own interests through the market as the motive forces of development. Development could result only from more productive workers, better division of labour and use of better machines. Adam Smith's model guided economic thought through the industrial revolution, but he himself did not live to see how the theory looked in the practice of its application. He died in 1790. David Ricardo (1772-1823) the greatest of Adam Smith's disciples writing in 1817 was to acknowledge "That the substitution of machinery for human labour is often very injurious to the interests of the class of labourers . . . The same cause which may increase the net revenues of the country may at the same time render the population redundant, and deteriorate the condition of the labourers." *(The Principles of Political Economy and Taxation,* Chapter 31, page 264, Everyman Edition.)

In the century and a half since David Ricardo wrote, there have been great changes in the nature and functioning of the economic system, and also in ideas about the type of system that is desirable; but already early in the nineteenth century economic analysis proceeding from Richardo gave rise to some doubts about the powers attributed to the market system to regulate itself for the best. Certainly the market left to itself does not necessarily use resources to the full; in particular it does not give full employment. The system is subject to the oscillations of boom and crisis. In many instances the market fails to allocate resources to best uses from a social standpoint. It leads to huge concentrations of wealth and economic power within the industrially developed societies, to widening gaps between the rich nations and the poor nations, and to political tensions of the most violent sort. Out of the complex of social, ideological and, in general, historical change and in contrast to the *laissez-faire* market model emerged a new model – the model of the centrally planned economy. Centrally planned economies, for example in Russia and Eastern Europe, have developed on the basis of state ownership of the means of production in contrast to the capitalist economies in the West based on private ownership of the means of production. However, in the private ownership economies centralised planning has been carried to considerable lengths in recent years within structures of a world economy regulated by market forces and the power of the 'universal commodity': money. In Britain after the Second World War, and in many other private ownership economies, considerable zones of economic activity came under state ownership or control and centralised planning to varying extents was undertaken, co-existing with underlying market relations and operating within a world market.

Social Models Do More Than Explain: They Organise

All societies possess, in some sense, models of their social and economic systems. The model may be myth. That is, what actually happens may be very different from what is supposed to happen. (Enoch Powell's model is different from historical actuality in the 200 years since Adam Smith.) It may not be a detailed model but merely an idea, a picture held in the imagination, a verbal description. Paradoxically, there is such a thing as the myth in reality; the myth takes over and in reality gives a society its cohesion, economically, legally and in other ways. Some of the things that follow from this fact are important for us. The way that the men and women, who make up a society, see themselves crystallises their relations and provides a mechanism for assigning functions and for judging whether or not functions are appropriate for themselves and others. In short, the idea that people have of their society shapes many of their day-to-day practicalities. In this sense it is reality of a very tough texture, at the same time this concept by which social relations are cemented may be 'myth', in the sense of a false or incomplete conception. Underlying circumstances change and are out of tune with the concept of social organisation by which men live; for example, technologies, economic relations and social needs change and people are motivated by new aspirations.

A society's consciousness of itself may be true in the sense that this consciousness in fact organises it, and false in the sense that for many members of that society it debars the fulfilment of realisable aspirations. Struggle for social change always implies a critique of the prevalent model of society. The battle of ideas is not mere talk, it is a process of refashioning tough strands in the social texture. Of course, the struggle is also and essentially a struggle about political power. However, political power, organisation and the ideas that unite or divide people in human society are closely interrelated. The power of a minority ruling class, for example, will require a social organisation that enables them to control sources of wealth and to protect their positions of strength by force, if need be, but these positions require also the support of ideas, belief in the necessity of the existing social structure, and become precarious as soon as a substantial number of 'the ruled' no longer accept the social model according to which the society is organised.

Models of economic systems tend to be both explanations and justifications. They say 'this is how things work, and this is why this way of going things is good'. There are also critical models: they say 'this is how things work, and look where it will land you'. Marx's *Capital* is such a critical model. The purely objective model ('this is how things are') is of only limited use in social studies since society is a system of consciously acting human beings who must always be considering the outcome of their actions. *Society is a system in which the decision-makers are within the system.*

Marx's critique displayed capitalist society as the inevitable expression of a fully developed commodity/market economy; he argued that such an economy must lead to great concentrations of wealth and power in the hands of a comparatively small number of firms and people. Marx's model also implied that the commodity/market economy was historically transient and that it would be necessary to develop new forms of social relationships for the organisation of social production.

Possibly the most influential model of the pure market system presented as an expression of political democracy was that of John Stuart Mill. His model presupposed "The instruments of production, the land and tools, would be divided fairly . . . so that all might start . . . on equal terms." *(Principles of Political Economy,* Book II, Chapter 1, paragraph 2.) Economic and social incentives would coincide in fostering individual initiative and freedom. Citizen would be linked to citizen through the free competitive market. Each would vote for the commodities he wanted by the payments he was ready to make and for the occupation he preferred by the remuneration he was ready to accept. The capitalist market system undoubtedly released tremendous productive forces in the course of the nineteenth century but the system as in Mill's ideal was far from coinciding with the system as reality. Nonetheless Mill's model remains an important 'social myth' in terms of which belief in the commodity/market system is expressed and in terms of which this system is accepted as the most suitable form for organising social production.

The market and free exchange freed man from the constraints and restrictions of feudal society: but up to a certain point only. The countries in which the industrial system first became well established and in which it provided a means of accumulating great national wealth were to enjoy a vastly different course of progress from that of the economically backward countries. In the 'third world' today the relative poverty of under-developed countries tends to increase rather than diminish by comparison with the industrially advanced countries. Mill's hope of equally distributing property has not proved realisable. With large-scale production has come accumulation of property and concentration of economic power in a few hands. Production has tended to be dominated by the interests of the owners or controllers of means of production. Competition has taken the form primarily of rivalry between competing capitals in which the over-riding consideration has been to produce more in order to accumulate more in order to produce more. The market has only distantly communicated the consumer's feeling. The theoretical freedom of every man to do as he likes with his own time and money has counted for little against the imposed necessities for the many to earn their living under circumstances over which they have no control.

Objectives In A Market Economy

Social systems are powered by the conscious, purposeful actions of men. But the system itself may express no purpose, in that the direction in which the system is going may have little to do with the conscious purposes of individuals or collectives of individuals. Yet it is the deliberate, conscious actions of people that cause the system as a whole to move and develop. An actual system may move far away from its ideal or hoped-for objectives. But the system still exists and will only be rejected when an alternative has been discovered and a way of changing over to it is seen and adopted by a sufficiently powerful social force.

Adam Smith taught the simple doctrine that each individual in pursuing his own advantage was 'led by an invisible hand to promote an end which was no part of his intention'. It was the job of the state to see that competition was allowed to run free. The social objective was the expansion of production and the best allocation of capital, labour power and other resources. The theory was that the market, unobstructed by monopolies or restraints of law and custom, could best do the job of allocating resources to needs. So let each man pursue his own interests, work at what he wanted, spend his money as he wanted, and the end result would be the best one to be had.

It is the decisions to buy and to sell that make the wheels of the market system turn. It is clear that the way these decisions are made will depend not only on what the participants in the market want out of life, but also on whether they enter the market backed by much or little money, many or few commodities. In Mill's ideal all men would play the market game with equal opportunities. In reality many are hardly able to get into the game at all. The opportunities of some are quite different from the opportunities of others. Particular institutions (for example, governments and banks) can deal themselves pre-arranged hands with which to play the money game. To appreciate the workings of the market system, therefore, one must take account of different types of decision-takers, taking into consideration how they are placed, both as regards access to resources and as regards the ends for which they will be using these resources.

It will be easier to see the essential characteristics of the model we require if we look first at a simpler model. Consider a village in which there are a number of craftsmen who together supply the needs of the village; that is, they supply one another's needs. Time has established a proper balance in the community between weavers, carpenters, masons, farmers and the like. Each works to supply the needs of the village community, in order to obtain the wherewithal to buy what he himself needs. Each decides to work in order to get the wherewithal, the money with which to be able to buy other men's products.

In a developed capitalist economy, by contrast, most people live by selling not products but labour power, which someone else uses in the making of the products. Within this system there is a market of a special kind between employee and employer. The employer acquires an accumulation of capital. This he uses to buy materials, tools, machines and other equipment and to pay wages for the labour he hires. The capitalist is an employer of labour producing on a bigger scale for a wider market. The object of his production is to make a profit. To do this he needs to find a market in which he can sell at prices exceeding the costs incurred by him in production. In the simple model, decisions to produce and decisions to buy are spread evenly through the whole community. (We need not argue whether such a democratic market has existed or could anywhere exist: the concept, however, is important because arguments often go on as if such markets exist here and now, whereas the actuality, given large-scale production and a worldwide market, is rather different.) The model that will serve better to point to the essentials of the actual market economy, must draw a sharp distinction between organisms controlling production, on the one hand, and consumers on the other. These are two very different types of elements. In physical terms the first are typically 'massive nuclei', enterprises using considerable accumulations of capital and employing large numbers of people, and the second are lightweight particles in the form of individuals.

The enterprise buys the skills, the labour time of a multiplicity of individuals, its employees. It buys all sorts of materials and machines in the market. It sells its products in the market. Without question it is these massive elements, the enterprises, that count in the market. It is their decisions to produce, to buy or not to buy, to employ or not to employ. that enliven or deaden the economy.

It is, of course, argued that their decisions are more apparent than real since what they do is governed by the market and the market is governed by final consumption, that is by the aggregate impact of the vast host of small elements in the market, the individuals. The ultimate force that powers the economy, so that argument runs, is the sum total of ordinary men and women in the shops deciding what they will buy or not buy.

The weakness of this argument is that the great majority of ordinary people depend, directly or indirectly, upon employment in the enterprises. This fact makes our crude, over-simplified model nearer to the reality than one might think at first sight. In an industrially developed country one may think of most of the small undertakings – the self-employed, providers of services, and such like – as being either, in some sense, adjuncts of the big enterprises or people providing facilities for employees of the big enterprises. (The worker's wife, the shopkeepers in the neighbourhood of the factory and many others depend for their living on the earnings of the factory worker.) The decisions crucial to the level of economic activity are those taken in the enterprises – to employ or not to employ. The motivation of such decisions again can be simplified without going too far from the actual. Typically any enterprise will aim to achieve the highest possible level of activity. Typically the motivation of the enterprise is to make profits – whether for private owners or to fulfil state targets. Normally the more the activity the more the profit. But, of course, the product must be saleable. It must, moreover, be saleable at a price that exceeds its cost of production. (There will be circumstances where a firm is in a monopoly position and by restricting output may be able to get overall a larger profit than it would get by increasing output: but we need not here be concerned with this case.)

We don't have to think very hard about this model to see that we are confronted with an ambiguous situation. If there is plenty of employment there will be a lively market for the goods on which employees spend their money and also for the materials and machines that are used in the course of the activities for which they are employed. So one might say good markets lead to better. But by the same token bad markets lead to worse. Without further analysis one may easily appreciate the danger if the system becomes unstable. Movement away from stability may tend to be cumulative.

It is also not difficult to appreciate how important a factor injection of purchasing power from outside the system could be. Loans, credit from banks, state purchases, subsidies and (working in the opposite direction) taxes are such factors that in the real world operate on the system. What we have been saying above relates to the overall level of activity in the system. It may also be that particular markets are over-supplied or under-supplied with specific and differing consequences for the several enterprises. Extraordinarily complex and subtle balances exist between the enterprises themselves and in relation to particular markets.

Furthermore, what are the bounds of the system? In the simple model we were thinking of a village. To what should we relate the more realistic model? In the actual world our enterprises sell in a world market. But for any one enterprise there are constraints of many sorts. National legislation, currency, import duties, transportation, language, custom – a wide range of factors act like frictional forces limiting indefinite extension of the market. Also, the vast majority of the world's population are only indirectly linked to the system and are not directly participating elements of the world system, either as employees or as entrepreneurs. We may think therefore of a system as a grouping of linked national systems.

Historically it is apparent that the typical enterprise tends to become larger and larger. (It is also a fact that the ownership of enterprises tends to become more and more concentrated.) One of the reasons for which enterprises over the last two centuries have, in the typical cases, greatly increased in size is that economies result from large-scale production. But, as is argued later on, growth in size now continues far beyond what is required for technological reasons. Other factors make for concentration.

Since, in the long run, few enterprises are able to determine the prices at which they sell, and must be guided by what the market will bear, the only sure way to increase profits is by lowering costs. And the only sure way to lower costs continuously and indefinitely is to improve productive techniques. This is easier for firms with big capital resources capable of undertaking specialised mass production. There are strong tendencies in the system towards production of more and more with smaller and smaller productive labour forces. This important aspect of things will be taken up again in Chapters III and IV. At present the point has been to clarify certain basic concepts and to construct a model of the market system which is sufficiently simple to provide a useful tool and sufficiently near to the reality to suggest what actual consequences might flow from technical change and from the scientific revolution generally.

To summarise, the market economy may be viewed as a system of large organisms, whose basis is industrial, producing goods to be sold at a profit on the market. Similar large organisms operate the financial apparatus. There are additionally numerous small organisms undertaking production and distribution which it is not convenient for the large organisms to handle themselves; but these small organisms are, in general, closely dependent on the large organisms. Allocation of resources is through the market. The system is energised by the pursuit of money in the form of profit going to owners and controllers of property (and in particular means of production) and of wages and salaries going to those who work for the owners or controllers of property. Incomes are spent mainly individually on consumer goods, but since both incomes and products in the main derive directly or indirectly from the large organisms, it is these that give momentum to, and determine the main characteristics of the economic system as a whole. The market and hence the system is worldwide – but, though the whole world is affected by the system, only a fraction of the population of the world is fully within the system. Within some of these (as in the Soviet Union) centralised planning has taken over many functions from the market. In others (such as India or Peru) large peasant populations sell to, but are not absorbed into the industrial market system whose elements are in these cases typically a few large state concerns or foreign private companies.

Models of Centrally-Planned Economies

The contemporary economic scene cannot be interpreted in terms of the *laissez-faire* market model alone. Rejection of *laissez-faire* pointed the way to planning as its opposite and natural alternative. The attack on *laissez-faire* came, however, from widely differing directions: (a) political attack from various shades of socialist and anti-capitalist opinion; (b) concentration of economic wealth and power into increasingly huge organisations favoured planned control within such organisations and co-ordination between them extending beyond national boundaries; (c) war, economic crises, various forms of social and economic instability, as well as external political pressures, each converted capitalist opinion to support various forms of central economic planning; and (d) starting with the Russian Revolution of 1917 the advent to power of new political forces with socialist or nationalist programmes designed to catch up with the advanced industrial powers brought into existence a considerable variety of centrally planned economic regimes.

Political organisation, property ownership, and forms of economic control differ widely from country to country; but in certain essentials there are surprising similarities in central planning by state agencies. What is more, though planning emerges in opposition to the market, it may be superimposed on relationships developed within a market economy, without radically changing such relationships.

The centrally planned system replaces demand on the market by planned production targets. These may be legally backed instructions to the producers, orders placed by central authorities or indicated targets which it is hoped to achieve by the influence of central controls or by indirect means such as investment controls, taxation and other secondary controls.

Planning co-exists with the market in a number of senses. The planned economy itself is a constitutent in the world market. Within the economy itself market forces may be left to operate to a greater or lesser degree, interacting, supplementing or conflicting with the plan in various ways.

Although *laissez-faire* aspects of the market economy are eliminated, the planned economy may remain a commodity economy in that a considerable range of goods are produced for exchange and private labour given in exchange for wages is 'socialised' by a system of planned exchange relationships separate from labour and outside of its control.

The similarity of the two models is announced rather emphatically by the similarity of their organisational structures – a nexus of large enterprises paying wages to their employees, with similar management structures and similar categories of employment.

By definition central planning is bureaucratic – that is economic decisions are taken by planners at the pinnacle of an hierarchical structure. The most marked differences are in the property forms. In the economies of Eastern Europe for example the means of production are, in general, state-owned in industry and for the most part co-operatively owned in agriculture. In the capitalist countries of Western Europe there are considerable areas of public ownership, but private ownership of productive resources remains predominant and public ownership is most commonly found in public utilities and public service industries.

Central planning is commonly identified with socialism. This is inaccurate, or else a tautology. If socialism is taken to mean state ownership or control of the means of production together with economic planning in the interest of the community there is no difference apart from the objective of serving the community. And this, anyhow, permits of many interpretations when one is speaking of a bureaucracy acting as proxy for the people. In the case of the planned economies of Eastern Europe and the Soviet Union, whatever one may think about the way the bureaucracy uses its powers, there can be no question that it is the bureaucrats that take the decisions and control the productive resources and allocate the product. The workers are separated from, and have no more direct control over, their products than they have in a capitalist society. If socialism is defined as "A state of things in which every member of society will be enabled to participate not only in production but also in the distribution and administration of social wealth". (Engels' article on Karl Marx published in *Volkskalendar, 1878),* then nowhere does a completed model for such an economy yet exist. Basic notions associated with socialism include (1) public ownership of the means of production, (2) a classless society in which people administer for themselves their social and economic affairs, and (3) production for use replacing production for exchange.

It should be noted that in this section I am dealing with models of centrally planned economies and do not equate these to socialist economies. There does not as yet exist a socialist society in Engels' sense of "Every member of society . . . participating in the administration of social wealth"; on the other hand there are a number of countries, of which the Soviet Union was the first and China is the largest, where all important means of production are publicly owned. Whenever a society is able directly to plan employment of productive resources 'going over the head of the market' to meet some social need, production for use is in some measure then over-riding production for profit, 'plan' is opposing itself to 'market' as the economic regulator. In this sense in the economies of the Soviet Union and Eastern Europe, there are important areas of production for use; such areas also are to be found as a result of intervention by the state or public authority in capitalist economies. On the other hand, the publicly owned economies still retain many economic relationships, criteria and objectives that are very similar to those of capitalist economies. (This would appear to be the main basis of Chinese criticisms of the policies of Liu Shao Chi and of Soviet economic policies which despite public ownership are described as 'capitalist'.)

An important question arises – namely, what is the relationship between plan and market? Clearly areas of planning exist within any enterprise and such areas of planning may be extended in political forms; however, the world market and the world money system in which the reality of the commodity economy finds its most powerful expression, remain as economic regulators from whose impact no area of the world is entirely able to escape. There is, as it were, a worldwide contest between 'plan' and 'market' in which the social relations appropriate to "production by freely associated men . . . in accordance with a settled plan," (*Capital*, Chapter 1, Section 4) are only gradually being discovered as this contest unfolds. The contest is one between practical alternatives, that is policies for dealing with specific economic situations, and at the same time one of ideas. "The categories of bourgeois economy . . . are forms of thought expressing with social validity the conditions and relations of a definite, historically determined mode of production, viz, the production of commodities."

Chapter II

The New Technology: Computers

Cause and Effect in Technological Change

Both science, as the power of control over nature, and techniques, as the instruments of such power, are, to a certain extent, independent of the social and economic circumstances in which they develop; but only to a certain extent. In other respects they are shaped by and bear the imprint of the socio-economic system. Technology is independent, for example, in that a method of doing something that has been perfected in one social situation may be taken over and used in another. But technology is dependent in that the economic exploitation and development of knowledge must await suitable socio-economic conditions and the ends that techniques are made to serve are dictated by these conditions. For example, the development of machine production presupposed the specialised division of labour in the preceding stage of manufacture (see page 60ff. below) and also presupposed the accumulated funds and expanding markets of developing capitalism.

Since the dawn of the modern industrial age the factory owners have always been faced with a problem of labour. Without a labour force no factory can run. This very fact gives labour a power that is always a potential threat to the owners of the means of production. On a number of counts those who run industry have looked for improved means of producing a greater mass of marketable commodities, a greater sum of values per unit of labour employed. At the time they have favoured those mechanisms and those methods of dividing out the functions and tasks of labour that most reduced the dependence of the owner on labour. This overriding importance of productivity, in the sense of power to produce marketable wealth in excess of costs, has given certain specific characteristics to the development of technology and to the organisation of technical workers employed in industry.

There are, therefore, complicated interactions between technical knowledge and skills, between the dynamic of the economy and the structure of the social system. The basis of the industrial revolution was the machine. But in the absence of suitable political and economic conditions machine production could never have developed and the form that its development took was largely dictated by the requirements of those who owned and ran industry.

The machine took over from the skilled handicraftsman and permeated by its influence all aspects of economic activity. It is for this reason that one speaks of the industrial revolution, that is, of a revolution in technology. Today the computer, and the associated electronic techniques of which it is a premier expression, is in an analogous way all-pervasive in its potential impact on economic activity. A study of what computers are and what they do is indispensable to an understanding of relationships between science, technology and economic activity in the contemporary scene.

Physical aids to calculation, for example the abacus, are ancient; machines to calculate are as old as other machines. Leibniz constructed a calculating machine in the seventeenth century. The idea of the computer as a general-purpose calculating machine had its origin in attempts to mechanise the tedious work of calculating tables. Charles Babbage (1791-1871), wrestling with the problem of designing a machine to calculate tables, was led on to see that a machine that could undertake virtually any calculation was feasible. From this we have advanced to the recognition that general-purpose machines can execute virtually any well-defined routine and by virtue of this power render automatic an extensive range of economic activities which are at present carried out by human labour. It is this capability that gives to the computer its far-reaching, pervasive significance. Before considering technology in the context of our present socio-economic system, we devote Chapter II to considering the computer and its significance for human activities. The following observations will serve as a starting point:

1. The technological revolution is inseparable from a body of new mathematical and scientific theory which is variously described as cybernetics, information theory or communication theory.

2. Its base in the economy (analogous to machine-making in the industrial revolution) is the electronics industry and associated scientific disciplines.

3. The digital electronic computer is the salient example of a technologically revolutionary type of equipment, but other forms of control instruments of this type may shortly be developed.

Information Processing

The revolutionary thing about the machine was that it replaced the skill of the human hand. The computer can replace the human brain in the performance of any well-defined mental routine.

Alongside the machine revolution and the computer revolution man's ability to harness power (steam, electricity, nuclear energy) has vastly extended. But this *by itself* is of less economic significance. The point is to *direct* and *focus* and *control* power. When a manufacturer buys labour power the point of the transaction is not physical power. Energy on its own he can buy much more cheaply in other forms. The essential of what he is buying is the brain of a man as an information processor. Such a man receives information in the form of instructions to make something with available instruments and materials. His brain processes this information and so guides his action in making the required product. The individual worker is, in fact, one of many in a social team and a constant interchange of information with others is needed. The revolutionary thing about the computer is that it is a universal information processor. The purpose of this section is to explore the nature of a universal information processor. This is far from being a simple undertaking, but without it one could hardly understand the changes that the computer will make, or could make, to economic and social relations.

Although it was to be roughly a century before the technical means of making the modern digital computer were to be found, the universal information processor in conceptual design was the invention of Charles Babbage. One of the few of Babbage's friends and contemporaries who really understood what he was getting at was Byron's daughter, Ada Augusta, Countess of Lovelace.

> "The analytical engine", she wrote, "does not occupy common ground with mere 'calculating machines'. It holds a position wholly its own, and the considerations it suggests are most interesting in their nature. In enabling a mechanism to combine together *general* symbols in successions of unlimited variety and extent, a uniting link is established between the operations of matter and the abstract mental processes of the *most abstract* branch of mathematical science. A new, a vast, and a powerful language is developed for the future use of analysis, in which to wield its truths so that these may become of more speedy and accurate practical application for the purposes of mankind than the means hitherto in our possession have rendered possible. Thus not only the mental and the material, but the theoretical and the practical in the mathematical world, are brought into more intimate and effective connection with each other. We are not aware of its being on record that anything partaking in the nature of what is so well designated the *Analytical Engine* has been hitherto proposed, or even thought of, as a practical possibility, any more than the idea of a thinking or of a reasoning machine."[1]

1. *Charles Babbage and his Calculating Engine,* edited by Philip and Emily Morrison, Dover Publications, 1961, p. 252.

What a computer does is much less than what a human brain does. Imagination, intuition, ability to interpret vague or imprecise instructions – these a computer cannot achieve. It is no concern of ours here to speculate whether man will be able to create machines more similar to brains as *instruments,* let alone as personalities. The implications of a powerful and speedy information processor are all that we need concern ourselves with – and these are far-reaching enough.

There is something in our cast of mind or training that makes most of us feel that in the sum total of human activity, information is but one aspect. We rate doing before talking, deeds above words, as if deeds were something very solid and real and information something subsidiary. Oddly enough, however, military men, who are seen typically as practical down-to-earth characters having no truck with theory, are very conscious of the importance of what they call 'intelligence'. Here the basic fact shows itself – that information is power.

Man's ability to process information, individually and collectively is basic to his power over other creatures on the earth. The power of man lies in his big cranium not in his muscles. It lies in his brain rather than in his senses. In language rather than in strength. The input of data to the central nervous system in man by sight, hearing, touch, etc., is not markedly different from that of other higher animals. Man's special powers are in what he does with the information that he receives, in the processing of this information. Here the experimental work of modern biologists is beginning to give us important new insights.

Professor J.Z. Young in his *A Model of the Brain* has studied in detail the working of the nervous system of the octopus and thus illuminated understanding of human mental activity. In addition to the power of the individual central nervous system, man has acquired the remarkable and unique facility of being able to transfer information of great complexity with rapidity from one human being to another and to process information collectively. Modern science represents an advanced stage in the collective processing of information by man. In this respect man is already enormously advanced beyond any other animals. Professor Young points out that for most animals the main means of transferring information is sexual. Obviously a screech or an expression conveys something from one animal to another, but basically an animal's ability to cope with its environment comes from the nervous system inherited from its two parents, a nervous system that "functions with rapid and precise feed-backs . . . designed by the hereditary instructions to provide precise information about the results of each action, whether it is good or bad for the organism, whether it yields pleasure or pain."[1]

1. *A Model of the Brain,* Oxford University Press, 1964, p. 289.

All this is true of man too; but in addition he has the inestimable advantage of supplementing his own experience by learning from other men's experience. Men receive information by direct contact with the environment of human society and also indirectly through other men. The information that other men pass on has been processed by them, abbreviated, simplified and given meaning. "By means of language and tools man constructs models of the world outside his own brain and outside his own genetic system."[1]

Meaning and Models

We live in and see the world in terms of a particular model that we inherit. But this basic, inherited model, depending upon what kind of creatures we are, is modified and added to by models that we create ourselves out of our experience and store in our nervous systems, in our memories. This is the process of learning, which in man may be either directly from experience or from information conveyed to us by other human beings. Speech – the use of words – is one way in which all normal human beings make models of the world. Thus J.Z. Young writes: "Words influence other people because they fit with the models that those others have in their heads. In his writing and art, his speech and his machines man manages to transfer outside his head at least some features of the information that is within it. The formation of such artefacts, available for the use of many, is our unique feature. The modern electronic apparatus that assists with communication of information and with computation is only the latest stage of a development that has been going on throughout the history of man."[2]

The more the nature of man is probed, and particularly of man in society, of social man, the more clearly we see the fundamental importance of information processing. If then we have found in modern electronic apparatus a means of universal information processing, for massive quantities of information at very high speeds, this cannot fail to be of tremendous significance. To call the computer a 'universal' processor is possibly to use too big a word. There are many forms of information processing that a computer could not begin to tackle. A computer could not, for example, write Hamlet. Yet Hamlet most certainly 'holds a mirror up to nature'. That is, in Hamlet, Shakespeare has distilled his own experience and made a model, a representation of human feelings and behaviour. A computer is universal in the sense that it can execute any algorithm. What is an algorithm? Originally it was the name for the rules of calculation using Arabic numerals – addition, subtraction, multiplication and division. Thus an algorithm became any

1. *ibid*, pp. 297-8.
2. *ibid*, p. 13.

calculation or routine process by which one set of pieces of information is transformed into another set of pieces of information according to a finite system of rules. The pieces of information are expressed in some code. This code might be an alphabet or a set of numbers or a set of symbols. We will discuss this matter further below and show that it is possible to translate any code or alphabet into a standard code or standard language. As an example of an algorithm we may take the mathematical formula $y = x^2$. The rule is, if the input number (i.e. the value of x), is, say, 4, then y has the value of 4 x 4; if it is 1.21, 1.21 is multiplied by itself giving a corresponding value for y of 1.4641; if $x = \sqrt{2}$ then $y = 2$ and so on. The rule here is take the input number and multiply this number by itself to give the output number.

All this, you may well say, is just a lot of mathematical trivialities. If the computer is an algorithmic machine and that is all it does, what is so world-shaking about it? There are, of course, I would emphasise, artistic and other forms of perception and action that go beyond mathematical relations of the kind which we are here discussing. The point I am concerned to make is that mathematical routines, though not everything, are more important for human activity than they may seem. Our capacity for mental arithmetic tells us something about our minds. The apparently simple, trivial process of receiving coded data, processing it and then putting out coded data in some new form, is quite fundamental to the activity of human beings, as social knowers and doers. Sights, sounds, sensations act upon our senses, some coming directly from the material world in which we live, some being codes, words, pictures, gestures, and the like, by means of which other human beings convey information to us. These sensations pass as coded messages along the channels of our nervous system to central points, and pre-eminently to the conscious activity of the brain. In the brain these codes are interpreted and generate further coded messages. These pass back along the channels of the nervous system to determine an output of action related to the input of information.

It may seem an exaggeration to say that all incoming information is related to action, although we are frequently aware of noticing only what we need to notice for the job in hand. The last thing that I am suggesting, however, is that there is some deterministic connection between incoming sensations and resulting actions. Indeed, it is the beings with the most complex powers of processing information that are least prone to predictable reflex actions in their behaviour, who notice more than most people. The fact, however, that is beyond dispute is that life is action, the activity of controlling the living organism, whether that control be of a positive sort leading to movement and change, or of a negative kind restraining movement and restraining the organism from changing its situation. It is in the nature of things that the incoming flow of informations *must* affect the behaviour of a personality and be a factor of importance in shaping the courses of action that, from moment to moment, and, from year to year, are adopted. It may be that the incoming information acts cumulatively and slowly over time, or it may be that reaction is sudden, immediate and specific. But all the way through, what one does is richly intertwined with the activity of processing incoming information.

At every moment throughout a living existence incoming information is being interpreted. We try to make out what it means. We look for patterns in it that we can relate to patterns already in our memories. When we have found these, we call up additional information related to these things or evoked in our minds by the incoming information. There is an interaction in our brains between what is already stored there and the new input of information. The input acquires meaning because it evokes past knowledge; it also adds to, modifies and changes our store of past knowledge. We have, to use Professor J.Z. Young's expression, 'a model in the brain' in terms of which incoming messages acquire meaning and which is always being added to and improved in the light of messages from our continuing experiences.

This process also takes place on a social scale and it is this with which we are here most concerned. The word 'model' will be used to describe in a wide sense all the representations of things with the aid of which human beings understand and interact with their environment. The models we make are both individual and social in the sense that they are products of communication and co-operation and at the same time means of communication. In this sense the range of models is very wide and there is much that we do not understand about them. In this category would be included all art and music; but even language in itself poses problems whose nature we have only recently begun to grasp with any clarity.

When we speak of the 'patterns' used by the human mind, we cover several forms of thinking process. In mathematical thinking it is necessary to draw a distinction between conceptualisation in general terms, in which mathematical concepts, terms and symbols may play a vital part, and detailed representation of relationships – formulae that may be calculated specifically. (See Mathematical Appendix Note 1.)

The instruments should be seen as of two kinds: (a) theoretical work achieved by the broadening out of mathematical thinking over the last century and a half and (b) advances in technology such as transistors, lasers, magnetic tape and innumerable techniques that make possible the processing of information outside the human brain. Of these the computer is singled out as the most appropriate generic representative at this point of time.

When we speak of patterns, we may often mean concepts in the most general sense. But in a more limited sense, for example, in the pattern of a letter of the alphabet or of a design on paper, precise definition should, one would think, be possible. It is interesting that this has proved one of the more intractable problems of computerisation. The work that is going on in this field will undoubtedly be important in defining the boundary of areas amenable to mathematical treatment. (An important field in which such work is being done is the theory of perceptrons, i.e. models of simplified networks of nerve-cells). We cannot here deal with these frontiers of new work, but we do need to have some general understanding of the distinction between mathematical models and models in a more general sense and at the same time to appreciate the very considerable power and versatility of the mathematical model.

Let us recapitulate; men acquire understanding and communicate understanding of their environment by making models of it. A model is a representation of something by means of some kind of code. In human life, these codes or representations take innumerable forms. A word is a model. We say 'chair'. A certain pattern of sound waves provides a code and communicates from me to you what the dictionary defines (using another code of visual letter patterns) as 'a seat for one person with four legs and usually a rest for the back'. A picture is a model. A doll's house with toy chairs in it is another kind of model, and so on. The study of these various models carries us into the heart of linguistics, epistemology, art and many other fields of study. We need to select and see the importance of the models that mathematics and computers handle.

Some writers classify models into various types; for example, iconic, analogue and symbolic. These classifications are not of basic significance, but some brief discussion of them may help towards a better understanding of how symbolic or coded models may be translated into other model forms. A symbolic model is a model made out of a set of mathematical symbols; it is a string of letters or numbers that can represent, for example, objects that actually exist in the real world.

An iconic model is one that, like a statue, reproduces the physical proportions of an object. A statue does not breathe, it has no blood in its veins, but it looks like a living person. A doll's house is another example of an iconic model.

An analogue model is a model that may not look at all like the thing it represents but behaves in an analogous way. For example, the addition of lengths marked on a slide-rule is analogous to multiplication. One can make a model in which the flow of liquid behaves analogously to the flow of incomes in an economic system or in which electric currents simulate conduction of heat in a building.

A symbolic model is a representation in mathematical symbols, that is a coding by means of numbers. We may very simply illustrate how an iconic model of a doll's house can be translated into a symbolic or mathematical model. Draw two lines through one corner of the doll's house at right angles in line with the walls where they run along the ground. Draw a third line rising up vertically through this corner. These three lines then provide a frame of reference which we may mark off in feet, say. Using such a frame of reference the eight corners of a rectangular doll's house 4 feet long, 2 feet deep, 2 feet high could be represented by the following eight triplets of numbers: (0, 0, 0), (2, 0, 0), (2, 4, 0), (0, 4, 0), (0, 0, 2), (2, 0, 2), (2, 4, 2), (0, 4, 2). Similarly other points – to whatever degree of detail – may be represented by triplets of numbers. (See Diagram I.).

DIAGRAM I.

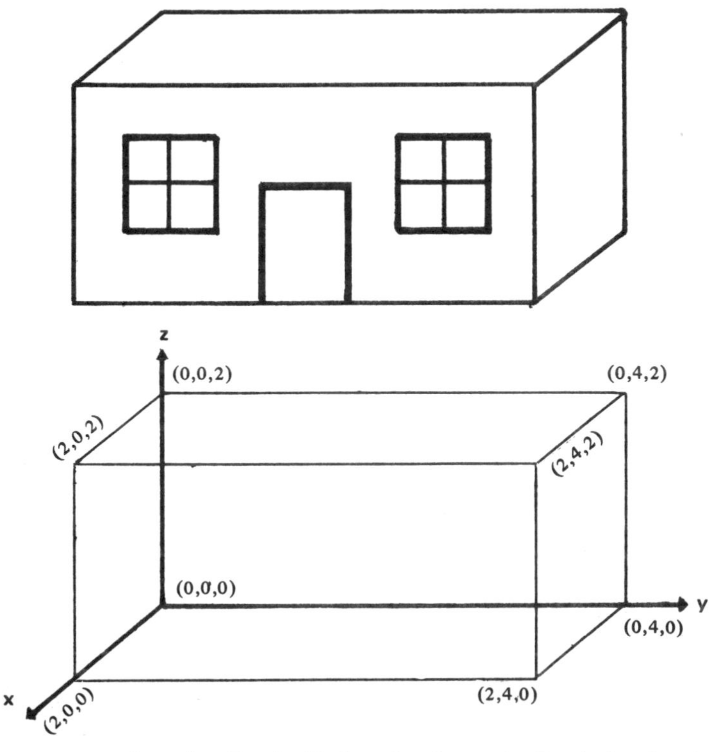

Representation of an Iconic Model of a house in Symbols, that is, in triplets of the form (a,b,c,)

An extension of this very simple method of finding a correspondence between numbers and a diagram, of translating numbers into pictures and vice-versa, enables a computer to print out animated cartoons depicting situations that are simulated within the computer by coded numbers. Similarly, an important application of electronics is the making of apparatus that simulates processes (as, for example, the heat flows referred to above). Electronic simulation of elementary logical processes in fact supplies the 'logical gates', i.e. the electric circuits corresponding to logical operations; these are the basic elements in the construction of general-purpose digital computers. Electronic simulation gives output results that are equivalent to calculations; for example, electronic machines simulate integration, differentiation, etc. – mathematical operations that are very widely used by scientists, engineers and others. (They would be used, for example, in calculating how far a body moves in a certain time, or how quickly a body moves). In this way such machines serve as special-purpose calculating machines and a general term for them is 'analogue computers'. It is a further indication of the power of symbolic representation that the general-purpose digital computer can simulate the behaviour of an analogue computer by representing each event, each state of the system by corresponding numbers.

The Newtonian Model

To illustrate a little further and a little deeper the link between mathematics and the coding of models consider a model of movement. For example, an object is moving through space, projected from the ground and making a trajectory through the air and landing again at some other point on the ground. (See Diagram II.).

One cannot cope with this comparatively simple happening without reference to some general model of the physical world. Here we have a universally used model created by the scientific endeavour of the fifteenth, sixteenth and seventeenth centuries – the Newtonian Model. This model is described in three simple laws. Yet it is rich in truth content, as is almost no other model. That is, it has retained, despite its simplicity, an ability to depict realistically a wide range of happenings in the physical world. It provides a framework within which scientists in all parts of the world can model physical happenings in a manner commonly intelligible to each other.

Neglecting air resistance, a model of the motion of a projectile can be deduced from the Newtonian principles in a few lines. This model for any given speed and angle of projection gives the trajectory. (See Mathematical Appendix Note 2).

With such models we perform experiments in the imagination. These are collective experiments in that people agree, as it were, to imagine

DIAGRAM II.

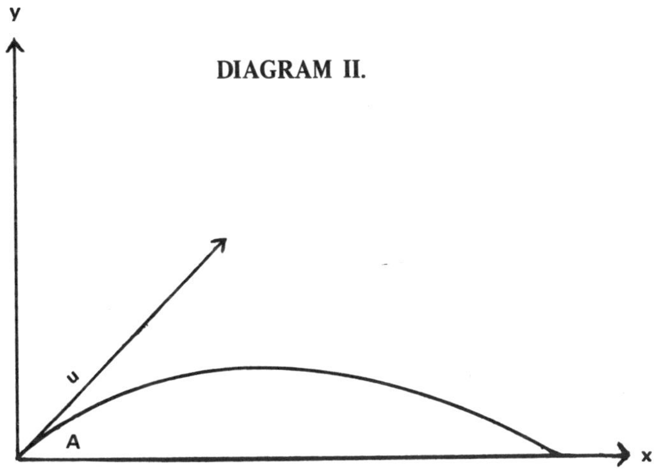

Mathematical Model $\left(y = x \tan A - \frac{g}{2u^2 \cos^2 A} x^2 \right)$ **of a Projectile**

In this representation

$$y = x - \frac{x^2}{8} \qquad \text{(i.e. } A = 45^\circ \text{ and } u = 16\text{)}$$

this gives the following table

x	y
0	0
1	0.875
2	1.5
3	1.875
4	2
5	1.875
6	1.5
7	0.875
8	0

things in the same way. This is the function that the commonly shared Newtonian model performs. Unlike the experiments we privately perform in our imaginations when we think of something moving through space, thus picturing in our minds roughly where it should fall, this model works strictly and precisely according to agreed rules, agreed units of measurement and so forth. It is settled in advance exactly how it is going to work and exactly how the findings are to be measured. This does not mean that these findings are necessarily more real than what we do in the mind's eye. A sportsman may in fact estimate the flight of a ball through the air far more accurately than a mathematician. His private model may be richer and more flexible in use. But there are, of course, also many areas in which the mathematical model gives degrees of precision far greater than individual human judgment (for example, the moon shot). There are also many problems that the mathematical model can handle which human judgment could not even begin to tackle. (The speed of the computer adds further scope, making it possible, for example, to calculate the position of a projectile more quickly than it flies – the basis of all anti-aircraft guns since the second world war).

The special point about the mathematical model is its precision and definiteness and its public character, in that it is a collectively understood and accepted model. The situation chosen by way of illustration is a limited one. In fact, the range of things to which precise computable models may be applied is limitless.

A simple model that corresponds to what actually happens in the real world is a powerful tool. Unfortunately such models are hard to come by. The model of the projectile is a good example of a simple model so long as we are prepared to neglect air resistance. When that is taken into account the simplicity of the model is lost. In fact the process of learning is, for humans, largely a matter of learning how to use models. We face a number of problems:

1. Does the model represent reality?
2. Is it simple to use?
3. Is it understood by and acceptable to others?

We may, and do, make models purely to amuse ourselves. Perhaps these are not models at all, just shapes, movements, ideas. Models that do not correspond to reality are creations we bring into being to please ourselves, fantasies, dreams. But generally – perhaps inevitably – there is some echo of reality even in the wildest fantasies. Why should we not seek aesthetic pleasure in the models that we make? Here, however, we are concerned with and will concentrate only on the practical aspects of models. We want them to represent reality. Our equations for the flight of a projectile are useful because we are convinced that corresponding to each point in time there is an actual point in real space where we expect the projectile to be. Our mathematical model is an algorithmic machine which processes numbers and for every time value gives us a position in space. It is useful because it represents the essentials of what actually happens to a projectile moving through space.

Here we have been able to find a simple relationship, and a simple rule by which to express it, and can give the calculating machine quite precise instructions in order to find the position of the projectile in the model. If the model, and therefore the calculations, were very much more complex, they could take into account the spin of the earth, the effect of air resistance and other factors. Such a model might be truer, that is it might represent more fully the reality with which we are dealing. But for many purposes we either would not, or could not, use such a model. We might not have the means of making the calculations. We might not have sufficient and sufficiently precise data to feed into our model. Learning how to use models does not just mean trying to cram as much truth content into them as we can but, rather, understanding what they do and what they do not. Provided we know the limitations of the more simple model it may give more power to act effectively in the environment than does a more truthful but more complex model.

There is in fact a very subtle and ever-present interaction between doing and knowing. We need constantly to build models of reality reflecting and representing how things happen with the greatest possible accuracy, however complex the models may become. Paradoxically we need to make these complex models in order that we may the more confidently use the more simple models that leave out important aspects of the reality. The point is that we should not have illusions about the simple models but should be alive as far as possible to their strengths and weaknesses.

As we use models we are constantly bombarding them with information from the real world that challenges their validity. A scientific theory is, in a sense, a model of reality. Many great steps forward have been taken in science because information that we feed into the model from reality contradicts expectations, proves the model faulty. But scientists do not start from a mass of facts and look for a model. They start with a tentative model or theory and then test it against the facts.

In order to understand reality we need a model in terms of which to interpret it. Very often we are at a loss to know what model to use. Often the work of the statistician amounts to guessing what shapes or patterns of figures might occur and then poring over masses of data to see if they do; or he may try to find devices that help to suggest patterns. He hopes to find mathematical relationships that he can express by simple rules, and he keeps testing his data for relationships which he thinks he might find in his data.

A model can only represent an aspect of reality and if one model handles one aspect well, whereas for other aspects other models are more convenient, why should not several different models be used? In principle there is no limit to the number of models that might be used. Since models can, by their very nature, represent only limited aspects or partial truths, one may properly reject the philosophy that looks for only one true model. There are, however, very good practical and social reasons for restricting basic models to the very fewest possible numbers. Commonly understood and commonly acceptable models act as a means of co-ordinating the work and communications of all those who use them. In science whole schools of thought tend to be defined by the fact that people accept and use the same basic models.[1] Where specialist basic research is being undertaken, the radius of understanding may be limited to scientific workers. For other purposes – and this is particularly true of socio-economic models – a wide and general understanding may be of considerable importance. Models – in the wider and more general meanings of the word – can co-ordinate the aims and actions of whole collectives of people. In a period in which precise mathematical models of economic and social situations become a possibility, the acceptability and intelligibility of the models used will become an important consideration.

'Abstract Machines'

The argument of the last three sections sought to establish two basic facts:

1. That model making and model using are fundamental, all pervading parts of human activity, and

2. That many very important types of models may take the seemingly trivial form of turning one string of numbers or letters into another string of numbers in accordance with a prescribed system of rules.

If a machine, given one lot of numbers, can stand in for the human brain in the work of information processing, and find the appropriate corresponding set of numbers to guide responses to given situations, and so guide actions, then we have at our disposal a very powerful tool. (A machine whose input and output are only numbers may seem at first blush to be of very limited use; but since number codes – see p. 46ff. below – may represent virtually anything, these limitations are more

1. See, for example, T.S. Kuhn's, *The Structure of Scientific Revolution.*

apparent than real). Such a machine – what Babbage called an 'analytical engine' – provides an immediately reproducible extension to brain power, much as the machine of the industrial revolution was an extension to the power of hand or limb that worked the tools. Unlike the biological mechanisms which have taken some millions of years to evolve, these extensions to man's biological powers are derived directly from materials that can be shaped, fitted and assembled in a period of time that on the scale of history is very short.

This section will deal with machines not from the standpoint of the engineer who fashions the materials used in the construction of machines, but from the underlying principles of operation by which machines can process information and build models.

To model the flight of the projectile we simply feed in a string of numbers representing points in time in order to obtain an output which is a string of numbers representing points in space. Thus:–

TABLE I. **Flight of a Projectile**
(launched at 30° at 160 feet per second)

Input: t = time	**0**	**1**	**2**	**2½**	**3**	**4**	**5**
Output: x = horizontal distance	**0**	**138.6**	**277.1**	**346.4**	**415.7**	**554.2**	**692.3**
y = height	**0**	**64**	**96**	**100**	**96**	**64**	**0**

We can prepare a computer program which models the situation far better than the few numbers above. It could give values for x and y against as many intermediary values for t as we may wish – that is down to several places of decimals. We can also arrange, with the aid of suitable peripheral equipment, for the computer to display in graphical or other visual form the movement of the projectile through space. This is just one of countless possible illustrations, but what I want to do here is to emphasis as strongly as possible that a string of input numbers, processed according to clearly defined rules to give us a string of output numbers, is a model. With suitable input and suitable processing this model may represent a dynamic situation of considerable complexity. Moreover, we have the means of translating its numerical output back into whatever form of representation may be most convenient.

The almost unlimited powers of mathematical model building and information processing that are now becoming available rest on the following foundations:–

1. The development of the mathematical/logical theory on which the conceptual invention of the computer rests.

2. The development of electronic technology making possible the simulation of elementary logical operations, (a) at very high speeds, (b) in a very small space (microminiaturisation) and (c) at low production costs.

3. The search for adequate formal or conceptual systems to provide the theoretical framework within which to collect data and make use of models.

Throughout the last century a great deal of work was done on the logical foundations of mathematics. This work showed that the main structure of mathematics may be deduced from a very small number of primitive ideas (such as *negation* and *alternation*, e.g. 'either this or that'). *Principia Mathematica* by Bertrand Russell and Alfred North Whitehead, written in the first decade of this century, brought to a conclusion a work contributed to by many and initiated, in particular, by George Boole's[1] *The Laws of Thought.* In a sense these mathematicians did in a theoretical way what Charles Babbage worked out in terms of practical mechanism. Without electronic speeds the analysis of mathematical procedures as a long chain of very simple logical steps would have been of little practical interest. (It is not until half-way through the second volume that Russell and Whitehead have made good all the logical links needed to prove that two plus two equal four!) Of course mathematics as a conceptual, intuitive, inventive activity is much more than logical deduction. It has moreover been shown that there are a number of operational problems in the field of mathematics for which no algorithms (that is well-defined routine procedures) can be specified. However, the general conclusion of the work that has been done on the logical foundations of mathematics and the study of the abstract mathematical theory of automata is that almost all mathematical operations, including even the most complex, can be performed as a sequence of very small elementary logical steps.

To represent ordinary calculations in terms of elementary logical processes means taking a great many bites of one cherry. We shall show below how many elementary logical steps are needed to perform a very simple addition sum. If we calculated in this way, things would go so

1. Boole was born in 1815 and died in 1864.

slowly that mathematical models would be of little use. In mental arithmetic, for example, we have learnt how to take short-cuts, how to carry through quite complicated mathematical manipulations, without even being conscious of the elementary logical processes on which the conclusions have implicitly relied. It is a curious fact that mathematicians have got on so well for so long without going down to the logical foundations of their work. They have in fact been able to create useful mathematical models using rules of manipulation that they instinctively felt to be sound and which have worked well enough in practice. But in the past the great thing has been to help the human brain find those short-cuts with the aid of which to make complicated calculations, to work intricate models.

With the computer we are, however, in a different situation. Long strings of calculations, which are out of the question for the human brain, admirably suit the computer. In a modern computer speeds for elementary operations are measured in nanoseconds. (There are 1,000,000,000 nanoseconds in one second; a computer that takes a nanosecond to perform an operation, will do in one second what it will take a man, performing one operation per second non-stop night and day, thirty-two years to do!). So if the computer takes 30 or 40 steps to do what we do all at once, still it is infinitely faster than the human brain.

Today a great deal of work is being done on the theory of algorithms, that is the theory of specifying routines. One conclusion already reached by the Russian mathematician, A.A. Markov, is that the rules defining any functional mapping (e.g. in a function such as $y = f(x)$, the value of y corresponding to any given value of x) can be translated into a very simple algorithmic procedure which he called the 'normal algorithm'. The meaning of this is far-reaching. It means that we can make a machine that can execute any algorithm – since we certainly could make a machine to execute the very simple procedure of the normal algorithm. (See Mathematical Appendix, Note 3). (Machines may be designed to execute *any* algorithm, the only constraint being time of operation and size of information store; but, as mentioned above, there are mathematical problems for which algorithms cannot be specified. However, the practical significance of such 'algorithmic unsolvability' is not great).

Abstract Models of General-Purpose Computers

A great deal of theoretical work has been undertaken on the abstract theory of machines – that is, their mathematical and logical structure. Here I will give only the briefest indication of this conceptual structure.

To define an abstract model of a machine it is necessary to define:–

1. A specified set of inputs.
2. A specified set of outputs.
3. The set of possible states of the machine.
4. A function to define how a particular state of the machine and a particular input determine a particular new state of the machine.
5. A similar function to define how input and existing state define the output of the machine at each stage of time.

These very abstract statements about the structure of general-purpose computing machines may in fact be made more intelligible by considering a homely example. Consider the routine used by a school child in adding numbers. The machine is the child's brain. The input is digits, the state of the machine is the number in his 'carry'. The output is the sum which is written down in a series of stages – first the units, then the tens and so forth. For example if he is adding the two numbers 49 and 72, the first input is the two numbers 9 and 2. He says to himself 9 and 2 are 11, put down 1 carry 1. The put down corresponds to the first output, the statement carry 1 means that his carry from nought becomes one. The next step is 4 and 7 make 11; take note of the fact that there is 1 in the carry, making the output 2 and the carry 1. The next step is an input of 0 and 0 and taking account of the carry results in an output of 1.

The point in making a deep study of the abstract theory of machines is that most complex processes can be built up by the structural linking of precisely defined routines as simple or simpler than the one that we have described. It is just such precisely defined, simple routines that the electronic digital computer is capable of performing at the extremely high speeds to which we have already referred.

Babbage's 'Analytical Engine' Was A General-Purpose Automaton

Charles Babbage was, as we have seen, the conceptual inventor of the general-purpose automaton. That is, he worked out thoroughly and in detail how one could be made. The principles of construction used by the designers of electronic digital computers today are similar to his. Babbage worked out how mechanical apparatus could perform the desired operation. By actually designing an analytical engine, Babbage elaborated the detail of his conceptions; but he never succeeded in completing it. Had he done so he would have built a digital computer with the same design structure as the modern electronic digital computer. But slowness and cumbersomeness of mechanical operation and liability to mechanical failure would have severely limited its value in application.

The use of cards to control the operation of the engine he took from the method employed by Jacquard looms to weave fabrics of complicated design.

> " . . . The Jacquard loom is capable of weaving any design which the imagination of mań may conceive. It is also the constant practice for skilled artists to be employed by manufacturers in designing patterns. These patterns are then sent to a peculiar artist, who, by means of a certain machine, punches holes in a set of pasteboard cards in such a manner that when those cards are placed in a Jacquard loom, it will then weave upon its produce the exact pattern designed by the artist."[1]

Babbage in fact had hanging in his room a portrait of Jacquard woven in very fine detail by one of Jacquard's own looms. Some 24,000 punched cards were used in making it.

The five constituent parts of Babbage's analytical engine correspond to the components of the modern digital computer, as follows:–

1. A memory or store for holding numbers. (For example our adding automaton needed to 'remember' from stage to stage the number in the carry. In practice the computer will need to take in and store the data on which it is to work; a set of instructions which it will have to follow; in addition, it will need to keep in its memory intermediate calculations needed to arrive at the results which it will in due course provide as output).

2. A mill. This corresponds exactly to the arithmetic unit by means of which, following the instructions, certain basic operations are performed on data. The name 'arithmetic unit' is not an altogether happy one since the operations performed by a general-purpose computer are the basic logical operations required in the execution of algorithms, i.e. well-defined routines. These will include, but are not confined to, ordinary arithmetic operations such as addition and subtraction; 'logic unit' or 'operating unit' or Babbage's 'mill' would be better names for this part of the computer but the term 'arithmetic unit' has probably come to stay.

3. A control unit to see that the engine performs its operations in the proper sequence.

4. Input devices to take in numbers and operating instructions.

5. Output devices to present the results of the transformation that the engine has carried out.

1. *The Life of a Philosopher,* p. 8.

Coding

Coding is the operation of translating one set of signals or symbols into another set. We shall here consider coding in its simplest form only. Information conveyed by means of a language may be done by books divided into chapters, which in turn are divided into paragraphs, which in turn are divided into sentences, which in turn are divided into words, which in turn are divided into letters. We shall concern ourselves only with letters and direct, straight-forward methods of coding letters. The translation of one language into another language – for example French into English – is an altogether different undertaking. The underlying structure of the languages in which human beings communicate is as yet far from being clearly understood. The work of Noam Chomsky has made appreciation of the nature and significance of this problem possible; but we are still far from understanding the processes of meaningful speech and are still far from making automata that can do more than translate stereotyped expressions. To make automata endowed with the power of meaningful speech, as human beings are, is a task that we do not even know how to begin to tackle. The 'languages' with which we are here concerned are strings of variously grouped symbols or letters. We are not concerned with the processes by which language structure generates significance.

To code language A in language B a correspondence must be established between letters in the two languages. That is, for each letter in the first language there must be a letter or group of letters in the second language which will be recognisable in whatever context it occurs. In fact, if we have a standard language and determine the correspondence between every other language and this standard language, it will always be possible through it to translate the letters of any one language into any other language. We shall look at coding in terms of a standard language and shall choose as the standard language what is in fact the basic language of the digital computer – the Binary System.

The Binary System has only two 'letters' – 0 and 1. The great advantage of this very simple 'alphabet' is that anything capable of being in two distinct different states can be used to represent a letter in the alphabet. For example, a light which can be either on or off gives a completely adequate simulation of a letter if we make 'on' correspond to 1 and 'off' correspond to 0 or vice-versa.

Consider now how to translate the letters of, for example, our 26-letter alphabet into the standard alphabet which has only two letters. As a matter of fact the 26-letter alphabet has considerably more than 26 letters, even if such refinements as capitals are disregarded. Spaces between letters are a kind of letter; their inclusion changes the meaning. For example, 'do the boys' is not quite, as Dickens knew, the same as 'dotheboys'. There are also . ; : , ' " ! and other commonly used punctuation symbols.

The amount of information that can be conveyed with one letter is known as a 'bit' – which is a contraction of Binary Digit. One letter does no more than fix one out of two possibilities. For example, if someone said they would use a light in the window to signal whether it was all right to visit, we might agree that light means yes and no light meant no. With two lights or one light displayed at two successive points of time, one can convey four pieces of information. One can do just the same with one's two letters marked on a piece of paper. For example, with the two letters 0 and 1 the possibilies are:–

0	0
0	1
1	0
1	1

With three places at which to mark one or other of the two letters there are eight possibilities as follows:–

000
001
010
011
100
101
110
111

Just such a signalling system serves to communicate input to and output from a computer, by means of paper tape, magnetic tape, cards and other means. For example, the Elliott 803, one of the earlier small computers, communicates input and output on 'five channel tape'. This means that the computer reads a piece of tape, on which a hole can be punched in any one of five positions; it does so by means of a photo-electric cell. So the signal is either (a) a hole punched or (b) no hole punched. In this way 32 different signals may be transmitted as shown in Table II.

TABLE II **Thirty-two Distinct Signals Punched on 5-Channel Tape (Col. 3) and Typed in 5 Binary Digits (Col. 2)**

0	0 0 0 0 0			.			
1	0 0 0 0 1			.			o
2	0 0 0 1 0			.		o	
3	0 0 0 1 1			.		o	o
4	0 0 1 0 0			.	o		
5	0 0 1 0 1			.	o		o
6	0 0 1 1 0			.	o	o	
7	0 0 1 1 1			.	o	o	o
8	0 1 0 0 0		o	.			
9	0 1 0 0 1		o	.			o
10	0 1 0 1 0		o	.		o	
11	0 1 0 1 1		o	.		o	o
12	0 1 1 0 0		o	.	o		
13	0 1 1 0 1		o	.	o		o
14	0 1 1 1 0		o	.	o	o	
15	0 1 1 1 1		o	.	o	o	o
16	1 0 0 0 0	o		.			
17	1 0 0 0 1	o		.			o
18	1 0 0 1 0	o		.		o	
19	1 0 0 1 1	o		.		o	o
20	1 0 1 0 0	o		.	o		
21	1 0 1 0 1	o		.	o		o
22	1 0 1 1 0	o		.	o	o	
23	1 0 1 1 1	o		.	o	o	o
24	1 1 0 0 0	o	o	.			
25	1 1 0 0 1	o	o	.			o
26	1 1 0 1 0	o	o	.		o	
27	1 1 0 1 1	o	o	.		o	o
28	1 1 1 0 0	o	o	.	o		
29	1 1 1 0 1	o	o	.	o		o
30	1 1 1 1 0	o	o	.	o	o	
31	1 1 1 1 1	o	o	.	o	o	o

In the righthand column the dots between the second and third channels are simply small holes in the tape that have no 'meaning' but are required to make the tape run truly – that is to keep it straight and to put the line that the computer is reading in the right place at the right time. The o's in this righthand column represent holes that have been punched through to represent 1 in the Binary Alphabet wherever it was required. Where no mark has been put on the tape, this represents a nought in the Binary Alphabet.

Hardware

The theoretical foundation on which the digital computer stands is the fact that, as we have seen, virtually any mathematical calculation, indeed, more widely, any algorithmic routine, can be reduced to simple elementary operations. The computer is designed so that it can perform a string of elementary operations on whatever numbers are fed into it. The job of the human programmer is to list instructions about operations to be performed by the computer and about the sequence of these operations.

It has been under consideration whether it would be of advantage to build into the hardware of the computer a capacity for directly undertaking some of the more complicated mathematical operations that are frequently used. However, as things stand, the computer does nothing more complicated than addition, multiplication and division. There are 77 operational functions that the Elliott 803, for example, performs – most of them very simple operations like exchanging the place of two numbers, making negative numbers positive and vice-versa, increasing a number by 1 and so forth. The computer designer has to combine a number of electronic gates capable of performing logical operations in such a way as to make the computer capable of performing the elementary operations out of which the programmer will build up the sequence of instructions by means of which more complicated operations are performed. There are additionally two kinds of operations of exceptional importance, namely (a) the loop and (b) the jump. (a) makes it possible with one brief programming instruction to repeat the same operation many times and (b) enables the programmer to make the sequence of later operations dependent upon the result of earlier operations.

Generally speaking, the work of the electronics engineer in building the hardware of the computer has not been integrated at the design stage with the designing of the programs. The programmers make the best use they can of the electronic hardware supplied. It is, however, the programs that give the computer its power and scope. If and when a richer integration of the software and hardware phases of the design process comes about, we may see considerable departures from what is at present the standard computer structure.

Computer circuitry or the logic circuits in the computer are in fact a network of logical gates. The developments that gave birth to the modern electronic computer at the outset used relays and switches to make the logic circuits. Vacuum tubes then came into use but their bulk, the heat and power used and their degree of unreliability limited the usefulness of such computers. Solid state components then took over – switching transistors, switching diodes, tunnel diodes and the like. Their very small size, the fact that no heater power and no warm-up time were needed, coupled with high reliability, gave a vast new potential. Advancing techniques in the production of these components – in the micro-electronic industry – is continuously and rapidly extending this potential.

Binary signals are used – that is signals that take one or two possible forms. 0 and 1 represent these two forms. In the physical apparatus, for example, inputs of zero volts corresponding to 0 and of ten volts corresponding to 1 may be used. The AND gate requires an apparatus with two inputs and one output which works in such a way that the output is zero volts unless there is an input of ten volts along each of the input channels. For OR the requirement is that there shall be an output of ten volts whenever there is an input of ten volts along either or both the channels. For NEGATION the requirement is that if there is an input of ten volts the output shall be zero volts and if there is an input of zero then the output shall be ten volts. Solid state components can be made to simulate, i.e. behave analogously to, these basic logical operations. They provide a physical means with which to operate on, and so to transform, incoming signals to give required outgoing signals. The apparatus performs operations analogous to logical processing and the output corresponds to the outcome of logical analysis performed by human brains. The steps implicit in analysis by brainwork have to be discovered before a machine to replace brainwork can be built and used.[1]

Combination of the simple logical processes that the computer simulates makes it possible to simulate mathematical calculations and algorithmic routines of very great complexity. What seem, when considered in isolation, to be comparatively trivial operations, when combined and structured, imply the possibility of calculating power that is practically limitless.

Information can be fed into the computer, translated into the form that it is most convenient for the computer to handle, operated on in this form and then put out after being translated back into the form that we require. The result will be exactly the same whether the operations are performed on the original language or after translation into some new language.

The number of logical steps involved in even the simplest mathematical operations is considerable and to represent a mathematical calculation as a string of logical processes is extremely cumbersome. (Reduction to normal algorithms would be even more cumbersome).

1. See Mathematical Appendix, Note 4.

This would be a most unpractical way of carrying on were it not for the fact that communications within the computer are at speeds approximating the speed of light and each operation is carried through with extreme rapidity. The Atlas, which is a powerful computer, averages three micro-seconds (i.e. three millionths of a second) per instruction (and each instruction involves a number of operations). The computer recently being built by Manchester University – MU 5 – will operate at about a hundred nanoseconds (a nanosecond, to repeat, is a thousand millionth of a second) per instruction.

Micro- miniaturisation has already gone very far and some hundreds of logical gates can be packed into an area of about one centimetre square. New developments will take miniaturisation even further. Since 1955 the size of calculating units has been reduced to one-thousandth of what it was and is continuing to decrease at this rate. In short, the long way round of breaking down calculation to its elementary processes is compensated for over and over again by speed and smallness of size in the computer electronics.

The built-in circuits in the digital computer as at present designed do nothing mathematically more complicated than multiplication and division. The functions that a computer may be directly instructed to carry out are, for the most part, fairly simple rearrangements. The computer must be so organised as to enable the human programmer to combine these simple operations so as to carry out complex transformations of considerable amounts of data.

It must take in and store in its memory (a) the list of instructions that it is to carry out and (b) the data to be processed. For example, the object of a program may be to find the square root of a number. The computer must have not only the list of instructions (a) but also the list of numbers (b) of which the user wants the square roots.

The memory of the computer is a device in which coded signals remain lodged for as long as may be needed in positions, 'addresses', in which they can be found. It will be necessary also for the memory to emit the signal that it has lodged in it, whilst still retaining the signal for future reference. (Technically, in fact, the construction of suitable memories created considerable difficulties when the earliest computers were being designed. The outstanding advantages of electronics for the communication and manipulation of information were not so readily matched when it came to the retention and storage of information. However, the original difficulties, technical and economic, are now rapidly being overhauled and looking to the future it is certain that new techniques, e.g. laser/holography, will bring the performance of input, output, information storage and information retrieval fully in line with the speed and effectiveness of communication and calculation within the computer).

Conceptually there is nothing complicated about the computer memory. It is like a set of cards arranged in a set order (each card has an 'address' written on it) on which numbers can be written or erased as often as one likes. The computer takes in a list of instructions placing each instruction in a particular address. Similarly it takes in data and puts each piece of data in a particular address where it can be found for future use.

In order that the computer may operate at all it must be controlled – there must be a control unit – so that it has 'on its plate' at any one time, the appropriate instructions and data on which it is to operate.

It must also have an arithmetic unit – which would be better called a logical unit – to be able to carry out such logical/mathematical operations as are called for by the various instructions.

It must also have a working area in which to tackle the job on hand. This is normally called an 'accumulator'. One may think of it as a writing pad on which a number is written down and on which other numbers, taken in accordance with the instructions from the store, are written down so that arithmetical or other operations may be performed on them. For example, if the operation to be performed is addition one needs to have two numbers. One will be the number already in the accumulator and another will be a number to be taken from the specific address in the store. We will call the number on the pad, in the accumulator, C (A) and the number to be taken from address N, C (N).

The computer may have different grades of storage. Some storage will be very quickly accessible and other storage may take relatively much longer to contact; a 'backing store'. (Big savings may be effected in the cost of constructing the computer by having some information stored in a manner that requires a longer access time. In this way the storage capacity may be increased without unreasonable increases in construction costs).

Finally, of course, the computer must have facilities with which to 'output' results. This output may be in the form of a binary code that can then, if necessary, be translated into the form required by the user, by means of peripheral apparatus outside the computer. The most used form of output is print at 500/1000 lines a minute; but many other forms, including visual display, are available.

Software: Computer Machine Code

The form of instructions will vary from computer to computer. But typically each instruction is composed of two parts, (1) a number that specifies the function to be performed and (2) a number that gives the address of the piece of data to be used in carrying out this instruction or, possibly, a further specification of the function. For example, for the Elliott 803 the instruction 30 5 would mean perform function No.30, which is 'Delete the number on the working pad, (the accumulator), C(A) and put in its place C(5)' – that is, the number to be found in address No.5.

If the instruction read 55 4 that would mean perform function No.55, but this is in fact a function that needs further specification. It is an instruction to double the number in the accumulator, C(A), as many times as the programmer specifies. The second number must be filled in by the programmer to say how many times it is to be doubled. For example, if the number 3 was in the accumulator the instruction 55 4 would mean double the number in the accumulator four times. Starting with 3 in the accumulator one would get 3, 6, 12, 24, 48. So the effect of this instruction would be not to bring any new number into the accumulator from outside but to change it from 3 to 48.

Like the 'abstract machine' considered above, the computer operates in well-defined time intervals. As each instruction is obeyed there will be a number on the working pad – the accumulator C(A) – and an operation will be performed on this number or, more usually on this number in conjunction with one number taken from the address specified in the instruction. As the calculation proceeds, the number in the working area, i.e. the accumulator, will be constantly changing, but it will also be useful to have some storage space in the computer in which to put interim results temporarily while going on with other parts of the calculation.

Part of the storage space will, of course, be used for the program itself, i.e. for the instructions. These will be carried out in sequence. That is, as soon as one instruction has been completed the computer will go on to carry out the next one, *unless* the instruction being carried out tells it to jump, either unconditionally or conditionally on some test (e.g. if the number in the accumulator is negative), to some other instruction specified in the jump instruction. In order that this important operation of jumping may be carried out, of course, each of the instructions themselves must have specified addresses.

The jump instruction is of crucial importance. It is used in 'the loop' referred to above, i.e. by means of it the computer can be made to repeat a particular operation many times over. Such 'iterative processes' have extensive and important applications. The jump instruction also makes it possible to use 'sub-routines'; that is, once some process has been programmed (e.g, turn miles into feet) these instructions can be used again and again by jumping to them and back again to other instructions as required.

Software: High-Level Languages

It is now possible to see how programming extends the power of the computer as a machine for carrying out routines. The hardware of the computer, that is the built-in circuits and integrated groups of circuits, performs certain elementary logical or mathematical operations. (With 'large-scale integration' and other developments in the production and design of electronic components it may be that the hardware will in the future do much more than it does at present. That is, computers may be produced with built-in circuits for performing quite complicated routines). Programming determines a sequence of operations built up out of the elementary operations simulated by the electronic hardware. Since, with the aid of these elementary operations, any mathematical calculation, any algorithmic routine can be performed, programming generates a potentially limitless extension in the power of the machine.

What is more, once a particular operation, calculation or routine, has been programmed, it can be used again whenever that same routine is called for. New routines can by built up. New structures are created in which other routines, already programmed, form 'building blocks'. This may be done by going from one program to another; the output of one program may be used as input to another program and so a whole series of routines may be linked together. Or bits of programs already written can be copied and used again as part of new programs.

From what has already been said the importance of *sub-routines* will be clear. A sub-routine is a program within a program. Any particular routine can be re-used. All the programmer has to do is to jump to the number of the first instruction in the group of instructions used previously to carry out this routine.

To program is to extend the power of the computer almost without limit. The chain of connections from which this extensible power derives is: (a) any routine for processing information may be built up from elementary logical operations, (b) the basis of all systems for controlling external environment is information processing, (c) programs can be used to write programs.

In view of (c) one has the concept of computer languages at different levels. The computer manufacturers sell not only the hardware but also sets of programs to go with the hardware, such as 'assemblers' and 'compilers'. Compilers are programs that translate more simple and convenient languages into the machine codes to which the computer directly responds. The most generally used so called 'high-level' languages are ALGOL, FORTRAN, and COBOL. These languages vary in a number of ways to suit different machines and so none of them is a complete 'lingua franca'.

COBOL instructions use words mainly; ALGOL and FORTRAN use expressions similar to those of mathematics. The following is an example of a very small ALGOL program:

Line number (for reference only)

```
1  BEGIN REAL SUM, X;
2     INTEGER I, N;
3  READ N;
4  SUM : = 0;
5  FOR I: = 1 STEP 1 UNTIL N DO
6     BEGIN READ X;
7        SUM: = SUM + X
8  END;
9  PRINT SUM/N, SQRT (SUM/(N*(N–1)))
10 END;
```

The explanation of this is as follows:–

The words *BEGIN* and *END* serve the same function as brackets. The declaration on lines 1 and 2 tell the computer that the numbers in addresses labelled I and N will always be whole numbers, whereas the numbers in addresses labelled SUM and X will be 'floating point variables' (similar to ordinary decimals or 'real numbers'). READ tells the computer to take in the next item of input and place it in the address shown (in this case N).

: = means give to address named on the left the value shown on the right.

A *STEP* B *UNTIL* C *DO* . . . means increase the number A by steps of B until C is reached and for each value perform the instructions given following *DO*.

PRINT means 'print out'.

/ means 'divide by'.

* means 'multiply by'.

SQRT means 'find the square root of'.

To simplify understanding and to help memory the address can be given names such as SUM; but certain words are reserved for the computer and may not be used as 'names' by the programmers; these reserved words are italicised.

To show what the program does we may make a table showing the contents of the addresses at each stage, assuming the INPUT DATA to be the following numbers in the order shown:–

INPUT DATA

4

7

5

1

3

Content of Addresses as Program is Executed

LINE ON WHICH APPEARS THE INSTRUCTION THAT IS BEING OBEYED		SUM	X	I	N
Line 3					4
Line 4		0			4
Line 5		0		1	4
Line 6		0	7	1	4
Line 7		7	7	1	4
Line 5		7	7	2	4
Line 6		7	5	2	4
Line 7		12	5	2	4
Line 5		12	5	3	4
Line 6		12	1	3	4
Line 7		13	1	3	4
Line 5		13	1	4	4
Line 6		13	3	4	4
Line 7		16	3	4	4
Line 9	(1)	Here the computer divides N (= 4) into SUM (= 16) Output 4.000			
	(2)	Here the computer takes the square root of 16 divided by N(N –1) which in the example is 4 x 3 Output 1.154			

The input data must be arranged in the right order to fit the program. Here the first number gives the number of items (in this case four) and the following numbers give the series to be processed (in this case 7, 5, 1, 3): The program calculates (1) the mean and (2) $\sqrt{\frac{\text{mean}}{N-1}}$. Once written the program may be used for any other series supplied as input.

Since ALGOL is a 'high-level language' the instruction SQRT is enough to obtain the square root. The compiler will have prepared sub-routines in computer machine code to calculate square roots; and the four letters SQRT written in ALGOL will be a sufficient instruction when translated by the compiler into machine code to call in the sub-routine for finding the square root.

Computing is still in a stage of clumsy primitiveness. There is a multiplicity of different computers and different computer languages. Each type of computer has differences and peculiarities as to size of store, speed of operation, types of backing store available, peripherals available for input and output and so forth. Most of these differences in computers imply knowledge of different programming instructions and varying devices in their use. All this makes for difficulty and complication. The writing of any new program is hard work, since any one mistake may cause the program to fail. But once a particular routine has been programmed it is a piece of work that may be taken over and used by others. So gradually libraries of programs and a store of experience will enable computer users to tackle more and more difficult problems more speedily, by placing their feet on ground already won by their predecessors.

This ability to program, to write and use sub-routines, to link program to program, and to use already written programs over and over again, gives the digital computer immense power. It compensates for all the tedious difficulties in the first place of writing down the routines as a faultless set of instructions. In time the difficulties of programming new routines may be reduced, but today, despite the fact that one single error will usually cause a program to fail, the advantages of using a computer are startling. As the stock of written programs increases (since any program can easily be reproduced), computer applications will become simpler.

For the most part computer users have their own individual computers or use of a variety of fairly small bureaux. Really effective pooling of knowledge and resources has yet to be achieved. It is probable that effective use of computing facilities will require the establishment of 'computer grids', analogous to electricity supply grids, not so much because they will be linked physically as a system of generating stations and transformers is linked (though it may well be that sources of computing power may be so linked) as because the expertise and experience for handling particular types of problems will be pooled. In this way a wide range of equipment will be available for flexible adaptation to the variety of problems that the system is asked to tackle.

At present actual operations within the computer are technically far in advance of the operations which produce input and output data. However, big advances may be expected in this field in the near future. There remains the even greater problem of collecting data, storing it and getting it into computer-readable form. Certainly the rapidly advancing technologies of the electronics industry have much to offer here. Difficulties, however, lie in the socio-economic system itself and these are the subject of the next part of the book. Greater co-ordination and a more widely spread common understanding of how the facilities of the computer might be used are clearly required. Not, however, until there is better agreement on what is to be done can the problems for the electronics engineers be properly framed. Once the problems are framed it is quite certain that very simple and rapid methods will be found for collecting most of the basic data required as computer input.

Only passing reference has been made so far to 'analogue computers'. These are computers that calculate results by imitating, mechanically or electrically, the way in which systems or processes behave. Computation in this way may be very valuable, particularly as it can give immediately meaningful visual results. In general analogue computers cannot work to such fine degrees of accuracy as digital computers and by their very nature they must be built for a special purpose. They cannot be taken for this reason as typifying the essential features of the technological revolution; but they represent rather an important aspect of the many-sided applications of electronic techniques in association with general-purpose automata. It is now time to turn to consider the impact of the general-purpose automata that have been described, and their significance in relation to the social economic system.

Chapter III

The Technology of Productivity in a Market Economy

The Social Impact of Technology

The electronic digital computer and conceptual thinking on the theory of machines, models, systems analysis, cybernetics, information theory and the new trends in mathematical thinking have been dealt with above as a prelude to discussion of technological change. We must examine, as well as changes in technology, changes in social behaviour interacting with changes in technology. As a starting point I look at changes that are actually taking place in the production process. This may be no more than a starting point; technology itself interacts with and is shaped by the social and economic structure in and by which it is developed. Moreover unrealised potentials – whether they act positively or negatively – may be dynamic factors in social change.

The starting point, however, remains the actual production process. Technical change here makes headway by immediately driving into and disturbing the older order of things. New advances are made in the natural sciences. New techniques become available. Production is re-organised. The pre-existing pattern of working life is radically altered as a result. At the same time men and women, particularly those employed in industry or sciences related to industry, become aware of new possibilities and begin to link to their political and economic struggles demands for far-reaching social reorganisation. The visions that men have of the incongruity between the possible and the actual themselves become a force making for change. But to quote the words of Frederick Engels:

> " . . . the final causes of all social changes and political revolutions are to be sought, not in men's brains, not in man's better insight into eternal truth and justice, but in changes in the modes of production and exchange. They are to be sought, not in the *philosophy*, but in the *economics* of each particular epoch. The growing perception that existing social institutions are unreasonable and unjust; that reason has become unreason, and right wrong, is only proof that in the modes of production and exchange changes have silently taken place with which the social order, adapted to earlier economic conditions, is no longer in keeping. From this it also follows that the means of

> getting rid of the incongruities that have been brought to light must also be present, in a more or less developed condition, within the changed modes of production themselves. These means are not to be *invented,* spun out of the head, but *discovered* with the aid of the head in the existing material facts of production."[1]

The computer has been selected in this book as the embodiment of a new stage in technological evolution. Or it might be more accurate to say, it embodies a technological revolution. To substantiate such a claim one must show that it alters the production process in general – not just for one or two particular products, but for all or almost all products. Its analogue, as was suggested earlier, would be the machine in the industrial revolution and I shall later refer again to the economic meaning of machine production. In essence, however, what the machine then did was to replace the tools and operations of the hand craftsman that had become more and more narrowly specialised as the labour of production was more and more finely divided in manufacture.

The word 'manufacture' is here used to describe a stage in the evolution of economic society. It was one of the important technical changes facilitating the emergence of capitalist society. By 'capitalism' I mean a mode of production in which private owners of capital and means of production employ workers for wages to produce commodities for sale in the market, the object and motivating force of production being realisation of a profit to accumulate more capital. Emphasis at this point is on the *economic* aspects of capitalism, but it is important not to forget that it is also a *cultural* formation of society with its particular values, customs and methods for doing things. The technical significance of manufacture consisted almost entirely in the organisation of production, that is, in the division of labour. In manufacture the craftsmen were brought together under one roof to make a productive team in which the job as a whole was broken down into a number of separate processes assigned to particular craftsmen. This division of labour defined very precisely a routine which the limbs of each craftsman followed, a routine which later the machine was to replace. The division of labour is not only tremendously important in the production process itself at this stage of economic evolution, but it remains today as an economic factor of paramount social importance, structuring the lives and the day-by-day practicalities of the majority of people in the community. In the fully developed commodity system of today the social process of production is articulated and split up so that each person's labour power becomes just one cog in a vast system external to him as a human being and seemingly beyond his control.

1. *Anti-Duhring*, pp. 369-70, Lawrence and Wishart, London, 1955.

Human experience is fragmented and occupations are defined in terms of their saleability in the labour market.

If we go back to the industrial revolution in Britain at the end of the eighteenth century, we may see that the machine as a replacement for the routine motions of the craftsman was general in its application. There were machines to spin yarn, machines to weave cloth, machines to shape timber, machines to cut metal, machines to strike hammer blows and so forth.

In all production some co-ordination and control is required. This in turn implies information and its processing. It implies well-defined rules and routines for operating machines and for linking and co-ordinating the output of one machine to supply the intake to another. These routines of brainwork are general to the production process and it is in this area in particular that the computer enters in to take over work for which man in the past has relied mainly on his own unaided powers.

The most conspicuous form of the new technical revolution of today is automation. Man's intuition was quick to recognise its revolutionary implications. However, even within the factory or at the point of production the forms of technical change are considerably wider than what is described as automation. Joan Woodward in an important survey of industrial organisation published in 1965[1] spoke of changes of two main kinds;

> "Those resulting from a radical rethinking of the manufacturing operations, the outcome being a more formal structuring of the decision-making process, and those that were entirely technical. Many but not all of the latter were associated with one of the three main streams of engineering progress covered by the term 'automation'."

The three types of automation to which she refers are the expansion of mechanisation by transfer devices, techniques of automatic control over manufacturing process, and processing of technical and business information by electronic digital computer. The routines of mechanisation to which the computer applies are in the first instance the routines of assembly and linking of operation to operation. The application of computer control to the assembly of products is as yet in its infancy; but development of this potential could be of far-reaching industrial significance. Automatic control may be over an individual machine (as for example numerical control or, indeed, the cards that controlled the Jacquard loom), or it may be over a whole process as in a chemical plant or a steel works. Finally there is the routine of the clerk eminently suited, in the soulless organisation of large offices, for being taken over by computer.

1. *Industrial Organisation: Theory and Practice.* Oxford University Press.

From the days when the American industrialist, F.W. Taylor (of whom more below) at the end of the last century had the vision of a factory in which no one man for any one moment stood idle, human work has been more and more ruthlessly organised as a mere appendage of the supremely valuable machines. But the very act of doing this defined the routine that the computer is so well adapted to take over. This, in itself, almost certainly implies a rapid fall in the number of men and women involved in the main economic processes.

At the same time, as Joan Woodward noted in her survey, new ideas about the co-ordination and management of work viewed as a whole have been developing. The technical changes were not only in the office or on the shop floor, but also in management science. All sorts of new mathematical techniques and methods of 'the systems approach' began to be adopted. These new methods clearly require more information and more analysis of information for advisers to build models with and thus to extract relevant measurements as a guide to management policy. Without the support of the computer it is hardly conceivable that these more sophisticated methods could compete against the intuitive judgments of the manager of earlier times. (The expression 'management science' should not be taken too literally; a manager may use advanced theory and techniques but this does not mean that the function he performs or the aims he pursues are scientifically objective in the sense of being independent of the economic interests that he, as manager, represents).

Natural science has become increasingly important in production processes. Trial and error and the rag-bag of hard-won experience are giving way to the guidance of scientists, laboratory experimentation and testing. Natural science, of course, has much directly to contribute to the productive process on many fronts quite independently of the computer, but the computer was a tool of which the scientist most readily and first took advantage. It enlarged his powers and extended his ability to call in and process information.

It may be that in time men may come to call the technological revolution, at whose threshold we stand, the 'scientific revolution'. The outlook of science and the methods of science, which have been developing in the womb of human society over the centuries, may become the commonsense of the future, the form in which man's relationship to his environment finds its natural expression. This may be the ultimate direction of change, but its midwife, in the present time, is undoubtedly the computer as a means of information processing outside the human brain. In those areas where the computer can imitate the human brain it acts with greater speed, it can handle quite massive quantities of data, and it can follow through routines of very great complexity. The scientific work underlying this information handling revolution of course embraces more than the computer. A crucial turning point came with the discovery of the electron by J.J. Thompson in 1897, at the Cavendish Laboratory in Cambridge. From this followed deeper understanding and control over the characteristics of the electron, opening the way to the science of electronics and its industrial application. The thermionic valve was invented by Ambrose Fleming of University College in London, and patented in 1904. In 1948 the transistor, with properties in practical use far superior to the valve, appeared upon the scene and since then numerous and very rapid advances have been made in the science and the application of electronics, especially in all the various forms of telecommunications which include radio, T.V., radar and telemetry.[1]

The social impact of these advances is evidently enormous in extending and shaping our awareness of the world and, in association with the computer, in extending our power to control our world. For example, this means that what is now mainly a broadcast receiving service for the mass of the population to hear and see events all over the world, is potentially also a broadcast transmitting service by which individuals and groups of individuals acting together could bring their influence to bear upon events in the world. A number of questions about 'feedback' *from* people *to* social organisations will be taken up in the last part of this book. Here we need only to notice some of the new concepts to which scientists are opening a way and some of the new possibilities for 'systems' in which individuals act.

Although it is the science and industry of electronics that provides the indispensable foundation for the current technological revolution, the computer is the instrument through which man's knowledge of and power to control the electron makes its impact upon the production processes and socio-economic life generally. The computer is an instrument that can, as we have seen, perform the following functions:–

1. it can receive information and issue *control* signals in compliance with any well-defined routine,
2. it is capable of handling and storing and analysing *massive* quantities of data; but there is a third function –
3. it can operate in 'real time', that is, it can receive information, interpret the changed situations that this information implies are *about* to occur, and take correcting action *before* they occur.

The significance of these capabilities of the computer may perhaps become clearer if they are considered in connection with the body of ideas about the interacting elements of organisms, that has grown up

1. For a clear and comprehensive review see *The Electronic Revolution,* S. Handel Penguin Books, 1967.

simultaneously with the computer under the general name of cybernetics. In the introduction to the essays Wiener published in 1949 under this title he wrote: "It has long been clear to me that the modern ultra rapid computing machine was in principle an ideal central nervous system to an apparatus for automatic control; and that its input and output need not be in the form of numbers or diagrams but might very well be, respectively, the readings of artificial sense organs, such as photo-electric cells or thermometers, and the performance of motors or solenoids. With the aid of strain gauges or similar agencies to read the performance of these motor organs and to report, to 'feed back', to the central control system as an artificial kinesthetic sense, we are already in a position to construct artificial machines of almost any degree of elaborateness of performance."[1]

The computer thus becomes the instrument for receiving information, analysing it and determining a course of action appropriate to this information. It can handle large quantities of information; it can store this information over time, it can process it very quickly, and it can give signals to cause apparatus to react immediately to whatever new situation the incoming data indicates, but it can do more than this. The computer makes possible not only the far more rapid and complicated control of systems, organisms etc., as they exist in nature or as men have created them but it makes possible also the creating of models to represent and simulate such systems and so to experiment with them, in order to see what happens under a variety of different circumstances. A human body, indeed any living creature, is a homeostatic system; that is, it keeps itself in the same state by constantly adjusting itself appropriately to changes in its surrounding conditions. It is now coming to be understood that there are some common principles in the interactions between component elements of an organism and between the organism as a whole and its environment, whether the organism be a living animal, a machine or a collective activity of men in society. The technology of electronics and the computer in particular is providing us with new powers of very far-reaching social significance for understanding and controlling systems.

Technological Revolution in the Forces of Production

We return now to the economic system on which technology impinges. This is dominated by productive enterprises which, to produce goods, require productive forces, falling basically into three categories:–

A. The tools and equipment with which an enterprise works (extending

1. *Cybernetics,* Norbert Wiener, M.I.T. Press, 1965.

equipment very widely to include not only machines and the motive power by which they are driven, but also the buildings in which the whole plant, the complex of productive instruments, stands).

B. The materials on which the activity of production is carried out.

C. Human labour, skills, knowledge, strength etc., – used to control the inanimate and non-human means of production so as to achieve the desired objectives of the production process – its subdivisions reflecting such division of labour as the tools and machines and the social structure dictate.

In capitalist society production is organised within separate 'enterprises', that is socio-economic organisms that function as a single unit comprising a labour force (of various skills) working on objects, generally described as material, with tools, that is, any equipment used repeatedly in the transformation of the material object of work.

A technological revolution expresses a relationship between science and society. What goes on within a science may be revolutionary for the work and understanding of the scientists within that field of work, without being revolutionary in the socio-economic sense. Technological revolution implies changes in techniques and in scientific knowledge that have impact on economic and on social life (the latter generally being the consequence of the former). The agricultural revolution, by which men husbanded animals and cultivated fields, was such a revolution, but occurring some eight to ten millennia ago is too remotely in the past to help our present understanding greatly. However, the industrial revolution is of great relevance occurring as it did in the Eighteenth and early Nineteenth Centuries when the market system of today was in process of development.

The foundations of modern science were laid in the Sixteenth Century (Leonardo da Vinci, Copernicus, Tycho Brahe), and Seventeenth Century (Bacon, Descartes, Locke, Galileo, Newton, The Royal Society, the mathematics of differential calculus). The Eighteenth Century saw the emergence from these foundations of important technical applications. It should be noted, however, that the influence of science in the industrial revolution was far more indirect and remote than it is today; it generated a cultural climate within which practical experimentation and ingenuity, rather than scientific analysis, discovered ways of developing machinery, steam-power, and such like. There was the smelting of iron from coke by Darby, Newcomen's steam engine, Hargreaves', Crompton's and Arkwright's inventions of machinery for cotton spinning, Watt's rotary engine and so forth. There were also the first beginnings of electrical science (Hauksbee's frictional electricity and Franklin's lightning conductor and the concepts of positive and negative electricity). All this was accompanied by new advances in economic theory (Adam Smith) and far-reaching socio-economic changes.

This development of machinery in the Eighteenth Century coincided with a socio-economic situation ripe for its utilisation. It coincided, in brief, with the emergence of capitalism. Ownership of land ceased to be the determinant of economic power; dominance passed to the owner of capital, that is of money wealth turned to ownership of financial institutions and factories which, by expanding their output of products, hastened accumulation of money. The capitalist market system was developing simultaneously with the new science and the new philosophy. Manufacture in the form of work divided up between many specialised skills (but still unsupported by machinery) was developing. Merchants were eager to supply growing markets. New methods in agriculture accompanied the dispossession of peasants of their lands. At the same time those seeking to undertake production and those seeking employment appeared in greater numbers; men ceased to be so firmly tied by the restraints of guilds and what remained of feudal rights. Science and the new knowledge it gave, changing social relations, changing economic relations all combined to speed the development and economic application of machinery in many fields.

With the development of capitalism the centre of gravity of political and economic power shifted, but it was still a class system, a social structure in which a surplus produced by the labour of the many sustained the power and position of a few; as such it did not differ from other forms of class society that it superseded. However, one altogether new feature entered economic relations, in that this new system was able constantly and rapidly to increase output; indeed its essential dynamic was concentrated on increasing the *relative* excess product, the surplus by which the total product exceeded the subsistance of the producers.

The machine of the industrial revolution was not just a tool or instrument like a powered tool we might use today, as we shall see when we turn to examine the nature of the machine in the next section. The simple economics of the situation was that the machine did the work of the skilled craftsman far more cheaply and far more rapidly. Extraction of the coal and the iron to supply the materials for the machine was already being developed. There were markets to be won overseas (where industry had not developed) for the enlarged supply of goods that the machines produced; and the new relations of production and distribution that the machine brought into being themselves enlarged the market at home. The wages of those who worked the machines, of those who produced the machines, themselves enlarged the demand on the market. The expansion of trade involved more and more people in the operations of trade, in the supply of materials to international markets instead of for local use, in return creating an international demand for the products of the machine. The economic impact of the new technique of production – machines replacing the skills of the craftsman – sent a series of shock waves through the economic system of the whole world bringing changes – different in form and character from place to place – but, by the end of the Nineteenth Century, changes everywhere in every corner of the globe.

The machine broke up, with appalling hardship in many cases, the old manner of life of the handcraftsman. For the future the typical seat of production was to be the factory in large industrial complexes near to coal and iron and means of transportation, in most cases by water. With the industrial revolution there was a rapid increase in population and the formation of what Marx called the proletariat, that is large numbers of people in the towns dependent for their existence on the sale of their labour power for wages. The changes of the industrial revolution for many meant ruin; but for others, for those who invested in the new methods of production, for those who benefited from the expanding trade, for the capitalist who had the capital with which to support the new enterprises, and for the bankers and financiers who gathered together and parcelled out the funds that industry and trade needed, the rapidly changing forces of the industrial revolution brought immense wealth. Men's attitude and outlook on life changed. The permanence and stability of the past was everywhere being undermined, trade and profit carried men to distant parts of the world and linked together what were once isolated communities. Money meant power and new political forces emerged. Machines for killing provided new means of domination of man over man. The machine changed the structure of economic life and the changing structure of economic life implied gigantic social and political changes. The fact of social transformation is beyond dispute. What we need to look at is *how*, in terms of our model of the economic system, the new techniques contributed to changed economic and social relationships.

Productivity And The Division of Labour

In opening up the connection between technology and the market society, the key is *productivity*. In this concept the technical is combined with the socio-economic.

There has been a good deal of arid controversy amongst economists about the definition of productivity and how to measure it.[1] In Salter's view 'only one type of productivity concept is measurable', this is output per unit of input and as a rule the input in which one is

1. A useful summary is to be found in *Productivity and Technical Change* by W.E.G. Salter, C.U.P., 1960, p.2, *et. seq.*

interested is labour. Output is measured by an appropriate index of volume and input in 'man hours, which may be divided into categories'. 'Output divided by man hours yields a measure of output per man hour'.

One of the examples quoted by Salter is bricks where in the U.K. in 1947 production per hour ranged from 540 in the least efficient plants to 2,120 in the most efficient plants, the mean being 1,360. In the industry as a whole the same number of bricks are made in Britain today as in 1937 but with less than two-thirds of the labour. Calculations of productivity are quite simply made by dividing quantity produced by labour time spent in production. The concept of productivity in this sense is straightforward but its meaning needs to be thought about; for example, productive labour time in a particular industry expresses the labour input at one stage of production only. It takes no account of the labour that has already gone into the production of the machines used or into raw materials or components.

The definition of productivity given by Marx is as follows: 'By increase in the productiveness of labour, we mean, generally, an alteration in the labour-process, of such a kind as to shorten the labour-time socially necessary for the production of a commodity, and to endow a given quantity of labour with the power of producing a greater quantity of use value.[1] Marx's *Capital* (Part IV, chapters 12 to 15 inclusive) gives what is still the most valuable theoretical analysis of the industrial revolution. Numerous descriptive accounts of the industrial revolution are available, but Marx's treatment, which is both theoretical and descriptive, is of particular interest, throwing light as it does on the inner workings of technological change in an economic system viewed as a whole. Marx, (1818-1883), lived through the high tide of the industrial revolution. For information on techniques of production Marx drew heavily on *On the Economy of Machinery and Manufactures* (London 1832) by Charles Babbage, whom we have mentioned as the inventor of the computer.

What was the great change involved in the industrial revolution which was associated with the rise of capitalism? Small-scale peasant agriculture plus independent handicrafts formed the basis of the feudal mode of production and also constituted the main basis of production in the Graeco-Roman world after the dissolution of the primitive communal societies and before the development of slave gangs as a productive force. But the handcraftsman continued to exist alongside the slave economy and also alongside capitalist economy as it developed right up to the present time.

The form of productive organisation within which capitalism first

1. *Capital*, Vol. I, Chapter XII, p. 303 in Allen and Unwin, 1938 edition.

developed was manufacture; that is the organised assembly of crafts, each specialising on a sub-division of the work task. This gave an advantage in productivity for which the technical basis (if one may call it such) was nothing new – namely, co-operation. That men working together can do things that they cannot do on their own is as old, at least, as the Pyramids. Also through trade there is a sort of co-operation. Through trade the skills and facilities of some are combined with the skills and facilities of others. Economic and social relations are established between widely separated peoples. New requirements and exchange of skills have an impact on the productive process.

Manufacture contrasts with the 'putting out system', the merchant, for example, putting out materials, or simply orders for goods, to craftsmen located apart from one another in a number of villages. Manufacture by contrast was a bringing together of craftsmen in one place. Marx quotes the case of 'wheelwrights, harness makers, tailors, locksmiths, upholsterers, turners, fringe makers, glaziers, painters, polishers, guilders, etc.,' coming together to make carriages by the combination of their separate skills. In other cases craftsmen making the same product would work together in one place, each on his own carrying through all the processes required to make his product.

With time obviously the nature of the productive activities in the 'manufactories' would change. A wheelwright would become, for example, a specialist in making carriage wheels and an upholsterer a specialist in upholstering the seats of carriages. In other cases the process of production would be divided up into component stages, and specialised skills and tools would be developed to tackle each process more effectively or more rapidly. Wire for the production of needles passed successfully through the hands of between seventy and ninety detail workmen, each working a separate machine, in the classic example given by Adam Smith at the beginning of *The Wealth of Nations.*

The motive force behind these changes was increased productivity and the motive force behind the increase in productivity was the desire to reduce costs, thereby putting the capitalist in a far stronger position to make profits from his undertaking. Since there were many capitalists no one could increase his profit by raising his price against the others. But if the capitalist cut costs and could still command the same price in the market, clearly he had that much the more profit. If competition in the market made it difficult to maintain prices then he could reduce prices, take sales away from his competitors and still be left with a margin of profit on each commodity sold. If he did not keep his costs down and make a profit to plough back into new production he could soon be out of business.

As the capitalist system of production developed, production became more social in a double sense: interdependence through the market became greater, there was social division of labour, and within each productive unit there was a finer division of labour. There also emerged a new activity of special importance, namely that of co-ordinating and managing the interrelated work of the participants in the productive unit in the factory. But there was also a second directing function, namely that of deciding the end products. This was determined by the people who put up the capital to support the undertaking.

So it was that management in the sense of co-ordinating the interrelatedness of the production process within each factory or productive unit came to be mixed up and merged with the directing authority whose central aim was profit, which in turn was governed by the market. That is, the directing authority aimed at selling the product on the market as profitably as possible. The profits would come not only from selling well in the right market, but essentially from keeping down the costs of production. One way to this would be increased productivity but another would be keeping down wages. The inverse relationship between wages and profits inevitably gave management within the capitalist production structure a contradictory relationship with labour. On the one hand, management sought to perform the function of harmonious integration of interrelated factors, but on the other hand, the aims of its operations necessitated the keeping down of costs, and in these the salient element, which management by its action might hope to change, was the wages paid for those very activities that management was striving to co-ordinate as smoothly as possible. This contradiction is, of course, still in evidence. It is the economic foundation of class struggle in capitalist society.

Prior to capitalism productive techniques tended to be highly conservative. Change, of course, there was; but suitable techniques once discovered tended in primitive societies to be preserved as rituals or, later, by force of social custom. In the period of capitalism the cultural superstructure and economic incentives of competition in expanding markets favoured technical change and indeed technical change of hitherto unparalleled rapidity occurred. The new cultural outlooks of science encouraged men to look for the reasons, the principles behind techniques that proved successful. 'Newton's contribution', wrote J.D. Bernal[1] 'lay in finding the mathematical method for converting physical principles into quantitatively calculable results confirmable by observation, and conversely to arrive at the physical principles from the observations.' And Bernal adds Newton's atomism was 'in unconscious harmony with the economic and social world of his time (1642-1727)

1. *Science in History,* pp. 340-3.

in which individual enterprise, where each man paid his way, was replacing the fixed hierarchical order of the late classical and feudal period where each man knew his place.'

All these processes were at work *before* the industrial revolution, before the machine had come upon the scene. The machine and new technology were to step up the pace. The division of labour had narrowly defined certain specialised productive processes, whilst these were still being carried out by the skills and muscles of worker-craftsmen. With the specialisation of skills went also specialisation of tools. The scene was being set for the machine to take over.

The Economic Significance of the Machine

To recapitulate, prior to the industrial revolution there was a considerable and important preparatory period. In it the socio-economic soil was made ready for industrialisation. Important factors were the accumulation of capital, the growth of the market, freedom from restraints of feudalism in labour and land; at the same time changes had been going on, in particular in the division of labour, which defined very precisely the problems that the machine makers were to solve. Processes of production were broken up into particular specialised routines. This was the essence of the matter. Once the machine, powered by steam and later electricity, replaced a particular craft skill it could do what no individual men or hosts of men in combination could ever do. But steam and the new uses of iron and steel were secondary and the machine primary. The technical ideas central to the form that the new machines took were quite old and long preceded the industrial revolution; in particular, gears and cog wheels derive, in a very direct way, from the watermill (already known to exist in 85 BC) and the mechanical clock (linked in its origins to the watermill and known in Europe already in the early fourteenth century).

We may start here from Charles Babbage whose studies of machinery Marx incorporated in his own work in *Capital* (Marx *Capital,* Volume 1, Part IV, Chapter 15). Babbage defines a machine as a union of simple instruments set in motion by a single motor. Marx sets this in its framework of economic relations: 'In manufacture, the revolution in the mode of production begins with labour power, in modern industry it begins with the instruments of labour.' Marx goes on 'Our first enquiry then is how the instruments of labour are converted from tools into machines, or what is the difference between a machine and the implements of handicraft?'

Marx identifies three components of developed machinery "the motor mechanisms, the transmitting mechanism, and finally the tool or working machine".

"The machine proper," he concludes, "is therefore a mechanism, that, after being set in motion, performs with its tools the same operations that were formerly done by the workmen with similar tools. Whether the motive power is derived from man, or from some other machine, makes no difference in this respect. From the moment that the tool proper is taken from man, and fitted into a mechanism, a machine takes the place of a mere implement. The difference strikes one at once, even in those cases where man himself continues to be the prime mover. The number of implements that he himself can use simultaneously is limited by the number of his own natural instruments of production, by the number of his bodily organs. In Germany, they tried at first to make one spinner work two spinning wheels, that is to work simultaneously with both hands and feet. This was too difficult . . . the Jenny, on the other hand, even at its very birth, spun with 12-18 spindles, and the stocking loom knits with many thousand needles at once. The number of tools that a machine can bring into play simultaneously, is from the very first emancipated from the organic limits that hedge in the tools of a handicraftsman."

With the advent of the machine the craftsman as the central figure in the productive process is replaced by the machine minder. This activity may still involve skills but they will be skills of a quite different sort. (In many cases, however, all that is required is an endless and boring repetition of simple operations; machine production as it develops tends more and more to be organised around the machinery, to which the worker becomes an appendage.) The craft of applying the tools to the material is replaced by the task of controlling the way in which the machine works the material. An essential part of the production process has been defined as a routine and machines are constructed to perform this routine. For some operations it is difficult to find a suitable machine and endless repetitions of minute parts of a process are undertaken by human labour pending the invention of a suitable or cheap enough machine. (A human 'assembler' or 'packer' attached to a mechanical conveyor belt is a particular example). In the main the routine of applying tools to the material used in production is taken over by the machine and the productive labour becomes typically labour time spent in co-ordinating, feeding and taking delivery from machines.

Figures can hardly tell the whole story but where they are available they indicate how immense was the change in productivity generated by machine production in the nineteenth and first half of the twentieth century. The following table is taken from *Political Economy* by John Eaton (Lawrence & Wishart 1963):–

TABLE III.1

Textile Output 1819-82

Period	*Production in 1,000 lb.*	*Number of workers*	*Production per worker in lb.*
Spinning			
1819-20	106,500	111,000	968
1880-2	1,329,000	240,000	5,520
Weaving			
1819-20	80,620	250,000	322
1880-2	993,570	246,000	4,039

Table III.1 shows increases in productivity four or five fold between the 1820s and 1880s in cotton spinning and weaving. In more recent times the increases of productivity in other industries have been equally remarkable. The following figures (from W.E.G. Salter's *Productivity and Technical Change*, pp 107 and 164) show increases in productivity in the UK and USA in the second quarter of the twentieth century:–

TABLE III.2 **Changes in Productivity**

	UK (1924-50) *Output per operative (1924 = 100)*		*USA (1923-50)* *Output per manhour (1923 = 100)*
Electricity Generation	372	Electricity	335
Chemicals	236	Rayon and allied products	1,217
Steel tubes	259	Canning and preserving	200
Cement	251	Cement	234
Iron and steel	152	Iron and steel	273
Cotton (spinning and doubling)	133	Cotton goods	203
Median (all industries)	160	Median (all industries)	198

Productivity as an Economic Objective

The concept of productivity we have suggested is fundamental to the understanding of contemporary economic systems. In earlier systems it had no such central importance. (It might be interesting to pursue, though we cannot do so here, the emergence of the concept of productivity in the history of economic ideas. See, for example, the comments already referred to of W. E.G. Salter in his *Productivity and Technical Change* C.U.P., 1960) It may be that productivity will be of no great importance for human society in a not too distance future. But at this moment of time it is very important. The objective of raising productivity is – for better or for worse – central to the economic aims of almost every community in the world. The concept of productivity is also needed as a means of understanding the motive power by which our present economic system is driven.

The concept as we have studied it so far seems simple enough and clear enough; but on a careful examination a number of problems arise. First, why attach to productivity of labour an importance above that of other factors? There are many factors of production – land, machines, materials for example – as well as labour. Why not measure the productivity of other factors of production also? Economic analysis does in fact present a mathematical model (see Mathematical Appendix Note 5) which by assuming all inputs to production with the exception of one to be fixed, calculates a rate of increase in production attributable to this one input.

Two points need to be noted: (1) the productivity of one factor is not independent of the other factors. If a certain amount of capital is given, then under those circumstances the productivity attributable to labour will be of a certain magnitude. If the capital used is different, then the productivity of labour will be different. (2) Formulae such as those given in the mathematical appendix do not correspond to anything that exists in actual economic systems except under most exceptional particular circumstances. Far more typical of reality is a fixed ratio between the amount of labour, the amount of material and the amount of machine time used in a particular productive process, depending upon the technique of production used. There are a number of different possible teachniques and a variety of possible combinations of factors of production. But the possibility of continuous change of any or all of the factors is such a rare phenomenon that one may as well regard it as non-existent.

There are circumstances in economic analysis when it is important to consider the different outputs resulting from different combinations of several factors used in production. So the above type of analysis has its uses; but not for our problem. We are here concerned with the social impact of technology in the production process as a whole. Particular types of production may be constrained by shortages of land or shortages of particular materials taken from nature. For present purposes we can regard these as constraints embedded in the natural circumstances to the changing of which the production process is applied. The productive factor of central interest for the theme we are pursuing is labour; our problem is to understand how changed social relations in production – and hence more generally – are induced by technological changes.

Assume that we know how to measure output. (In fact, this is full of difficulties, some of which are mentioned later.) Also assume, for the time being, that labour is all of one kind and input of labour can be quite simply measured by time. Suppose productivity is to be measured for cotton cloth and that x yards are being produced per worker per day. What does this mean? It certainly does not mean that to produce x yards one day's labour time is sufficient. The statistic from the supplying factory tells only how much additional time has been worked in this factory in transforming the raw materials that it received into the finished cloth to be supplied. Maybe the supplier only carries through the process of finishing and hemming; or maybe he also undertakes the weaving. The actual breakdown of costs working back from the price paid in the shop might be somewhat as follows. One quarter retailer's charges, 10 per cent wholesaler's charges, 65 per cent manufacturer's price, of which 10 per cent is profits and overheads, 5 per cent for finishing, hemming etc., 20 per cent weaving, 10 per cent spinning and 20 per cent raw cotton. The productivity of any one manufacturer means only productivity in one stage of production. Output per worker employed will mean something quite different if the material that the manufacturer buys in has been processed or has not been processed to a more advanced stage. Modern machinery, technical know-how and many other factors will moreover raise productivity, but the provision of these supports to production will, naturally, involve additional costs. By using machinery the weaver, for example, is drawing on work done by others when he buys cotton yard. All the way back down the line to growing the cotton and mining the ore labour time has been put in by others.

One could, of course, go on to enquire, in the case of cotton cloth for example, how much time before the cloth came to the finisher was put in by the weaver and before the cloth came to the weaver how much time by the spinner, how much time spent in the transportation of the raw cotton, in its growing, in the making of the tools and machinery and so forth, until all the labour at all the stages making up the chain of production processes had been accounted for.[1] In addition

1. The concept we are considering and some of the theoretical difficulties in it are presented in Piero Sraffa's treatment of 'dated labour' in his *Production of Commodities by means of Commodities*, C.U.P., 1960.

to theoretical problems there will also be countless practical problems in making such a calculation. The attempt to do so brings one up at once against, for example, the fact that every national economy is no more than one component of a total world economy.

It is, however, possible – without expecting or requiring a high degree of precision – to make some estimate of overall productivity. To do so (1) the volume of output must be measured in some meaningful unit, (2) some estimate must be made of the capital stock at the beginning and end of each period (in the form of fixed capital and in the form of stocks of materials etc.) and (3) some estimate must be made of imports in relation to exports. This gives a measure of the volume of production in a given period of time. This divided by the number of productive workers yields a measure of productivity. There may be some difficulty about estimating volume of output because of price changes, for example, but assuming that this difficulty can be overcome, it is possible to measure, however roughly, the productivity of an economy considered as a whole, but whether such measures are worth much more than what our intuition tells us is doubtful. It is clear that industrially advanced economies – such as those of Western Europe or North America – are able to produce a vast mass of material goods. Many of these goods are of great complexity. From decade to decade productivity has clearly increased, in the sense that a given quantity of goods of approximately the same kind are produced with a smaller and smaller productive labour force.

The measures of productivity that are introduced may be misleading for a number of reasons. There are the difficulties of actually measuring volume of output. There is also the problem of assessing the quality and suitability of output and there is the important question of how the products are distributed between different sectors of the community. Are the communities in which massive quantities of consumer goods are produced necessarily well off? The mere fact that the national product and national productivity are measured has tended to exalt the measures – the Gross National Product (GNP) and National Productivity (GNP divided by numbers employed) – into the central objective and yardstick of economic achievement. What is much more useful, and here the computer enters the picture, is the measurement of the relative productivity of different plants and industries. We shall take this point up in Chapter IV.

Productivity and Profit

There is another angle from which we look at productivity, which we noted briefly above; that is, in relation to the decision making processes of the separate entrepreneurs. By entrepreneur I mean the man in a market economy in charge of the firm or unit of production, who on the one hand engages labour and pays wages and on the other supplies commodities to the market, receives money in exchange and with this renews the production cycle, engages in new investment, pays out dividends to shareholders, and so on.

This aspect of things – that is, productivity seen through the eyes of those who manage individual enterprises or firms – is far more important for our enquiry. The entrepreneur's pursuit of higher productivity is the mainspring of economic change in the market system. In reviewing the course of economic history the generalised concept of overall productivity has some interest; but for the particular firm seeking to maximise profits it is the main lever to success, and as such is so energetically pursued as to become the main mechanism of socio-economic change in a commodity economy.

Profits made in the market by keen bargaining or speculative acumen and luck are always profits made at someone else's expense. In the modern jargon, it is a 'zero-sum game'. The hard bargaining that gains for businessman 'A' x pounds implies for 'B' a loss of x pounds and x - x = 0. We need to look elsewhere for processes capable of changing the economic structure more fundamentally. An entrepreneur runs a business for profit. His profits will come from his ability to sell what is produced for more than he has paid out on production. If profits made at someone else's expense are ruled out (for example, by selling products at abnormally high prices or buying materials at unusually low prices) what means of increasing profits are there? If an employer can keep down the wages, he will save costs and increase profits. It is well known that employers try hard to keep wages down and have done so throughout the whole history of the market system. But as a worker has to live there is a physical limit to depression of wages. And in most societies a level of wages regarded as 'fair' becomes established, putting employers more or less on a par in what they pay for their labour. The only remaining strategy for reducing costs is therefore that of increasing labour productivity.

By definition the technological changes that we are interested in are those that affect the production process. The production process in its essence is the application, on a social scale, of man's power to control the natural world. Man uses his powers to grow food, make clothes, provide shelter and to provide scope and freedom to live, each man according to his own vision. In the market system a very simple mathematical model gives the main essentials of the production process, i.e. $W = f(T)$. This states that the output W is a function of time (T) spent in productive labour. Assume we have solved the problem of measuring the volume of output and that productive labour has been reduced to a homogeneous form; that is, so much of any one man's labour can be expressed as equivalent to so much of any other's measured in time. For the entrepreneur (e), $W = f_e (M,P,T)$, meaning that his output is a function of the material M, the plant P, and the labour time T. (I am using f with subscript e, f_e, to indicate the particular functional relationship that interests the entrepreneur.) If p_1 is the price at which he sells each unit of his output, p_2 the price he pays for his materials, p_3 the price he pays for his plant and p_4 the price he pays his workers in wages, then his profit is $Wp_1 - (Mp_2 + Pp_3 + Tp_4)$.

If (a) we leave aside gains and losses in the market that change the distribution of income but not the total to be distributed and (b) exclude two particular forms of (a), namely changes in wages and price advantages due to monopoly, then changes in profit can only be due to changes in productivity.

Of course not all fixed plant is used in one production cycle. However, every manager has his own means of estimating to what extent fixed plant is 'consumed' during any production period. (Depreciation is designed to represent this; in some cases rental charges and other devices may be used also). Having allocated part of the cost of plant and machinery attributable to each batch and having paid for raw material, the entrepreneur must deduct these costs from receipts for sales to arrive at receipts attributable to the production processes carried out in his factory, his 'net product'. From this surplus over and above what he has paid for the products of others, wages of the workers engaged on his own production, must be deducted, before he can arrive at his profits. If labour productivity has been increased; that is, if workers employed to produce each batch of products are reduced, total wage payments per unit of product sold will decrease and profits increase. The surplus going to profits as an absolute amount and relative to wages, may increase at the same time as wages increase, if there is a sufficiently great increase in labour productivity.

The search for increased labour productivity is thus the driving force in production for profit. It is important to notice here that we are excluding the profits of monopolists who can avoid the pressures of competition by controlling sources of capital or by obtaining protected markets. It must also be clear that no moral judgment is being passed concerning the entrepreneur's search for profit. He is driven by the nature of the system in which he operates to do this or be defeated by his competitors. If he merely avoids incurring losses but makes no profit, he will have no resources for new investment in new equipment with which to increase productivity and lower unit costs and he will be unable to compete against others who have.

Increasing productivity is the one sure road for the entrepreneur to expand profits in the sense that he is not just 'robbing Peter to pay Paul' or enjoying the fruits of some temporary good fortune. But all the same the road to better productive techniques is a stony and treacherous one. First attempts at innovation tend to be costly failures. Any entrepreneur who has the slightest excuse for not following it will be tempted to stick doggedly to his old routines. It is also very obvious that anyone with capital who can become one of those privileged few who operate the financial apparatus of the market system will find money-making there a lot more sure and easy than it is in the field of production. However, the law in finance is 'to him that hath shall be given'; the finance house with far-reaching connections and big capital can do more for its customers, and its sheer size makes collapse less likely. Finance however lives on borrowed light; the basic strength of an economy is in production. Financiers put their money where production prospers; so again we come back to the fact that the ultimate motive force of a market economy is increased productivity. In the last analysis the success of the individual enterprise depends upon ability to raise productivity.

Technical Change and the Social Structure of Capitalism

We have seen that inside a system based upon private capital accumulation the forces acting in support of new, that is improved, production techniques are very strong. But they meet many social and economic frictions that delay their action, and to some extent distort them. Within the capitalist market system the competition of many entrepreneurs was most effective in encouraging technical change. The freedom of the market established itself against the restrictions and economic traditionalism of feudal society because, ideologically, it seemed to offer what the most enlightened spirits wanted: freedom to use man's growing command over nature for the good of man; and because, economically, the new methods put growing power into the hands of the new people who were developing the new forces. As capital was accumulated and the owners of capital became free to employ whom they wanted, where they wanted, on what they wanted, methods that increased productivity were bound to prevail. However, throughout the history of the market system the way for the innovator has never been easy.

Innovation means introducing new methods. New methods are untried methods. What is conceptually sound will have to overcome a string of practical difficulties that cannot be foreseen. A good idea will not become a profitable idea until the practicalities of application have been sorted out; and perhaps not even then if it conflicts with the full exploitation of existing plant.

Invariably the capitalists with the big resources are in the more favourable position. They can afford some experimental failures; even better they can wait and watch others fail, coming in when the others are running short of funds but in sight of a solution. At that stage the heavy investment of capital, which in the nature of things cannot begin to yield profitable returns for some while, will be much less risky.

There is no doubt that the large companies are responsible for most of the expenditure on Research and Development. The twenty largest firms in the USA, UK, France and Italy accounted for a half of all such expenditure in 1963-4. But there is much evidence (and some of it from those who are advocates of the old-fashioned competitive market like Professor J. Jewkes, cf *The Sources of Innovation,* 1958) that most new inventions come from the small companies even though they are made into a commercially viable product by the giants. Thus 'Terylene', says Jewkes, 'was invented in a laboratory running on a budget of £20,000 p.a. in 1940. £4m. was spent on pilot plant development and £15m. on new plant for the first major commercial development'. It is in ways such as these that technology and the structure of capitalism interact and conflict.

Once a new plant has been installed and is operating smoothly and profitably, its owner will, very naturally, abhor the idea of further innovation. In the competition between different productive techniques there will tend, therefore, to be a certain leapfrogging, as those who successfully go over to new techniques suddenly overhaul those who were in the lead before.

The man with the new technique will be able to produce the same product as others in the industry with lower costs. This gives him the two major advantages of (1) making a bigger profit on every unit that he sells and (2), when the market gets difficult, winning customers from his competitors by reducing prices whilst still making some profit on every unit that he sells. Generally, the larger the scale of production on a particular plant the lower the unit cost and, for many new techniques, relatively higher expenditure on fixed capital means that unit costs drop quite sharply up to the point where plant is being used to the fullest possible extent. (Because high-capacity usage of mass production plants, broadly referred to as 'economies of scale', reduces cost, it is rather generally assumed that modern technology necessitates ever-larger giant industrial organisations. In fact this is not so. Employment is individual plants does not increase but more generally decreases with the introduction of more advanced techniques. The size of firms increases, but this is related to market power and not to scale economies. This question is further discussed in Chapter IV.)

Each producer is anxious to get larger markets. This gives a great impetus to the extension of sales by leading producers going outside the home market and selling throughout the world. The need for large markets, the need for big reserves of capital, from which to support innovation, to buy the successes of others and to weather bad times, strongly favour greater and greater concentrations of wealth: 'To him that hath shall be given'. In a market system innumerable small firms continue in existence, some of their number going broke, new firms appearing ever hopefully. But the trend is always for more and more of each nation's business to be done by the very big firms, themselves constantly decreasing in number; and in the world at large a similar pattern is established giving an economic predominance to the economically advanced nations, which it is virtually impossible for the economically backward nations to counteract by merely playing the market system according to the rules of the market. And, one may add, the advanced nations rarely play the economic game according to the rules but use the sheer power of wealth and military might to bias the rules in their own favour.

Capitalism economically armed with machine production, and through the agency in particular of large firms with strong financial backing, invaded and set up its markets in the four quarters of the world. But capitalism is essentially commodity production, that is, production of exchange values (goods and services for exchange in the market) carried to its fullest extent. This was the system that liberated new productive forces and new freedoms for individual initiatives; but human society, by letting the development of the exchange system run free, let loose forces which – like the sorcerer's apprentice – it could no longer control. The commodity or exchange value system is often presented as if money were merely a convenient go-between by means of which men, through the market, expressed the uses to which they wished the production of industry to be put. To many today, however, the reality of this system is becoming more apparent and the products available on the market reveal the essential motivation of the commodity/money system, namely, to produce the maximum surpluses of exchange value, to accumulate capital and *not* primarily to meet needs. I shall argue that effective use of the resources of science and technical knowledge today requires the focussing of these resources more directly towards the uses we wish them to serve. The time has come, in my view, to subject traditional economic rationality which measures performance in terms of money and exchange values, to a searching critical analysis and to enquire whether there is not another kind of economic rationality better able to assess the use of resources and the satisfaction of basic human needs.

Free enterprise commodity production enjoys from its youth, the days of its emergence from feudalism, a reputation it no longer deserves. It has in fact become an obstacle to many of the forms of innovation that human society most needs. Research and development into productivity favourable to profit making, rarely addresses itself to the priorities of social need. Furthermore recession, military and other government policies, misdirection of capital – for example into property speculation – and monopoly distortions due to the concentration of economic power in a few hundred firms serve as formidable barriers to innovation.

The price paid for social regulation by market forces in terms of inability to plan socially has been heavy. Alongside the advances in technology and the social ideas and formations that it liberated, there were untold hardships for those, such as peasants and handcraftsmen, whose interests were trampled underfoot by the new forces.

> "In a capitalist economy (at all events in its Nineteenth Century versions)", writes E.J. Hobsbawm in *Industry and Empire,* "businessmen will be dynamic only insofar as this is rational by the criterion of the individual firm, which is to maximise its gains, minimize its losses, or possibly merely to maintain what it regards as a satisfactory long-term rate of profit. But since the rationality of the individual firm is inadequate, this may not work out to the best advantage of the economy as a whole, or even of the individual firm. This is partly because the interest of the firm and the economy may diverge in the short run or the long, because the individual firm is to some extent powerless to achieve the objects it would wish to, because it is impossible for the accountancy of the individual firm to determine its best interests, or for other analogous reasons. All these are merely different ways of expressing the proposition that a capitalist economy is not planned, but emerges from a multitude of individual decisions taken in the pursuit of self-interest.
> So long as satisfactory profits were to be made in the old way, and so long as the decision to modernise had to emerge from the sum-total of decisions by individual firms, the incentive to do so would be weak. What is more, the general interest of the economy would very likely be lost sight of."

It is now time to turn to ask what the new technology of our times, in particular the computer, electronics and science-based industry, may be expected to do to our present social structure and economic relationships. Before looking to the future we will approach the present as we approached social and economic changes in the past. We shall look at present applications of computer technology from three points of view successively:–

1. The computer as a means of production and as an instrument of increased productivity.
2. The computer as an aid to co-ordination, planning and decision-making within firms or within large social organisations.
3. The computer as a means of social planning, co-ordination and communication affecting very many aspects of social relationships,

as a means of co-ordination and communication between organisms and communities, at the local level or national level or internationally.

NOTE: The history of social and economic change through the last two centuries of the capitalist epoch will help the reader to understand the issues confronting man as he makes his history today and tomorrow. There are many texts to which the reader may go; amongst these the following I have found particularly valuable –

Studies in the Development of Capitalism, chapter 7, by Maurice Dobb (George Routledge & Sons, 1946).

Industry and Empire, E.J. Hobsbawm (Weidenfeld & Nicolson, 1968).

Science History Technology by H.J. Fyrth and M. Goldsmith (Cassell, 1965).

Men, Machines & History, S. Lilley (Lawrence & Wishart, 1965).

Chapter IV

The Current Impact of Computer Technology

The Computer as a Means of Production

To call the computer a new type of machine is misleading. For lack of a new word – as often happens – the computer is constantly referred to as a machine; but it is as well to remember that it is as different from the machine of the industrial revolution, as that machine was different from the craftsman's hand tool.

The computer is an information processing and routine controlling device. It serves as a means of production in a number of ways, for example:-

'numerical control' replacing the skilled operator in charge of the machine tool which can be programmed to produce a multiplicity of shapes to very fine tolerances, for long or short runs as required.

as an aid to writing control programs for numerical control.

in 'Computer-Aided Design' to speed and simplify the design process.

in transfer automation controlled by computer to feed the work from one machine to the next.

in monitoring and controlling processes in manufacturing, chemical, steel-making and many other industries to optimise output, control quality, and regulate the input of materials, that is to economise in the use of materials and to improve the quality of the output.

in stores control and warehousing; the computer being used to arrange stock, to select and to monitor stock levels and to indicate when additions to stocks are to be ordered.

to replace routine clerical work in banks, in accounts departments and indeed anywhere where routines to be followed by clerks can be precisely specified. (Data required in computer-readable form to operate these routines at the same time provides information for control, co-ordination and decision-making referred to below.)

To some extent the computer makes it possible to improve the quality and increase the speed of production, but its most important economic function is that the processes by which man adapts nature to his needs and, in particular, the production of material goods can be made more and more automatic, and so require less labour time from men and women themselves.

The social and economic consequences of this one fact are immense and incalculable. Since it is out of the thoughts and understanding of man himself, his actions and reactions to a changing world, that the future will be shaped, one cannot, naturally, attempt to predict what it may be. But it is clear that new scientific knowledge and new techniques must result in considerable social and political instabilities, since they are radically changing the central core of the economic system, the basic processes and relations of production. Under such circumstances it may be wrong to assume continuation of the market system as we know it or even of a market system with a much higher degree of centralised planning superimposed. What we shall do at this stage is to study the direction of present trends, not in the hope of calculating from them what the future holds, but the better to assess the problems and possibilities facing those who will make the future.

Statistics cannot tell us whether, within the market system, new techniques mean unemployment or, if so, on what scale. There is plenty of evidence of the big reductions in labour requirements for a wide range of economic activities in recent years. Some are directly attributable to computers and automation, some due to better organisation, others due to improved techniques in which computers and electronics are but one factor amongst many. *The Board of Trade Journal* (19th May 1967 and 20th August 1969) records deliveries of numerical control equipment which show that, in one quarter in 1968 alone, these equalled total deliveries in the whole decade to 1965. Along with automatic control of machine tools in the engineering industry there is the development of transfer automation. This is particularly important in the motor industry where it has resulted simultaneously in great increases in output and reduction in manpower. The Ministry of Labour *Manpower Study No. 4* of 1965 estimated that the use of computers in offices would lead to a reduction of 22 per cent of labour in the area of work to which electronic data processing was applicable. (At the same time clerical, professional and planning work is tending to increase the white-collar element in most production units; overall increases in productivity may therefore carry with them increased white-collar employment.)

As examples of the general increase in productivity a number of industries may be cited. For example, containerisation is likely to affect both Docks and Shipping; the McKinsey report to the British Transport Docks Board in June 1967 suggests that ships, and hence crews, required on the North Atlantic could ultimately be reduced by more than 70 per cent and in the Port Industry the reduction in dock workers handling general cargo could be as high as 90 per cent of the total employed using break-bulk methods. Erik Christensen[1] indicated the sort of productivity increases that were taking place in the engineering industry with the introduction of numerical control and transfer automation; he instanced numerical control of a turret lathe leading to a 76.7 per cent saving in direct labour and transfer automation giving increases in productivity ranging from 100 per cent to 500 per cent.[2]

Of course, against savings in direct labour must be set the labour that goes into making the more technically advanced equipment. However, not all improved techniques require more expensive plant and in the case of electronic apparatus production costs are falling (faster, probably, than prices). National Coal Board Reports and Accounts show that the use of power loading machinery in deep-mined coal increased from 20 per cent to 74 per cent between 1965-6 and 1968-9. Productivity in the coal industry in the United Kingdom increased by 50 per cent between 1950 and 1969. In the Docks between 1962 and 1968 employment fell by one-sixth but tonnage handled increased by one quarter. In the railway industry over the same period, employment fell by one-third. Between 1964 and 1968 the number of seamen in British ships fell by one eighth but the volume of shipping increased by one quarter. The new 400,000 tonners actually have smaller crews than the old 40,000 tonners. Over the period 1961 to 1968 sales through supermarkets doubled whereas the total of retail sales overall increased very much less, by 50 per cent.

Statistical measurements of productivity, particularly of overall productivity, are difficult to make. Some theoretical problems have already been mentioned but, in addition to these, productivity should be measured when optimum use is being made of capacity. It is rarely possible to measure productivity under such conditions and measurements of actual productivity will tend to be less than potential productivity. However, the general trend can be deduced from some of the overall indices that are available. The National Institute of Economic & Social Research shows an increase of 40.7 per cent in output per man hour worked in manufacturing between 1963 and 1971, the increase between 1966 and 1971 being 24 per cent.

Between 1966 and 1971 the gross domestic product in UK increased by 11 per cent, industrial production and manufacturing by about 12 per cent. Over the same period, according to the economic editor of

1. *Automation and the Workers*, Labour Research Department, 1968.
2. Another first-rate account of the impact of computer technologies in engineering, is to be found in *Computer-aided Design* by M.J.E. Cooley, published by the Amalgamated Union of Engineering Workers, TASS Division.

The Times[1] population aged 15 and over rose by 1,338,000, but the working population fell by more than 750,000 and the number actually employed by more than 1¼ million, with more than 2 million dropping out of the labour force altogether – and this was on top of a rise in registered unemployment of 434,000. Thus more than 2½ million people – more than 10 per cent of the working population – were not employed in June 1971, but would have been employed if there had been no increases in registered unemployment and in the inactive population from 1966. Clearly the ratio of product to producers is rising fairly rapidly and unused productive resources are increasing. It is also worth noting that there is a relative decline in the numbers employed in manufacturing industries (for example, this was 40 per cent of all employed in 1961 as against 38 per cent in 1969). Employment in professional and scientific categories, on the other hand, is tending to increase (e.g. by 40 per cent between 1959 to 1969 against an overall increase of 5 per cent in employment over the same period).

The following figures are calculated from the statistical appendix of the National Institute Economic Review:-

Overall Input and Output Per Person Employed in UK Industry (1949 = 100)

	1949	1954	1958	1963	1968	1970	1971 (3rd quarter)
Output per person	100	114	118	138	168	176	188
Overall output	100	113	117	126	163	169	170

The following figures are quoted by Dr. J. Kuczynski in *Scientific World* 5/1970:–

Increase in Productivity in Manufacturing in USA

Five year periods	1950/4 – 1955/9	1955/9 – 1960/4	1960/4 – 1965/8
	11.6%	13.4%	16.3%

Source: *Long Term Economic Growth 1860 – 1965,* US Department of Commerce, Bureau of Census, Washington DC, 1966. Dr. Kuczynski states that the rate of increase in productivity in the USA was higher in the 1920s but argues that the impact of new technology is currently most startling and rapid in its consequences in the military field.

Under-utilisation of capacity, unevenness between individual firms, retention of obsolete plant and many other factors make it difficult to measure in a meaningful way the consequences of technological change,

1. *The Times,* 2 March, 1972.

but no one associated with modern industry (cf Dr. Schon's Reith Lectures 1970) would suggest that the consequences of technological change are today not far more disturbing to structural stability than they ever have been before.

In any one country levels and distribution of employment must be greatly influenced by public financial, social and military policies and also by the relative success of this country in winning markets for its products overseas. Nor can one isolate the effects of changing techniques in individual firms. The firms introducing automation and computer techniques most rapidly are generally the richest and commercially strongest, using the new techniques to increase their strength and extend their markets. The striking increases in labour productivity that automation may bring need not result directly in dismissals, if reduced costs enable the firm concerned to extend its markets sufficiently rapidly. But even so there may be a less obvious reduction in employment in that new labour is taken on at a very slow rate. It is likely – and this is what lies at the basis of the social crisis in the United States – that in a highly automated market economy the key economic activities and the well-paid jobs would be confined to a smaller and smaller fraction of society as a whole. An increasingly large part of the community would have to seek a living on inessential, secondary work, usually not well paid. More and more welfare and other expenditures from public funds would be needed to sustain the economic functioning of society. The owners and controllers of the major industries would become decreasingly dependent upon the productive labour force.

It is because the implications of automatic control over production are so far-reaching, because it is something so different in kind from all that we know on the basis of past experience, that one cannot, in any simple way, produce statistical or factual analysis to show what is happening. The processes of social change generated by the new productive forces are likely to be not obviously discernible on the surface. Some of these have been explored by J. E. Meade in his book, *Efficiency, Equality and the Ownership of Property* (London, 1964).

> "To the engineer automation in industry means the incorporation into a productive process of a particular type of control mechanism. In the economists' jargon this implies, I suspect, a high rate of technical progress with a marked labour-saving bias in it. Automation will certainly increase the output per head which will be produced by the aid of the new automated machinery. But it could conceivably reduce so much the amount of labour needed with each new machine of a given cost that the total demand for labour was actually reduced. This could happen if, in spite of the net accumulation of capital equipment, the new labour required with the new

automated machines was actually less than the growth of the labour force plus the labour made redundant by the scrapping of physically worn-out old machinery. In such a case to absorb the new and the redundant workers in the next best uses (for example, on machinery previously considered obsolete or in uses which need no machinery such as domestic service) might require an absolute reduction in the real wage rate on efficiency grounds." (pp. 25–26)

The essential trend in industry generated by computer control is towards marked reductions in the productive labour force. Plants will, more and more, run themselves with comparatively few operators. The proportion of maintenance, scientific and technical staff will increase. Overall the number of people attached to a productive plant in relation to the volume of output will fall sharply. The number of people continuously tied to the productive process will be a declining proportion of those involved directly or indirectly in it. The computer will replace human labour in industrial production, in process control, in clerical and other data handling jobs unevenly. In some areas it will be more easy to make use of the computer. In some areas labour shortages or high costs of labour will provide a strong stimulus to its introduction; in other areas introduction may be delayed for opposite reasons. But it is quite clear that the process is going on, driven by the basic motive force of the market system, namely increased profits from decreased production costs.

In the main it is easier for the large firms, with very big capital and research resources, to make the most rapid progress. They can maintain a diverse team of experts capable of tackling the many-sided problems that arise. They can afford to experiment and to learn from their experience.

The overall direction in which the industrially advanced countries – the USA in particular – are moving would result in fewer people being in basic employment, that is, the main social needs and activities would be met by a relatively smaller labour force, and unemployment, open or disguised, and occupations of secondary social importance, would increase. Present trends, if prolonged, would mean that the owners of industry become less and less dependent upon an industrial labour force, which would be reduced to negligible proportions in the not too-distant future. It should be noted that this is not what I expect will happen; in fact all sorts of social and political forces will be generated as the technological revolution proceeds, causing social upheavals and political struggles which in turn will result in as yet unpredictable, but fundamental, qualitative changes in the way work is done and the way the affairs of society are arranged.

In this section I have been concerned to deal with broad trends. It is the general underlying processes, the new situation developing in production and economic activity overall, that is giving rise to the most important social consequences. To study in greater detail the particular forms that technical change is taking and the economic consequences of these changes, case by case, would require a very lengthy treatment[1]. In the next section some highlights of current trends are briefly surveyed.

Present Computer Trends

Computers began to be commercially available outside the laboratory in about 1951-2. These computers used vacuum tubes to simulate the logical processes and were, by present-day standards, slow and cumbersome to program. In about 1958 this first generation of computers made way for a second generation using transistors, operating at much higher speeds and supplied with programs to translate high-level languages such as ALGOL, COBOL and FORTRAN into the language in which the machine itself worked. The next phase, around 1963-5, made use of integrated circuits, that is, groups of logical gates produced as one piece and very small in size. Today the most modern machines – spoken of as fourth generation – use even larger combinations of integrated circuits (medium-scale integration), have still higher speeds, larger memories and backing stores and combine a wide variety of peripherals to provide a system that can be used by a number of users at once, with access 'conversationally' to the computer. (A conversational system is one in which the user can instruct the computer to extract information from its files, to process this information, to give answers and submit itself to further questioning.) In 1970 there were about 100,000 computers in the world. In three to five years this figure may have doubled. Ivan Berenyi[2] quotes the following figures for individual countries:- 'United States 62,500; West Germany 6,100; United Kingdom 5,900; Japan 5,900; USSR 5,500; France 4,500; Canada 3,000; Italy 2,700; Scandinavia 1,500; Netherlands 1,100; East Germany 500; Poland 420; Czechoslovakia 200; Yugoslavia 180; Hungary 120; Rumania 50; Bulgaria 30.'

Of course, the size and function of computers may differ considerably; costs may range from a few thousand to a few million pounds. A review made by the French organisation C.O.T.A.T. (College of Advanced Techniques and Territorial Development) for their Second International Symposium on Data Processing and Regional Planning

1. For those interested in pursuing the detail, in addition to the books referred to above, *Social Research in Automation – A Social Science Research Council Review,* (Heineman, 1968) provides a useful introduction together with a bibliography; and as already mentioned S. Lilley's book *Men, Machines and History,* (Lawrence and Wishart, 1965) gives a useful account of the main computer applications in industry at the time it was written.

2. *Scientific American,* October 1970, p. 104.

estimated that the total of data processing installations in Western industrialised countries is expanding at an exponential rate of about 30 per cent a year. The value of data processing equipment in use in the United States has increased over the last decade from approximately £800m. to £12,000m. Rates of increase in Britain and Western Europe have been similar. In value terms – according to the C.O.T.A.T. estimate – the equipment in each of these countries was about one-twentieth of that in America (the estimate from *Scientific American* quoted above by numbers gives each of these countries about one-tenth the American stock – presumably the European computers were on average smaller).

The heaviest use of computers has been for data processing by industrial, commercial and financial undertakings. I have already mentioned, and shall deal further with, the use of computers directly in production to control machine tools, to link the output of one machine as input to another, in the control testing and monitoring of whole industrial complexes, in steel manufacture, non-ferrous metals, chemicals, and so forth. It is not such uses, however that devour the main bulk of computing power. It is rather the use of general-purpose computers to take over such laborious clerical processes as payment of wages, invoicing, stock control and recording. This type of application has been attractive because one can calculate the cost of doing by computer jobs hitherto done by hand. Management has argued to itself that the computer is an instrument of the future and it will be good for their status to be seen to be using computers. Such lines of thought have possibly caused estimates of savings on clerical labour to be over-optimistic. Certainly many computer installations are not as yet paying their way. Possibly too many firms have tried to pour new wine into old bottles. In introducing the new techniques they have not been able sufficiently to adapt existing procedures to the new possibilities. "It is perfectly true," writes Michael Rose[1] "that computers can successfully absorb the task of the large office and perform them at less cost and with greater reliability than a team of clerks. What is more disturbing is the extent to which users' evaluations of the machine have remained fixated on the advantage of office automation in the face of accumulating evidence that the really significant gains from computerisation derive from a more adventurous use of the machine." However, despite much evidence of failure to use computers effectively, demand for more and more computers still presses on relentlessly. Few are prepared to take the view that the computer is a passing fad. The potential of electronic information processing appears too certain to doubt.

1. *Computers, Managers and Society,* Penguin 1969, p. 78.

Despite the fact that the growth rate is continuing at approximately 30 per cent per annum, C.O.T.A.T. in the report referred to above regards it as inconceivable that this rate of expansion will be sustained into the future for more than a few years. The most rapid growth rate that it is prepared to contemplate assumes a decline to about 14 per cent by 1990. Even so, such a growth rate would carry the turnover of the data processing industries, in such countries as France, Britain or Germany, from about 0.5 per cent of the gross domestic product in 1969 to 1.5 per cent in 1975 and 5.7 per cent in 1990. On these assumptions data processing equipment would account for about 10 per cent of all investment by 1990.

During the last fifteen years electronic calculating speeds have increased tenfold every five years, the size of the calculating units have been decreased to one-tenth of what they were every five years and the cost of calculation to one-twentieth or one- thirtieth every five years. In the face of technological change of such impetuosity it is hardly reasonable to think that we can get answers to questions about the future by extrapolating present trends. At best they throw some light on the next three or four years. Beyond that extrapolation can hardly be useful. We need to look more deeply into the meaning of the information revolution in the context of economic and social activities.

It is useful to begin by looking at present applications, only if we do so critically and ask not only how these new powers serve the needs of various types of organisation and activity, but also whether this new potential should cause us to question the appropriateness of existing forms of organisation and activity.

In industry and commerce the point is not merely to do now automatically by computer what we did before by hand, but to consider what types of organisation would be appropriate to automated information flows. In many cases even quite small steps into the future are proving very difficult. It is clear to every business management that the mass of information about wage payments, invoicing, stock levels, production progress, and such like, that is now handled by computers as a matter of routine, provides the raw material that is needed for a management information system. In theory, up-to-the-minute information in computer-readable form is available, but few managements have succeeded in devising for themselves really practical information systems. Many problems, which it seemed at the outset might be left to the information technician, are turning out to be far more complex than was thought because they involve social or political issues; that is, they cannot adequately be solved without going outside the boundaries of the firm to contemplate far-ranging changes in the structures of social organisms.

In science computers are being used to carry through more and more complex calculations and to serve as aids to information storage and retrieval. Typical of this type of use is computer-aided diagnosis in medicine where an information system provides statistical data and carries through statistical tests to show the diseases with which particular symptoms are associated and the likelihood of this association under particular circumstances, patients' medical history, etc. They are also being used to simulate experimental conditions. In fact, computer simulations of experiments in chemistry, for example, may be more 'realistic' than experiments conducted in a laboratory. The laws of interaction of molecules may be sufficiently well understood for them to be built into a complex simulation of a long chain of processes whose outcome would be very difficult to determine by setting up an experiment with actual molecules. One could, for example, simulate the consequences of an explosion. An article in *The New Scientist,* 30th April 1970, by Dr. Vahl describes the computerised chemical system known as BISON. "This", he writes "is a research system consisting of a self-consistent, field molecular orbital program for large diatomic molecules; a properties program for the same systems; a graphical display program which plots and automatically paints charge densities; a transition probability program; a spectroscopic constants program; and a crystal-field integrals program." The systems are designed so that the experimental chemist "can ask of them truly chemical questions such as 'What is the dipole moment of CaO?'; 'What are the vibrational levels of VCl_2?' and 'What are the transport properties of alkali vapours?' "

Simulation, in the sense of applying known laws to a complex set of interrelationsips, may also be most fruitfully used in a number of other fields. For example, economic situations or social planning situations may be simulated by means of computer models, drawing on pre-prepared information and formulae held in a data bank. Situations may be simulated for learning purposes in many fields, as is already done in teaching people to fly. Also new information handling techniques, such as those being explored by the Open University, will make whole courses of learning available when desired to be played back visually through screens such as are at present used only for television. If the reader has grasped the basic idea of what the computer does, he will be able to imagine for himself the various directions in which applications are possible and likely. Applications in real life situations will, of course, constantly run into unforeseen practical difficulties. To date, for example, apart from rather costly laboratory applications, big batch processing jobs have predominated and it has been difficult for the occasional user to get his needs met or to try out new possibilities. For him long delays and high costs have made computer applications unattractive. In the near future this situation may change rapidly with the general extension of time-sharing systems allowing the user direct access, by means of a terminal for example, to the computer and the data and preprepared programs comprised in the system. Better use of known systems and techniques is likely to develop; but new principles of applying electronic techniques to information processing (that is, something other than the electronic digital computer embodying Babbage's principles) have still to appear.[1]

Intra-Firm Planning and Mathematical Programming

Preceding sections have dealt with the computer and other electronic equipment as means of production, that is, as an improvement in productive techniques in the traditional sense. This chapter deals with production techniques, if such they may be called, that are new in kind. The activities to which I am referring are variously described by such names as 'operational research'. 'management science', 'economic cybernetics', 'the systems approach' and so forth. It is easy to see that these new techniques are applicable to social organisations outside production and are applicable to the activities of whole societies or to any component parts of them, and not merely to firms with their limited economic objectives. However, it is in relation to the firm within the market system that I first consider them, since these new techniques undoubtedly affect productivity, profitability and organisation.

The style of thinking used in operational research is not completely new and it is not difficult to find isolated instances of similar methods being used in the past. (For example, Charles Babbage analysed mail handling and transportation as an operation system and his recommendations encouraged Rowland Hill to introduce the penny post.) What is new is the extent to which it is now feasible to use such techniques. This is partly attributable to a widening of mathematical thinking and a more general use of mathematical models beyond the physical sciences to which they have been mainly applied over the last three centuries. It is also due to the new information processing powers provided by the computer; in the past the massive calculations involved in the study of systems having many interrelated elements ruled out practical applications which today the computer makes feasible.

Operations research was born immediately before and during the second world war. The revolutionary event that gave birth to these new

1. The reader may collect for himself many examples of advance being made from the current general and scientific press. As background reading I would recommend:–

   Information, various articles from *Scientific American,* W.H. Freeman and Company, 1966.

   Automation: its uses and consequences, John Rose, Contemporary Science Paperback, no.9., 1967.

   Computers, Managers and Society, Michael Rose, Penguin, 1969.

techniques was that scientists and mathematicians began to adapt scientific methods of investigation and experimentation to problems other than those of the natural sciences. They were asked to look at such questions as the size and formation of a convoy likely to reduce losses from submarine attack to a minimum; or the depth of detonation and pattern of depth charges most likely to destroy an attacking submarine; or the location of radar equipment to give maximum coverage from some fixed quantity of available installations.

One particular problem – apparently extremely simple – perplexed some of the finest scientific and mathematical intellects, took some years to solve and in the end gave birth to a new branch of mathematics – linear programming. This was the now-famous transportation problem. It is worth pausing to consider this problem. It provides a prototype illustrating the elements of a now widely used technique to improve the use of resources within economic organisations considered as a whole. It also demonstrates to what an extent the emphasis of mathematical model-making has been related to the problems of physical science and how difficult it is to discover appropriate mathematical techniques to apply to situations of a new kind. Over the centuries very refined, crisp and neat techniques, particularly those of the integral and differential calculus, have been evolved for dealing with problems of physical science. When faced with new areas in the biological or social sciences or in economics we have to grope for new methods in order to handle what seem very simple problems. It is probable that in these new areas altogether new styles of mathematical model-making will be required.

It is indeed right to regard the mathematics of social and economic model-making as being at an embryonic stage, in which methods and achievements are still very primitive. Much of the apparent sophistication is spurious, amounting to no more than the lifting of advanced techniques, developed for the physical sciences, and the attempt to find uses for them in the economic and social sciences. The real mathematics of the social and economic sciences may turn out to be very different in kind, founded on their own fundamental theories in much the same way as a great deal of the mathematics of the physical sciences is rooted in the Newtonian model. If it is indeed the case that the mathematics of the social and economic sciences is still at a very primitive stage, one may expect very rich fruits to be harvested as the new mathematics advances.

The transportation problem in its original form was this. At the outbreak of war merchant vessels are to be requisitioned. They are distributed about the world at a number of different ports. When they have been requisitioned for Admiralty use they will be required to be differently distributed. Which vessels then should go to which ports in order to reduce costs or sailing times to a minimum in getting the vessels into their new positions? The problem involves a number of *constraints,* that is, the total of available ships and their original distribution. It is also necessary to give a mathematical definition of the objective that is being pursued; this is called the *objective function.* In this case the objective is to make the total of miles sailed by all ships as small as possible. (A simple example is worked through in Mathematical Appendix Note 6.) Obviously with large numbers of ports and large numbers of ships the possible number of routings soon becomes astronomical. It is necessary to find some methodical routine for finding the best solution reasonably quickly. Even when the mathematics of the underlying situation are understood, it turns out that the required routine is pretty laborious and in most real problems it is impossible to get useful results without the aid of a computer. But fortunately, although the apparently simple transportation problem turns out to be much less simple than it might appear, it is also of much wider and more general application. Where appropriately simple linear relationships exist between the various factors, problems of allocating resources, using available supplies in proper combinations and relating a product most suitably to available equipment can be expressed in terms of a linear programming problem of which the transportation problem is a particular example. The linear programming problem in its general form is, broadly speaking, a problem of allocating resources. A particular product requires particular materials or particular production capacity of which supplies are limited. These constitute the constraints. These will be expressed in mathematical form as a number of simultaneous equations or simultaneous inequalities, (which by a fairly simple mathematical device may be transformed into simultaneous equations). The kind of situation that these equations represent may be illustrated by a number of products A, B, C, etc., in making which capacity on a number of machines I, II, III, etc. is required. The time for which machine I is required for product A plus the time for which machine I is required for product B plus the time for which machine I is required for product C etc., must not exceed the limit of production time for which this machine is available. Constraints on machine II, machine III etc., may be similarly defined. Within these constraints the objective might be to minimise costs or maximise profits and if costs per unit or profits per unit are known, it will be possible to express this aim as a mathematical function known as the *objective function.* (For an example see Mathematical Appendix Note 7.) Within this general idea of linear programming there are many ways in which the general linear programming model may be adapted to special circumstances. There is for example integer programming in which solutions must be in whole numbers. (For example, if the products were ships a solution which defined the optimum production programme as 2¾ tankers and 7 1/5 liners would not be meaningful. One is only interested in the best of the whole number solutions.) Another adaptation is parametric programming which enables one to consider what gains would result from changing the constraints; for example, if one knows what additional profits or savings would result from additions to capacity or increased supplies of a particular material, then one knows how much it is worth paying to change existing constraints.)

Another type of situation that can be represented by linear programming is that which is analysed by the 'theory of games'. The theory of games in its simplest form represents a contest between two persons. Each player is in a position to adopt different strategies which may bring him different gains or losses depending upon the strategy adopted by the other player. Each player will assume that his opponent will study his own strategy and will seek to gain the greatest possible advantage. The problem is to find a mixture of strategies which will give a player the best chance in the long run of making gains. In fact the relationship between the players can be expressed in matrix form and reduced to a particular case of linear programming.

Linear programming is also used as a planning technique in the Soviet Union and in other countries with centrally planned economies. Indeed the idea of linear programming was very fully developed by the Russian mathematician, L. V. Kantorovich, as far back as 1939. However, for a long time the mathematical techniques being developed in the capitalist countries were criticised and resisted in the Soviet Union and it was not until some 20 years later that the ideas of Kantorovich and other pioneers of mathematical methods began to be applied in Soviet planning.

Linear programming is, in fact, one particular way of looking at interrelated factors in a system considered as a whole. I have pointed out that it has many widely differing applications; even so, it is a very limited way of looking at a system, applicable only to particular types of factors and relationships. Engineering and scientific research are also concerned with the study of systems. A biologist may study bacteria, an engineer an internal combustion engine or even a component such as a valve as a system of interacting parts. An engineer, for example, may study a machine with a view to improving its efficiency, that is measuring input and output in some standard units and trying to increase the ratio of output to input. If it were possible to apply similar methods of study to whole organisations, the pay-off might be very considerable. Most of the mathematical methods applied to intra-firm planning are attempts to do this, though not always very clearly seen as such. Most go-ahead organisations apply a considerable amount of money to laboratory research; few apply much to systems research. If, as a result of work in a laboratory, the output of a particular machine is doubled, it will increase to some small extent the output of the whole organisation. A more effective integration of an organisation as a functioning system might be expected to give very much greater increases in output and, at the same time, to identify those areas in which the returns to detailed scientific research are likely to be greatest.

There is always a certain resistance in individual, privately-owned firms to research work since it is costly and unpredictable. There is no guarantee that useful results will in fact be useful to the firm paying for the research and it may often be felt to be more profitable to rely on harvesting the fruit of other people's research. In this event the firm's policy may limit research to such levels as are necessary to create a scientific awareness in the organisation and to be able thus to pick up quickly and to understand work of significance being done elsewhere. It is possible that systems research is slow to develop because most firms prefer to rely on the fruits of work being done elsewhere or because thinking at administrative and policy levels is resistant to change, – and systems research is about fundamental organisation change! However, whilst the long-term and ultimate implications of mathematical and systems planning techniques, backed by the computer and electronic technologies, may tend to be incompatible with a private ownership market system, there is no question at all that there are ways in which they may be applied to the short-term aim of increasing profitability and the productivity of resources in the organisation viewed as a whole.

Mathematical and programming techniques are also applicable to other organisational problems, to social planning and co-ordination for example, where there are objectives other than the maximisation of profits. The simple objective of profit maximisation and cost minimisation simplifies the task (as in the case of the profit-oriented firm) of defining the objective function. The main problem in the application of mathematical programming techniques to social planning is the definition of measures of the 'good' that is to be maximised. There is already a danger of an 'optimisation mania' developing before any adequate means have been devised for defining what is to be optimised and how decisions on ends to be pursued are to be made to rest with those who are most affected.

At the present time most methods of studying interactive systems limit themselves to particular aspects. Linear programming is one such method. Linear programming, as we saw, dealt in the main with a given situation at a given point of time. Dynamic programming (pioneered by Richard Bellman, a mathematician with the Rand Corporation) deals with multi-stage processes. Richard Bellman writes "These are composed of sequences of operations in which the outcome of the preceding operations may be used to guide the course of future operations. Two types of operations may be distinguished immediately: those in which the outcome is completely determined and those in which it is not determined but is predictable by means of a probability distribution."[1]

A probability distribution defines the range of possible events and the possibility of any of the possible events occurring. It is not at all difficult to program a computer to simulate a sequence of probable outcomes. In the deterministic model a particular input determines a particular output. In a probabilistic model the outcome of a given situation may be one of several possible outcomes, some more likely, others less likely. The probabilistic model can simulate sequences of alternative outputs indicating a number of possible future situations and the relative likelihood of each of them.

Another group of methods widely used by management today are those of network analysis, 'project evaluation review technique' (PERT), and the like. The point of network analysis is to show the sequence of interconnected stages in a complex process. (A very simple example is given in Mathematical Appendix Note 8.) Operations forming part of a wider process may, in some cases, proceed simultaneously, in other cases only after the completion of preceding operations. The linkages between stage and stage may be measured in terms of time, cost, capacity used and in many other ways. If one is measuring capacity the network analysis will show where the bottlenecks are. A common use of the network is to analyse time taken. If a time is assigned to each operation it will be found that one particular 'path' in the network – the 'critical path' – determines the time for the completion of the process considered as a whole.

Many computer programs have been written to find the critical path and analyse other aspects of the flow of work through a network of interconnected operations. The usefulness of such analysis is obvious. The main danger and difficulty is that data on time taken, costs, capacity available, and so forth, may be uneven and inaccurate leading to very misleading conclusions. An over-centralised management that tries to use network analysis may be in for trouble if communications with and between the people who carry out the operations are poor.

Advantages of network analysis are, on the one hand, that it is easily broken down to focus on detail and, on the other, that detail may be omitted and only the main stages shown. It is a method of studying a system that enables one to move from the particular to the general and back again to the particular. What is shown as a single operation may itself be studied as a network; for example, the network for servicing an individual machine might be the 'detail' of a much bigger network that

1. *Modern Mathematics for the Engineer,* edited by Beckenbach, Mcgraw-Hill, 1956.

dealt with the flow of production in a factory as a whole.

Network analysis is a sort of 'skeleton modelling' of the operation of a system or organisation. But one may, of course, make models in other ways, models that more fully represent the functioning of an organisation. It is, for example, often possible to make computer models simulating the process of production, the intake of materials, the input of labour working on these materials and so forth. Such models of production processes are valuable ways of locating areas in which the greatest production costs arise and of assessing the consequence, for example, of changes in costs of materials or changes in direct labour time on a particular product. Computer modelling opens up an immense potential since it makes it possible to test alternative courses of action experimentally 'in the imagination'.

One particular aspect of the flow of goods through the economic system has received a great deal of attention – namely, inventory control. The inventory, or stocks, are goods that appear to be moving more slowly than, for example, components on which work is actually being done. Much capital is tied up in the form of stocks: stocks of raw materials to be used, stocks of component parts awaiting assembly in the finished product, stocks of finished goods, stocks in the hands of the distributor. If the average level of stock holding could be reduced, capital would be saved and the rate of profit considerably increased. There are also factors that encourage stock holding. If there is an inflationary trend and prices are tending to rise, it may be profitable to hold stocks. This is a purely speculative consideration. On the other hand, there are considerations related to production and sales planning. If production is held up for lack of a component or a material this will be far more costly than warehousing or interest on the capital tied up. In producing components or finished products long runs will usually reduce unit costs considerably. For example, if the set-up costs of a machine are £100 and the labour and material per unit produced is £1, the unit cost per item in a run of 100 will be £2 whereas in a run of 1,000 it will be only £1.10. If stock can eventually be sold it may be more profitable to produce it in long runs and hold it for a considerable time. On the other hand, dead stock is dead loss. Mathematical models can fairly easily simulate the different kinds of situations that may arise; and there are a number of devices, for example 'exponential smoothing', by which automatic decisions on stock levels may under certain circumstances be safely entrusted to a computer.

The position of the wholesaler or supplier who buys in stock is different, but the same kind of problems arise for him. To hold too much stock for a long time will be costly and the stock may deteriorate in value; but if the supplier has not got stock readily available to meet his customers' demands he may lose a lot more than the profit on the unsold items. He may lose the continuing trade of that customer. He would like to know when the customer is likely to come to him. This may be a random, erratic process. 'Queueing theory' is a widely used technique to help with such problems. The 'queue' is a model of a situation that occurs in a great number of contexts. A customer presents himself and joins a queue. He is served in some prescribed order. It takes a certain time to serve him. The ideal is to have as little queueing as possible with as few people as possible serving the queue. The problem is to find a balance between two evils – either long queues or the wasted time of having staff waiting for customers. In addition to users waiting for supplies or customers waiting for stock, the queueing problem arises in a wide variety of economic contexts. The maintenance of machines may be seen as a queueing problem: the breakdown of machines may be seen as a random sequence of events leading to a queue of idle machines waiting to be serviced by the maintenance staff, the cost on the one hand being loss of production and on the other the wages of maintenance engineers. The problem of providing capacity for telephone callers is a classical mathematical problem dealt with in probability theory and queueing theory. Goods wagons in a marshalling yard provide another situation of the same type. For example, one might regard the wagon as the customer and the locomotive as the server – the problem is to arrange the arrival of locomotives at the marshalling yard so that the combination of waiting time by wagons and non-working time by locomotives gives a least-cost or most beneficial result in such other terms as may be specified, e.g. maximum use of locomotives with the proviso that wagons do not wait more than one week.

Programming problems in general are problems of provision for the future. Sometimes one may safely assume that events in the future will go on very much as in the past. For example, one might assume that the number of goods wagons coming to the marshalling yard would average the same as in the past and that the distribution of times of arrival as between days of the week and hours of the day would remain much as before. The problem then is to deal with the same situation in a more effective way. The stockholder has to make assumptions about the future. He is holding stocks to meet future demands. The production planner has to make assumptions about the future. He aims at organising production so that the sequence and grouping of production runs is as efficient as possible. Almost invariably this means making some assumptions about the future. Production planning, stock holding and forecasting of future market situations interlock and interrelate closely. Programming is inseparable from forecasting.

Mathematical models of many kinds are used in attempts to forecast the future. One can only be certain about what the future holds when the future becomes the present. But whether in words, in imagination or mathematically, models of the expected future are indispensable to human action. Mathematical models used to forecast the future may assume that a system operates in an unchanged environment, save only for changes in the structure of the system itself. In such a case one is forecasting, for example, the consequences of an improved organisation. In other cases one assumes that trends from the past continue into the future. One might, for example, assume that seasonal fluctuations continue whilst demand, averaged over the year, continues to increase at, say, 5 per cent per annum. Or one might assume that demand in the future will be like demand in the past on the assumption that the near past will have the greatest influence on the future but the more distant past will still have some influence, although the further away past events are the smaller their influence. (The technique for estimating the future on this basis is that of 'exponential smoothing' referred to above; exactly the same technique was long used by weather forecasters before it was rediscovered for application to economic situations.)

Of course it is also possible to build expected events into the model of the future; for example, one might add on to the general trend of demand the consequences of some known decision. If it were decided to allow old age pensioners to travel free one could include in one's forecast of future travel loads a step up to reflect this isolated decision. In forecasting the future one is always making assumptions about change or absence of change. To get ideas about what might or might not happen it is always of value to study past experience. In this way all the complexities of collecting basic data and making statistical analyses of this data have an important bearing on forecasting. Trends, correlations and models of processes occurring in the past may suggest a continuance of these processes into the future together with rates and forms of likely change.

The power of the computer to collect and analyse statistics is, therefore closely related to the problem of building models to simulate economic organisations. The ideal, from which most attempts fall far short, is to simulate the operations of economic organisms considered as a whole. Such models help to show the effect of changing costs, and to measure the consequences of new processes for costs, production times, etc. One begins to approach a situation in which economics may become an experimental science, experimenting – as the chemist already does – with computer models simulating real-life situations.

The objective of all these various forms of model-making, some representing the system as a whole, some only limited aspects of the system, is more effective control. Data and statistics combined with the modelling of systems provide a management information system. The computer and the associated mathematical techniques for model-building and programming create the possibility of management information systems of undreamed-of power and effectiveness. The efforts so far made in this direction have been stumbling and confused. The centralised administrations of profit-oriented firms tend to concentrate on the provision of information for top management. Undoubtedly the computer, plus mathematical programming, increases the productivity and profitability of the firm in a quite new way. At the same time organisation by centralising authority in an elite – what Eugene V. Schneider described as 'industrial bureaucracy' – militates against the full development of a well-articulated information system. It will be argued in the pages that follow that the potential of modern science and technology can only be fully realised in a system in which decision-making and information are widely diffused.

The techniques that have been discussed in this section have been developed largely in pursuit of centralised control in large firms whose objective is to maximise output and minimise costs, or, what is usually the same thing, except in certain monopoly situations, to maximise profits. That is, to say, the concepts of commodity production for a market have to date underlain most applications of new technologies and computer or mathematical methods. In the market, products with widely differing characteristics are unified as values forming part of a single product (what on the national scale is today called the GNP or Gross National Product). Economic activity conceived in these terms is given just one objective in the case of the firm to maximise profit, i.e. the excess of economic values produced over their costs of production, and in the case of the national economy, to maximise the National Product. In what respects technology moulded to such economic objectives may or may not serve social objectives, is a question that is reserved for discussion in Chapter V; but before concluding Chapter IV, I turn, in the next section, to the important question of how the new computer and mathematical techniques may be applied to planning, control and co-ordination of firms and other economic organisms that make up the national economies considered as whole systems; that is I now turn from intra-firm planning to inter-firm (or inter-enterprise) planning.

Macro-Planning and the Market System

The computer affords a powerful aid to centralised co-ordination and control. It provides a means of storing and analysing information of unprecedented power. It provides a means of statistical analysis and model-making. It is a formidable instrument for process-control and

1. *Industrial Sociology – The Social Relations of Industry and the Community*, McGraw-Hill, 1957.

mathematical programming. Though its potential as a tool of national planning has yet to be developed, this potential undoubtedly exists. The existence of this technological potential coincides with very marked pressures towards centralised planning in all parts of the world.

Centralised planning is, one might almost say by definition, bureaucratic planning in that it implies decision-taking at the centre by a bureaucratic élite. Adam Smith's arguments against planning and for the free market were dictated by the impossibility of a Sovereign, however wise, being able to understand the million-fold complex relationships of an industrial economy. The new electronic information technologies make conceivable some control processes that two centuries ago were totally inconceivable. Moreover, defects of the *laissez-faire* market system not then apparent are now very apparent. There are today very strong pressures in the direction of centralised planned control of national economies to turn them into integrated machines for production of values. Such centralised planning was dictated in the Soviet Union by the exigencies of constructing advanced industry in what had hitherto been an economically backward, mainly peasant economy. In former colonial or semi-colonial territories the pressure of similar economic considerations combined with the desire to support political with economic independence point the way to centralised economic planning. In the capitalist West such pressures are also very strong. The traditional philosophy of private property and private enterprise militates against centralised planning; but many new factors, repeated abandonment of *laissez-faire* principles, and the non-functioning of the *laissez-faire* system, its inability to bring available resources into full employment, the tendency of the labour force required in production to decline, the concentration of economic power and activity in one or two hundred very large firms – all these factors make an integrated social and economic plan indispensable to the survival of the existing social order. The resultant phenomenon is describable only by a contradiction in terms – planned commodity production!

Planning, which in one sense is the essence of socialism, assumes in this contradictory form a strange new political and social significance; it emerges as the central policy not for revolution but for the preservation of existing orders of society. It may therefore be necessary to make very clear distinctions between 'centralised bureaucratic planning', on the one hand, and on the other 'the conscious regulation of production by freely associated men' requiring consequently co-ordination between a number of economically interacting organisms. In this section we are concerned only with the former and, in particular, with the centralised planning of a number of large commodity-producing firms or enterprises. Consideration of the extent to which techniques dealt with may have applications in other social systems will be deferred to Chapter V. One must, however, at once observe that the nightmare picture of a highly planned social machine in which men and women are no more than cogs, have no part in the shaping or direction of the machine, alienated from and unable to influence its purposes, is an actual possibility. It is actual in the sense that it is technically possible; one may hope that it is not actual in the sense that the human society still has power to resist and prevent such de-humanisation of life. However, it would not be difficult to draw up a blueprint for a 'computer-aided bureaucracy' so supplied with information that it could inform itself on the instant of anything it needed to know about people, economic equipment, resources etc. This picture of extreme centralisation in a computer-aided bureaucracy is an extrapolation of present trends, not a forecast; its usefulness is that it may perhaps enable one to understand better some implications of present trends. Having drawn attention to these possibilities, it would not be useful further to pursue speculations about the more distant future. The purpose of this section is to look at present applications of the computer. From this it is already clear that the general fear of data banks with detailed information about individuals' private affairs is well enough founded. Seeing such uses, many wish that the computer had never been invented and advocate a world from which the computer has been abolished. Such policies are not only unrealistic and utopian, they attempt to destroy the technology of information processing that has an indispensable part to play in any democratic restructuring of society. The target of attack should not be the computer or, more generally, the underlying technology of electronics in information processing but the nature of the authority and the socio-economic structure that leads to such abuses in the development and application of information technology.

Whilst economic planning has long been associated with socialism and the planned economy is contrasted with the market system, there are, as has already been suggested in Chapter I, also many essential aspects of economies with centralised planning that are identical with the market system to which they are contrasted. That the two systems could be species of the same genus is suggested by the comparative facility with which centralised planning has been superimposed on the market in time of war. The essential difference, already mentioned, is that the rule of the market is modified by administrative decisions as to prices and quantities of goods to be produced.

In the contemporary world there can be no doubt that a belief in planning extends far beyond those who are proponents of socialism. Keynesian theory led to the advocacy of planned investment within the capitalist economies in answer to the massive unemployment of the 1930s. The exigencies of war demanded considerable measures of central planning in the use of resources and gave rise to methods of control that some felt could usefully be applied to peace-time situations. Public control through nationalisation of basic industries became extensive in Western Europe following the second world war. Financial policies of subsidy and taxation have long been used by public authority in attempts to guide the flow of national income in directions other than those which the market system would determine if left to itself. The question is what forms may planning (as applied to the national economy as a whole) take in the future and what relevance has it to the computer revolution?

Planning might be defined as 'the regulation of construction, production and distribution to satisfy social purposes'. But two groups of questions arise: (1) what are the means of regulation and are they effective? (2) how are social purposes expressed and who decides what they are to be?

The problem is first to see what forms planning may assume within the framework of a market system. Consider at what points the freedom of decision left to the elementary units (individuals or enterprises) in the market system can be replaced, curbed or redirected as a result of conscious decision outside of and independent of the market system. Typically one thinks of the planner as 'the state' or 'public authority'. Public authority we need not at this stage define more precisely; it might be a democratically controlled body, a dictator or a centralised bureaucracy, a national authority or a local authority. We are leaving aside for the time being all questions about who speaks for society, how the social structure relates to the economic structure and so forth. We may conveniently think of the forms of intervention by public authority under the following heads:-

1. Laws, rules, administrative measures and the like, applying to economic and social activities.
2. Measures such as subsidies or social services paid out of taxes that effect a redistribution of values produced.
3. The nominees of central or local authority running enterprises which produce goods or services, that is economic values for which money payments will be received on sale.

(The above division is that used in a study by the Italian economist Silvio Leonardi titled *Democracy of Planning* – Democrazia di Piano; he concludes that there is a marked trend towards planning in almost all countries today, the pressures supporting this tendency being political as well as economic.)

1. Even the pure market economy requires laws or customs to safeguard conditions of free competition. But all sorts of legal measures

may be taken to deflect the workings of the market system. For example, people may be forbidden to put up buildings for industrial purposes in certain areas or they may be forbidden to sell products that do not meet specified standards of quality. The repercussions of such measures on the market system are probably not considerable. But laws may also be passed which strike at basic principles of the market system; for example, price controls. If there are more buyers than sellers at a given price, there will be strong pressure to evade the purpose of a price control by linking sales with goods that are not price-controlled. Further legislation may be required to stop the loop-holes in black markets and the like. A running battle, of a similar sort, goes on within the market system over taxes and their evasion. Possibly a system of rationing may need to go with price controls. What then are the consequences for allocation of productive resources flowing from the rationing system? Experience of war economy taught a good deal in a pragmatic way about what can be achieved by use of legal or administrative directives and also gave a fair amount of information about side-effects.

2. Again with redistributive measures one of the main problems is to assess side-effects. The essential principle of redistributive measures is that public authority taps the money-flows at certain points. Indirect taxation, for example, siphons off a part of money payments made by the buyer to the seller. Income tax siphons off income payable to individuals or enterprises. Here, once again, the difficult questions are: what are the repercussions and where does the real cost fall? As there is never a reliable blueprint of what would have happened if public authority had followed a different tax policy, there is room for a good deal of argument. One of the great strengths of physical science is that it is able to model alternative situations with considerable precision and to test the consequences of changing the control variables. (One may calculate, for example, what happens if one changes the angle at which a projectile is launched.) If it becomes possible to model more adequately the essentials of economic situations, it may become possible also to assess more accurately the consequence of alternative public policies. The computer puts such possibilities within range.

There is no question about the feasibility of making computer models to simulate systems such as, for example, the production activities of a firm, or traffic flows in a city. A number of such models have been made and some large firms are using such models to simulate alternative courses that the development of their production activities might take. Clearly such models cannot simulate every feature of the wider economic or social life and their success in construction and use depends upon making meaningful abstractions so as to simulate only the essential interactions. Work is proceeding on the theory and practice of building such models and as time goes by they will become more useful. Nothing in principle prevents the construction of such models also for national economies considered as a whole. Work has been done in this direction (for example by the Department of Applied Economics at Cambridge). A particularly important type of model – the 'input-output model' – is considered more fully below. The complexity of the flows of goods and payments between all the various industries in a national economy is great and to be effectively simulated requires the power of the computer to handle massive data speedily.

Financial policy is another type of 'redistributive measure'. Most central banks are under direct public control and steps may be taken by governments to control the policies of privately owned banks. The money system is in many important respects distinct from the system of production and distribution. It is best therefore to think of financial policy, even where it is not firmly controlled by public authority, as an external control operating on the market system. To make credit available is to make purchasing power available. The immediate effect of a change in financial policy is a changed distribution of purchasing power. The repercussions of such changes are generally very far-reaching and hard to determine with precision. Credit policy will affect the level of investment undertaken by a large number of enterprises. At present the computers used in banking are in the main to replace and do more speeedily what previously was done by routine clerks. But there are potential uses of computers as instruments of financial control and information – for example computerisation of commercial payments and documentation – which would be of great significance. This potential might be the tool of highly centralised bureaucratic planning or, under other circumstances, a means of making information about economic transactions more generally available to the community.

3. The running of some businesses by public authority has always been regarded as necessity. (For example, almost all roads.) A striking feature of the contemporary market system throughout the capitalist world is the extent of the increase in nationalised industry. Sometimes the difference may be solely one of ownership, the publicly-owned enterprise operating in pursuit of profit in just the same way as the privately-owned enterprise. It is, however, also possible for governments to influence the general course of economic activity by the strategy they apply to the publicly-owned sector. Publicly-owned industry may provide goods and services free of charge or at prices below those that it could command if it entered the market with the sole object of maximising profits. This may however distort the whole structure of prices and incomes.

In general the use of the controls available to public authority has been clumsy and inefficient. Political dissatisfaction with the market system left to itself has compelled almost all governments to make some show of programming and planning. The results have almost always provoked violent criticism from one quarter or another. It is not possible to say even whether these criticisms are well founded for a number of reasons: what is sauce for the goose may not be sauce for the gander. The interests of those who own and run industry are very different from the interests of those who are employed in industry. But in addition to the class conflict over the distribution of the product there are widely differing views over what constitutes a desirable economic system. There are those who see planning solely as a means of pump-priming the system so that industry may be free to pursue its own aims and interests within a generally raised level of economic activity. And there are those who see public intervention as a constantly expanding system of administrative controls replacing the control exercised by the market as a means of making the capitalist system work.

Much economic intervention is ad hoc and localised. This is true of all types. For example, isolated measures of protective legislation sometimes have, in the wider workings of the system as a whole, consequences contrary to those intended. An important computer potential, yet to be developed, is the modelling of interactive systems as a whole, so as to reveal the repercussions of isolated actions on one another and on other parts of the system. (Models that attempt to simulate national economic systems as interactive wholes have not so far been very successful.) More generally, the computer makes possible data banks, statistical simulation and modelling techniques of a kind that have not in the past existed. The heart of the technological changes that are taking place is what we called earlier the 'information revolution'. New possibilities of monitoring the economic system as a whole and possibilities of effective dissemination of information create new instruments of regulation and control.

Taking the potential of the computer and the information revolution together, one may certainly say that the means of regulating a national economy viewed as a whole, now exist. The stumbling block is rather in the second of the two questions raised above, namely, 'How are social purposes expressed and who decides what they are to be?' In the Western capitalist societies the public administrations are by long tradition bureaucratic, that is they consist of an elite working in separation from and keeping their thoughts and reasonings secret from the masses of the people. Also their ideas and outlook have been shaped for societies in which the role of the administration is tutelary and passive rather than creative. The voice of the people is expressed circuitously by the election of representatives to Parliament or to local authorities, these representatives exercising control, if at all, only in a very general way by laying down guiding principles through legislation, etc.

If the administration assumes a more positive role, whose interests will it represent? The major issue involved in any departure from the market system begins to emerge: namely, if regulation is to be deliberate and conscious, as opposed to regulation by the market, how are the interests of those whom this regulation is to serve to find expression? In attempting to find some answer to this question, I shall, in Chapter V, consider some of the structural changes that might be necessary to enable members of a community explicitly to choose the purposes to which economic resources should be directed. In the absence of such structural change those powers of central planning that an administration of the existing form may assume are likely to be directed bureaucratically, that is to ends selected by the administration itself. Most probably these will coincide with the outlook of those who already hold the most powerful positions in the existing system by which economic decisions are taken. In general these are the leaders of the largest industrial and financial organisations. For reasons further considered below, production in their scheme of things is always predominant over consumption.

The orientation of economic policy to production for production's sake dates back to the industrial revolution. At that time there were already growing national and international markets, and the habits, experience and technical apparatus required for trading were well developed. There were also considerable accumulations of wealth in the hands of individuals, a developed credit and banking system, and freedom from restraints on trade and employment. What the new technology of the industrial revolution did was to cheapen very greatly the costs of production and at the same time to encourage large-scale and specialised production, as a means of realising lower costs. The existing market provided a starting point towards enlargement and extension more or less without limit throughout the world. From the big market came big profits for those who, by the cheapness of their products, could have mastery of it. Cheap production implied large-scale production and much machinery and capital. Accumulation of resources opened the way to accumulation of profits. So the governing objectives of the typical producer in a period of industrial expansion was to produce more goods in order to produce more capital with which to produce more goods, to get more profit, to provide more capital and so on ad infinitum. In the main, production was for a market either of consumer goods bought with wages earned in the productive process or of producer's goods used in this same productive process. Those who bought at first from outside the system tended to be drawn into the system.

The great social purpose of the market as a means of allocating resources – however rough and ready this allocation – to the most suitable uses was certainly realised in the sense that capital and labour shifted to those uses where profits and prices were highest because demand was strongest. Undoubtedly through the market some expression was given to the choices and tastes of the consumers both in final consumption and in productive consumption. But the market cannot be said to have served as an effective instrument by which the members of society could determine the broader objectives towards which they wished the economy to move. The only broad objective the market served well was the expansion of production. If in fact it was the will of the people in industrial societies of the last two centuries to hasten the extension of productive forces at more or less any cost, with scant regard for other social consequences, then indeed one may say that the market provided an effective economic means for attaining this objective.

It must, however, be noted that – whatever the reasons for this – market forces on a world scale have not sown seeds of industrial growth evenly through the whole world. The growth of new industrial economies has been stunted and overshadowed by industrial powers that had already emerged in the last century to positions of dominance. The world market has brought the whole world within the orbit of the industrially advanced economies without however automatically causing the under-developed countries to follow the sequence of events through which the industrial countries have themselves passed. So the advantages of the market system as an instrument for attaining *major* social objectives are today called into question on all counts. It is a system that is powered by the pursuit of profit. Profit is a by-product of production that takes no account of the nature of the product, and profit flows fastest to the largest concentrations of capital.

In general the consumer has little say in a direct sense about what is available for him to buy. In a seller's market he is of course in a weak position; but the more usual situation of the market finds the seller pressing by all possible means to enlarge sales – and therefore attentive to the user's tastes and wishes. At the same time the seller tries energetically by advertising to mould tastes towards the purchase of his products; Professor J. K. Galbraith in his *The New Industrial State* goes so far as to suggest that the producer decides what the consumer is to have before goods even appear on the market. The citizen as seller of his labour-power does not find in the market a mechanism through which to express his ideas on how his energies should be spent. In most actual situations his labour is regarded as no more than a commodity that he must sell; he therefore finds himself in a weak bargaining position. Apart from the fact that through the years there have usually been fewer jobs than people in need of jobs, the individual worker for whom a job is a condition of tolerable existence is just one of many items to be bought by the employer. That the labour market, left to itself, fails to meet the objectives of a tolerable society has long been recognised. By the formation of trade unions, by legislation and by other means, countervailing controls over the labour market have been introduced.

To summarise, the majority of individuals have an influence over the market that is so remote as to be negligible (whether it be the market in which they sell their skills as workers or buy goods as consumers). For the most part their only choice is between goods that have already been produced or between occupations in which the objective and form of work has already been prescribed. Within the market system production has come to predominate over consumption. The purpose of production is almost everywhere conceived as that of enlarging the volume of the product; there is little or no regard for the nature of the product, if only it can be sold.

Planning superimposed upon the market system confronts a number of problems. An economic system comprises a large number of interactive elements – there is a complex structure of prices in terms of which costs are determined and exchanges of goods effected. Administrative intervention at one point may have repercussions at other points that are hard to predict. Private ownership and the social outlook that goes with it may result in conflict between objectives determined by planners and those determined by the management of individual firms. There are a number of such frictions in the working of any plan which, though they persist, may diminish in the course of time. There are, however, more fundamental features that vitiate the market economy and the centralised planned economy alike. Existing forms of centralised planning are, in effect, economies in which a planning organisation is superimposed on market relations. It is the defects in these market relations themselves that require careful consideration: in particular, the relations of enterprise to employee and the relationship between enterprises. The dynamism of market relations is increased productivity where productivity amounts to the blind pursuit of higher production of abstract, generalised exchange values. Labour once bought and sold for wages has no part in the control of the productive process which is entirely subordinated to the motivations of the large firms and enterprises. For these firms and enterprises there is no motive or criterion of achievement other than the expansion of the surplus of exchangeable values over costs.

The planned economies of the Soviet Union and Eastern Europe have almost as much as the market economies concentrated essentially on the economic purpose of increasing the national product measured in terms of generalised exchange values. Russia was an economically backward country with a very small industrial centre and the first social purpose of the new economy was to develop industry as rapidly as possible. A centralised bureaucratic administration directed the resources of the country to this end. At the present time the inadequacies of over-centralised planning are being felt in the economies of Eastern Europe. It is only in Yugoslavia that thorough-going attempts to decentralise the decision-making process have been made. These attempts are still far from being fully successful, politically and economically and, though the advance of industry in Yugoslavia has been rapid, it remains at a level of development far below that of the United Kingdom. So the problem of how social purposes are to be expressed in a planned economy resting on an advanced industrial basis is nowhere illumined from actual experience.

Centralised planning in the Soviet and other Eastern European economies where the factories and other means of production are publicly owned, has mainly focussed attention on setting production targets for different branches of industry and ensuring that the targets of different sectors of industry are in balance. In a market economy the allocation of resources to different branches of production is achieved by the rise and fall of prices. If shortages develop prices rise and the consequent rise in profits attracts resources to this branch of production. Where there is over-supply prices fall and capital and labour tends to be withdrawn. The process works, but only crudely and over time, so that attempts are being made within the market economies to study the relationship of industries and to indicate desirable targets ('indicative planning'). In the planned economies of Eastern Europe the enterprises are obliged to direct their resources to the ends prescribed by the central planning authority.

Centralised planning implies model-making. It means specifying what particular enterprises are to produce, to whom they are to sell, on what terms and so forth. It may, of course, be that some areas are left to the market to control. Whether this is so or not the planner must have some model, however rough, to show the links and interactions between various economic activities and the interactions between what is planned and the market in areas where market-regulated exchanges continue. In the laissez-faire economy objectives are determined by the market, the justification for this being – putting it very crudely and over-simply – that what is profitable is also socially beneficial. Wherever planning or regulation by non-economic forces enters in specific objectives must be determined. I do not here propose to examine at any length the problem of who determines objectives and how they are determined. But it is fairly evident that decisions on objectives are made operative at those points in the social and economic organisation at which the activity of planning is centralised. One must ask how far such administrative centres can adequately represent the views and interests of a wider community. Such centralised planning superimposed upon or developing out of a market economy naturally tends to be central planning directed towards and measuring its achievement in terms of production targets, expressed in terms of exchange values produced. That is, the commodity, exchange value relations of the market economy in a very natural way may pass over into and continue as the underlying principle of centrally planned economies.

Planned economies based on public ownership of the means of production, of which there has been extensive experience in practice, in Eastern Europe and the Soviet Union in particular, all take over from capitalism a pre-existing structure of production relations as established through commodity exchange. In the commodity economies the generalised measure of value is money. But there are other generalised measures that take the form of economic indices, as for example indices of volume of production. Highly centralised planning inevitably tends – precisely because it is centralised – to concentrate on such generalised measures. This diverts the focus in a very practical way from the particular uses to which products are to be put. Centralised decision-making, since from the centre the economy as a whole is seen only in generalised terms, reinforces the importance of the units in which overall targets are measured. It is in such ways that planned production apparently motivated primarily by the decisions of the plan-makers, may retain structural characteristics very much like those of exchange value producing capitalism, the commodity/money system in its most fully developed form.

It is hard to imagine any future conditions of social life on this earth that do not call for co-ordination of economic activities between widely diverse communities of men and women. But it is by no means essential that all economic activities should be measured and related to one another in terms of generalised exchange values, that is in terms of the measure applicable to commodity-producing economies such as those in which we today live and which prevail over the greater part of the modern world. This point is of importance since, in seeking solutions to social needs, it would be a mistake to regard the economic relations with which we are most familiar as being necessarily inherent in the nature of things. The kind of relations that are fundamental to such planned control are well illustrated by input/output models. In various forms these are extensively studied and used both in the planned economies of the Soviet Union and Eastern Europe and in the capitalist economies. Input/output models display the relationships between different branches of industry, what the various industries take from and supply to each other. The input/ output model for a whole national economy shows also the resources that are fed into the system as a whole and the output destined for consumption outside the system. Such models to be realistic must be complex and require an extensive data base and powerful computerisation. (The principles of the input/ output model are briefly outlined in Mathematical Appendix, Note 9.)

Input/output analysis at the national scale tends predominantly to use overall indices or value terms to express relationships between industries. Flows of goods in real terms, that is, specific quantities of specific goods, as yet have been shown only crudely and to a limited extent. Ultimately, however, computerised information systems showing the concrete content of flows between different centres of economic activity may be of profound significance to the reshaping of economic structures in the future.

Input/output tables have been published for the American economy dealing with some 200 sectors and work is in hand on tables that will cover 500 to 600 sectors. In Britain since the second world war (see for example *Economic Trends,* 1968) and under the stimulus particularly of the practical and theoretical work of J. M. Keynes, more and more detailed national income statistics have been collected and a good deal of work, particularly at the Department of Applied Economics at Cambridge, has been done on input/output analysis.

The uses of input/output analysis are fairly obvious. If for example – as happened during the war – one particular industry, say aircraft, is to be rapidly expanded and others contracted, one may use input/ output analysis to work out the repercusssions on other industries, to see where bottlenecks are likely to arise, to see where there will be labour and other shortages and where surplusses. Large individual firms also use input/output analysis in estimating possible future demands for their products or their competitors' products. For example, input/ output analysis could give some indications of probable demand for a new material by looking at existing demand for materials for which it might serve as a substitute. Input/output analysis may, therefore, be used to foresee consequences of change and also to co-ordinate the balance of interchanges between industries.

We have now taken matters as far as we can go without beginning to look to the future and to enquire into some of the inter-relations between technological change and changes in the socio-economic structure. The potential that the computer gives in a purely technical sense for centralised control is very considerable; but it would be wrong to conclude from this that centralisation of social and economic power is an inevitable consequence of technological change. Everything points rather to the necessity of resolving the social tensions to which the centralisation of power and decision-making is giving rise. The computer may help bureaucrats to cope with the increasing cumbersomeness of social administration but it cannot, in itself, generate a new social structure – let alone a better one. The computer as the most revolutionary example to date of electronic information processing suggests, however, possibilities of a richness, speed and quality of inter-communication between human beings such as never before could have been dreamed of. Moreover far-reaching changes in technology invariably serve as midwife to changes in social structure. It is now time to enquire what the nature of these changes might be.

Chapter V

Future Economic Systems

Models and the Future

A plan is in a sense a model representing desired or possible courses of economic development. The computer greatly enlarges the possibilities of collecting, storing, retrieving and analysing the massive data needed as input to models of whole economic systems. The computer makes possible the representation, by means of models, of the numerous relations linking the component parts of an economy as a whole. It also – and this is probably its most important but as yet least developed potential – makes possible rapid, accurate and convenient communication of information, knowledge and scientifically precise analysis.

The aim, so far, has been to try to understand the situation in which we find ourselves. Now we turn to the future. This is the interesting part. In what frame of mind do we look to the future? The point is not to predict it but to create it. But creating implies predicting – in a certain sense. If, with a great mathematician of the past, we believed that:-

> "... *The morning of creation wrote*
> *What the last dawn of reckoning shall read* ... "
> *(Omar Khayyam Stanza 73)*

the job of looking at the future would be just making an accurate deterministic model. If I thought things were so, I, for one, would not waste time on models and analysis. Why spoil the story by looking at its end?

But absolute determinism is itself unthinkable; to decide what to think or not to think about it is, in itself, to refute it. However, a world without some relative determinism, some areas of determinism would be equally unthinkable. Man's ability to model what is unvarying in the environment, i.e. the element of necessity, alone makes control of the future possible. Insofar as the models we make have a deterministic framework corresponding to what is unvarying in the environment, we are able to regulate reality by adjusting what is variable and to get the results we want – or something approximate to them. We seek after what we can create, and are free to do so inasfar as we understand what we cannot change, and those aspects of our total situation that are unvarying and necessary.

What is required, then, is to throw light on the context, the framework in which the future will be shaped. We may assume that certain things happen or do not happen and ask, "What then?" For example, what is likely to happen if the basic economic structure of a 'large firm plus market system' remains unchanged? We may explore possible or desirable changes in the socio-economic structure. To understand the possibility of changes implies understanding how and why these changes might come about.

Analysis in a social system is not simple observation. Insofar as analysis makes what is possible clear and convincing it itself becomes a powerful force for change. A man is starving. He sees food out of his reach. He spots a ladder. At once he is roused to action and he goes to take the food. The analogy holds for social change. Ideas, once they grip and convince, are powerful spurs to action. Analysis is a means of revealing goals and paths to them. Indeed, social changes come about as a result of struggle for new ideas, that is by displaying their 'truth' in the double sense of correspondence with the facts of reality and the desires of people.

Looking at the present, what striking or significant features are there to help demarcate areas of possibility? What are the key problems of the present out of which change is likely to evolve or explode? Clearly any complete answer to this question would have to focus attention on the problem of political power, the role of political ideas and organisation and of social structure in effecting political change. Here the focus is a more limited one namely the relationship between technology and socio-economic structure; but in making this restriction I on no account wish to suggest that the problem of political power is unimportant but rather that the discussion I am here embarking upon is auxiliary to wider discussions.

What is basic for our present purposes is the scientific/technological explosion. We understand more deeply and so can harness as never before the molecular, atomic and electronic structure of matter. This extends our power to synthesise materials, to release new forms of energy and most important, perhaps, of all, as we have seen, to use the electron in the analysis, storage, collection and communication of information. This may make for us a world in which human command over natural forces is at once greater and more subtle, and a world in which also the links and shared consciousness of the human species could acquire altogether new qualities. Understanding of the bio-chemical, genetic and neural structures in living creatures advances rapidly. There are many evidences of the continuing advance of scientific theory and of technological advances in the field of practice – new plastics, new man-made textiles, new medicines, new techniques of production and processing, new kinds of tools such as the laser (that is light so much more coherent, monochromatic, directional and intense than ordinary light that it can drill, cut or communicate with unprecedented power and accuracy). There is the atomic pile, the supersonic plane, the moon rocket, and much else besides. How will they affect the way we work together and how we decide on what to work?

Changing Relations of Labour to the Production Process

The technological changes that affect the pattern of life for the greatest numbers of people are those that directly alter economic processes, particularly in production but also in offices, transportation and communication, etc. The advance of automation or, more generally speaking, of new methods of production will go on and will involve less and less direct labour and more and more machine-controlled processes. Possibly, or probably, it will gather momentum. The economic motivation by which these changes will be governed include (a) reduction in costs of production and (b) improved quality of production or production of products that it would be impossible for direct labour to create. There are a number of examples in micro-electronics; optical and photolithographic techniques are today used to produce integrated circuits, that is combinations of transistors and other components so small that 100,000 transistors can be fabricated on a chip no bigger than a postage stamp. Using these techniques economies of size are also economies of cost![1]

Insofar as production is automated, insofar as new scientific techniques for resources allocation are introduced, insofar as systems planning becomes important in the phasing and arranging of production processes, the relationship between human labour and its product cannot easily be measured in the traditional way. In the days when most goods were produced by individual craftsmen one could say with some precision how many hours of human labour were required on average to produce a particular product. For example, some cobblers might work faster than others but on average one might say that it takes so many hours to make a pair of boots. A cobbler had tools. These were the products of other craftsmen and to each year's work by the craftsman himself one would need to add a number of hours of toolmakers' time, of tanners' time and so forth to estimate the hours of labour time put into the production of the materials and tools used by

1. A useful summary of present micro-electronic technologies can be found in 'Large-scale Integration in Electronics' by F.G. Heath, *Scientific American*, February, 1970 and *New Scientist*, 21st July 1972, pp. 689-93.

the cobbler in the course of the year. A reasonably good estimate of the labour time required to produce a given quantity of boots would be possible. So, for most craft products, quantitative measures of labour time embodied in each would be meaningful.

For advanced machine production the relationship between labour time and product is not so simple. Similar products are produced by different processes requiring very different plant, machinery and materials. In many areas of production the contribution of direct labour is much smaller; often the more efficient and cheaper method of production is the one in which direct labour makes up a smaller part of the total costs. Nonetheless the concept of productivity of labour retains a meaning not so different from that which we studied in Chapter III. In money terms the cost of a product may be divided into (a) direct labour, (b) materials, (c) machinery and other fixed capital.

Clearly labour and also machinery and other materials were used in the production of (b) and (c) and similarly, labour, materials and machinery went into the production of these commodities at a still earlier stage. In this way one can imagine a chain of labour inputs or 'dated labour' (to use Piero Sraffa's[1] term) stretching back into the past. For example, if for a product currently being produced direct labour accounted for one-third of the value and means of production already produced by others for two-thirds, and if the same ratio held at the previous stage and at all previous stages the labour content of the product would be:-

Latest stage	33 per cent
2 latest stages	56 per cent
3 latest stages	70 per cent
6 latest stages	91 per cent
After 10 stages	over 98 per cent.

One concludes that in advanced machine production it remains possible in some rough and ready way to assess the labour input in different commodities. Prices and costs derive, albeit somewhat circuitously, from the social relations between people engaged in the production processes.

However, as automation and scientific innovation advance, the measurement of the cost of specific products in terms of the labour required for their production becomes less and less possible or meaningful. Scientific work carried out far away from the industry it benefits may be the crucial factor leading to a great simplification and

1. Piero Sraffa's *Production of Commodities by means of Commodities*, C.U.P.

cheapening of production. Organisations will spend more and more time on research work, exploration of possibilities, scouring the world for scientific and other information in order to keep at the forefront of technical change. Good production planning, stock control and the like will benefit a number of different products simultaneously and it will be very hard to know to which product to attribute costs incurred in this way. At the end of it all one may have plant running with a small team of maintenance and supervisory engineers capable of producing massive flows of products. Once the plant is in existence the unit cost of each product may be very low and the owners of the plant will have a huge productive potential operated by a few hundred people and capable of supplying several millions of users. Production more and more ceases to be analysable in the old economic terms.

In such an economy do costs, as at present conceived, continue to be meaningful? When the craftsman himself ceased to control the process of production and was replaced by the worker selling his labour time for a wage, there still seemed to be some correspondence between work put in and payment received. With the development of machinery the worker became more and more separated from his product and wages were determined more by subsistence requirements plus the fruits of collective bargaining. Although the connection between wages and the direct product of labour became somewhat tenuous, it at least seemed in a broad way true that there was a direct relation between the prices for which products sold under normal market conditions and the resources directly used in their production. The changes in technology and the organisation of economic activity that are at present taking place point towards a situation in which the wage contract can no longer meaningfully be represented as a payment related to output contributed – and indeed a situation in which prices in general cannot be said to have any significant correspondence to resources contributed to the production processes.

Unless social and political measures are taken to counteract present trends, the results of increasingly automated production on the relative shares of wages and profits are likely to be overwhelming. Professor Meade, in his *Efficiency, Equality and the Ownership of Property*, discussed from the standpoint of marginalist theory the impact of technological advance on pricing and distributing mechanisms (e.g. his discussion of the marginal product of labour on pp. 24/6). His conclusions which follow the paragraph we have quoted in Chapter III strongly reinforce the arguments of the preceding paragraphs.

> " . . . Automation might well cause output per head to rise relatively to the marginal product of labour. In this case efficiency pricing would require that an increasing proportion of output accrued to

property owners and the distributional dilemma would to this extent be intensified." (p. 26)

Under such circumstances, market regulation of economic relations must tend to become more and more arbitrary. On this account, as well as others referred to earlier, capitalist economies will require central control planning and investment support by the state in order to maintain the socio-economic structure in a form broadly similar to what it is at present. Within the existing socio-economic framework, the trend towards a science-based automated economy is bound to continue. It is equally certain that it will create sharper and sharper tensions. How can this not be so if technical advance is the harbinger of unemployment and worsening conditions of life and each giant organisation arbitrarily adjusts its pricing and investment policy to serve its particular interests?

To sum up, the direction of change is towards the replacement of human labour in direct production. The direction is towards plants which, once built, require less labour and lower running costs. Within the existing system of large commodity-producing firms, the tendency will be for the whole socio-economic framework to function as a machine for the production of economic values, in which science is increasingly harnessed to production and organisation and a decreasing proportion of the population is engaged directly as a labour force in production processes. This is the direction of change if the logic of the system is accepted; but beyond the technico-economic logic of the system, lies the question of its social consequences and political acceptability.

Projection of Increasing Automation in a Market System

Making projections is, in a sense, a device for understanding the present. What is immediately happening may not seem significant. Imagine that it goes on happening for twenty or thirty years; then we see the implications enlarged, as it were. A trend taken forward as a prediction may be silly or misleading; as an illumination it may be useful. A 3 per cent increase of population in a year may not seem startling. The implications are clearer if one says that in twenty three years – say, a generation – the population will double. To 'extrapolate' (i.e. to assume that a present trend continues indefinitely into the future) is not a reliable way of forecasting. Changes in one part or one aspect of a society or of a natural system interact with changes in other parts, and extrapolation as a prediction is usually nonsense even in deterministic systems.

Human societies and economies are systems in which the observers are within the system. This is a fact of which we need constantly reminding; we need to consider how this affects the system. Human observations are likely to precipitate actions that materially affect the development of the system. Man is acting and reacting all the time to what he sees and feels. The results of his actions may be quite different from what he intends. We may, as men, act individually or in small groups counteracting one another and producing results desired by none. The market system discussed in earlier sections is a system whose elements are millions of individuals acting as individuals. It is a worldwide system, whose rationale is the working of the laws of the market. But this system is a sea in which also swim some hundreds of big fish in the form of large organisations engaged in production, finance, communication, distribution and other activities. These big fish can, in some measure, influence the course of events, but their actions too will cancel out one against another and the deep-running tides of the sea they swim in are determined by market forces that they cannot control individually, despite their relatively large economic power. This remains true even when whole national economies are planned, but remain tied to the operations of the world market.

Projection of present trends assumes more and more automated production within a market system dominated by centralised organisations. At present the world economic system is unified by a market that is not within the purposeful control of any community of men. Imagine that the trends apparent in the present are projected into the future. The hundreds of very large organisations as at present may grow larger and fewer. The remaining giant organisations will employ only a fraction of the populations in the already industrially advanced countries now serving as their social and political bases. These countries already have complicated taxation systems by which public authority takes a substantial part of the revenues that the big organisations generate. Advancing technology will enable them to generate still larger revenues whilst the fraction of the population that they themselves employ will continue to decline.

Those who control the giant organisations will have great power and influence over public affairs, for it is they who control the fountains from which flow the whole of social wealth. Their power to produce wealth, using the advancing discoveries of science and aided by an infinitely extensible army of electronic slaves, will make it quite easy for them to supply bread and circuses at least to the populations of their own communities. What, under such circumstances, will be the meaning of the wage contract? The oligarchs who administer the giant organisations will need some people to staff their factories, their offices, their distribution centres. But not many. They could pay them high wages and still have vast revenues for themselves (provided the market system still functions adequately – and this is a question that needs looking at). Economic theory would suggest that the giant organisations need not pay their employees well, since the numbers seeking employment will vastly exceed the number of jobs offered. But a simple extrapolation from the present is so abhorrent to sense that one cannot even think of such a future without imagining that the masters of the giant economic organisations must be guided in their decisions by political rather than economic considerations. (As indeed they often are at present.)

Extrapolating from the present we assume desire for power, privilege and status to be strong motivating forces. We assume that people, who have found no cure for the syndromes of ambition, are still heading these organisations. What about all the other people that society no longer needs to use to support itself? Class tensions as they have occurred in the history of man through various forms of society have typically been due to exploitation, that is one class has extracted from another class the work necessary to maintain its wealth and power. Slave society needed slaves to support the slave owners. Capitalist society needed workers to work the factories. Landowners needed peasants to till the land. The masters of the automated science-based organisations will need more good scientists and a number of administrative, maintenance and standby staff to take charge of a productive capacity using comparatively few 'productive workers'. But this productive capacity would be capable of meeting the needs of communities many times greater than the community of people engaged in basic productive and economic activities. One must assume that the powerful masters of these giant organisations would pay and treat well the few that they employ, not for economic reasons but to secure their loyalty. One must assume that they would readily pay vast revenues to society at large to escape the danger of hostile separation and attack from a populace dependent upon but no longer necessary to the centres of economic activity. And to whom is the huge flow of goods from the centres of production to be sold? Already in the last half-century the market-based industrial system has proved incapable of spreading industrial growth through the under-developed populations of the world. The market for production goods outside the already industrially advanced countries has been slow to expand. Extrapolation does not suggest widening markets amongst the billion or two of the world's population that at present lack a substantial industrial base.

The technological revolution is rendering meaningless not only the wage contract but also the market system itself. The only possible market to support the explosively expanding productive capacity is one artificially created by taking away from the firms that produce the major goods and services more and more of their revenues to give to the population at large to spend so that these goods and services may be purchased. To do any such thing is totally contrary to the practice or theory that capitalist society inherits from its past. What is more the economic climate in which such measures will need to be taken will certainly be most unfavourable – fears of competition from abroad, inflation at home and campaigns against, rather than for, public expenditure. In a capitalist society the outlook of capitalism is bound to assert itself powerfully; and, so far, the predominant element in public expenditure that takes up the output of industry has been military.

The economic motive force of capital is profit. Through many generations capitalist society has been haunted by the fear that a declining rate of profit might destroy its dynamism. But now what? If the logic of the market system is being undermined, so too must that of the rate of profit. The purposes to which resources are allocated must tend increasingly to be a function of somewhat arbitrary divisions of economic power between financial empires.

Such implications of the technological revolution as we are considering are obviously very far-reaching. Even the most cursory consideration convinces one that this must be so; but the spate of economic writings includes very little that comes to grips with these issues. The few that do fully confirm the conclusion that the technological revolution is disrupting the pre-existing socio-economic structure.[1]

The value of trying to see where present trends are leading is that it reveals the incompatibility between the economic model, on which economic activity is at present based, and the changes in the nature of economic activity to which the technological revolution is leading. We are trying to make do with a socio-economic model that does not fit the times, and – to make matters worse – the system seems to have not a safety valve but a 'danger valve', so to speak, since the unused potential tends more readily to be converted into means of destruction.

Social Models and Models in the Natural Sciences

Once again it is necessary to draw attention to the fact that social activity differs from activity in the natural sciences. In the natural sciences men model a system looked at from outside, as it were. In reality, of course, the observer is not outside the system that he observes and the act of observing has in some sense an impact on the

1. Those who have faced up to these questions include pre-eminently Professor J.E. Meade in *Efficiency, Equality and Ownership of Property,* to which reference has already been made, and J.K. Galbraith in *The New Industrial State,* Hamish Hamilton, 1967. Their standpoints differ and mine from both of them. Professor Meade's critical comments on Galbraith are in the *Economic Journal,* June 1968. Relevant also is Michael Kidron's analysis *Western Capitalism Since the War,* Weidenfeld and Nicolson, 1968, in which the role of arms expenditure is the basic theme.

system observed. In atomic and sub-atomic physics this fact, indeed, needs to be taken into account. Since Heisenberg's 'uncertainty principle' was propounded in 1927 it has been increasingly clear that the division between the natural and social sciences is not an absolute one in this respect. But the difference of degree is striking enough to make it very important for our present purposes. Social activity takes place within the system to which the activity relates. In society men can only act together at all by having a commonly shared model in terms of which to express and interpret their relationships. The crisis of economic society, to which an extrapolation of the trends started by the technological revolution points, can only be overcome insofar as men arrange their relationships differently. This implies evolving a new model for socio-economic relationships which (a) corresponds to the real, historical context in which new economic relations are to be established and (b) corresponds to the aims and hopes of those who feel the necessity for change and are actively striving for change and (c) is clearly understood and so has meaning to those through whose actions the new socio-economic relations become effective.

New models of socio-economic relations will be built out of analysis, debate, controversy and political action; that is, struggle for new ideas interacting with social struggles to give effect to them. Because the model of a new socio-economic structure is a real historical creation it is wrong to ask of any economic, or political or sociological theorist that he tell his readers what the brave new world will be like. It will be as the brave new men make it. Analysis itself is partisan. It reflects the personality, the inner forces that make the writer the kind of person he is. But he deludes himself if he thinks he can create or foretell the future. All he can do is to help others to see what he sees, to tell what he knows, to find answers to other people's questions. The motive forces of change will be big collectivities of people unified by common ideas, by a common model of the kind of socio-economic structure they are seeking to create. They cannot choose just any structure as the whim takes them. If they allow themselves to be carried away by fancy, the facts of historical circumstance will bring them back to reality. New worlds are built within definite bounds of historical possibility. The blueprints for the new order begin to be sketched as the old order displays its inadequacy. One of the marks of inadequacy is an increasing complexity of social and economic relations as ad hoc remedies are found to patch up deficiences that come to light in constantly increasing numbers. The complications of social life can be compared to the complications of an out-dated scientific theory.

The Ptolemaic system, for example, succeeded in predicting the position of the planets almost as well as the new Copernican system, but the complication involved in doing so became exceedingly great. Of it Professor T. S. Kuhn writes:[1]

> "Given a particular discrepancy, astronomers were invariably able to eliminate it by making some particular adjustment in Ptolemy's system of compounded circles. But as time went on, a man looking at the net result of the normal research effort of many astronomers could observe that astronomy's complexity was increasing far more rapidly than its accuracy and that a discrepancy correct in one place was likely to show up in another."

A major theme of Kuhn's book is, as we noted earlier, the power of scientific models (which he calls paradigms) to act as the means of organising the collective work of scientists. This power is of great value but it makes for difficulties in breaking away from an old model, and organising work within the framework of a new model, until the old model has become discredited. There is a certain analogy for the socio-economic model with which we are concerned. There is, however, the major difference that those who are concerned with the scientific model are, generally speaking, a smallish group of scientific specialists, whereas those concerned with the socio-economic model may be – and in modern societies tend to be – the whole community.

We are, I believe, at a stage in history at which we must fight for a new system of ideas, a new social model. This will be difficult because of the resistances that man sets up to changes from an old model. Kuhn has shown this very clearly in the case of the scientist. (Kuhn makes no suggestion that he is interested in the analogy of social revolution, but if there is validity in his findings as applied to the history of science, we cannot escape asking whether this is not also how things work in the organisation of society at large.)

We have already seen how socio-economic models serve as organisers. To suggest a new system of social ideas is also to suggest social change and such a task is bound to meet formidable difficulties. Some of the difficulties are due to social inertia to historical change (a complex topic of study in itself), some to the difficulties of finding new models grounded in scientific fact, acceptable to and seen to be sound by those who wish for change. In such a task we cannot afford to be driven to despair by failure and rejection nor, even more obviously, by the taunt that the 'new system' has nowhere been shown to work.

It is necessary to look for a new outlook on the world. For myself, Marx, as the most penetrating critic of the system of ideas on which capitalist society is founded, has been and remains the most important influence; but there is today a great wealth of new thinking originating from philosophical starting points of wide variety. But much of the

1. *The Structure of Scientific Revolutions,* p. 68.

more widely publicised thinking about the future is very superficial, quick to speculate about possibilities without solid theoretical foundation and rich in new terminology outstripping new ideas.

Much is crystal-gazing suggested by projections and extrapolations of current trends coupled with blindness to the forms and possibilities of change in socio-economic structure. Books like those of Herman Kahn (not Kuhn) and A. J. Weiner (not Wiener), for example their book *The Year 2000*, are useful only in that they may frighten us into taking action about over-population, growing inequality, pollution or the possibilities of human genetic control. Others are simply pretentious guesswork. For example the valuable work that Norbert Wiener did in developing the idea of cybernetics has given birth to a multiplicity of pseudo-sciences. Much of the new terminology of the 'futurologists' is attributable to a rather simple fact of the present and the past, namely the desire to turn new knowledge into a specialist commodity. At times the creation of new disciplines is little more than the defining of a particular type of scientific labour power within the general process of division of labour in the commodity market.

On the more positive side, it may be useful to mention one or two authors who appear to me to be of great importance and from whom I have derived great value in thinking about the process by which men form models of the world in which they live – models as instruments of understanding, as intermediaries in what we do and as means of human co-operation. From Professor J. Z. Young, whose work *A Model of the Brain* I have already referred to, one obtains an understanding of the physical basis of perception/thought/action. The action of the external world is translated into signals channelled through the nervous system. The unceasing flow of messages and reactions to them is co-ordinated by the central nervous system. In this, in our brains, the messages of the physical world are interpreted by means of pre-existing models which themselves are tested and developed by the process of learning, so as more finely to fit our purposes as living beings. Professor Young sets out with great clarity and with great sensitivity the scientific basis of these processes and of the relations between physiology and other aspects of human enquiry.[1] In particular he points to the unique capacity of the human animal to communicate experience to other humans verbally.

It is in this field that the scientific work of Noam Chomsky is of particular importance.[2] He writes:

1. The wider aspects are dealt with fully in his more recent *An Introduction to the Study of Man*, O.U.P. 1971.

2. He himself has made a most valuable summary of his work in *Language and Mind*, Harcourt, Brace and World Inc., 1968.

> "There seems to be no substance to the view that human language is simply a more complex instance of something to be found elsewhere in the animal world. This poses a problem for the biologist . . . – the appearance of a qualitatively different phenomenon at a specific stage of complexity of organisation. Recognition of this fact, though formulated in entirely different terms, is what motivated much of the classical study of language by those whose primary concern was the nature of mind. And it seems to me that today there is no better or more promising way to explore the essential and distinctive properties of human intelligence than through the detailed investigation of the structure of this unique human possession." (p. 62)

If I may use terms that express my own way of thinking, I would say that Chomsky's great contribution is the study of the processes by which men make and communicate to one another verbal models.

Claude Lévi-Strauss, a French anthropologist, is also concerned with language and society. "Qui dit homme, dit langage, et qui dit langage dit société". ("Who says man, says language, and who says language says society.")[1] Lévi-Strauss is spoken of as a 'Structuralist'. For him the structure of human thought and human society provided the main key to understanding. His main field of study has been so-called 'primitive man' and it is his findings in this area rather than his philosophical position that are of particular interest. His book *The Savage Mind* reveals the gigantic achievement of early man in the arbitrary classification of his experiences. Inevitably – when one thinks of it – 'arbitrary' classification must precede 'rational' classification. We classify as best we may and find, as it were, the things we classify sorting themselves into some sort of order that is more than arbitrary. This first sorting, however arbitrary, provides some analogy, some model that advances the description and the understanding of other things. Primitive men provided, as it were, a set of models in terms of which to understand, explain and perform as a society, in society and in the world of nature. It is in terms of shared structures, shared models, that human beings communicate and that human society has cohesion. The models, thanks to which human beings understand reality and organise themselves in society, are crucial instruments of social change. The battle in which new models are forged is, in fact, the struggle of men for new ideas against old ideas, for new ways of life against old – the struggle for social progress.

It is not at all by chance that Levi-Strauss, an anthropologist analysing man's pre-scientific mythmaking, is concerned like Chomsky

1. *Tristes Tropiques*, quoted in Edmond Leach's book about Levi-Strauss, Fontana, 1970, p. 37.

with the social origins of language. What is of special interest for us is what Lévi-Strauss calls the 'science of the concrete'. Traditional African thought "can be seen as the outcome of a model-making process which is found alike in the thought of science and in that of pre-science". The words are from African anthropologist, R. Horton[1]. The idea of homeostasis used by the physiologist (cf J. Z. Young) reappears in these writers as a principle of social control. Basil Davidson gives the first chapter of his study of African "Structures of Belief" the title "A Science of Social Control" and throughout this book *The Africans* there runs the central concept of an ideal equilibrium between man and man, and man and nature.

This same concept of homeostasis reappears in yet other contexts in the work of Norbert Wiener. Physiologically homeostasis is the equilibrium of body temperature, heart rate, blood pressure, etc., which the sympathetic and parasympathetic systems of the human body maintain so that life can continue. Wiener notes (as also J. Z. Young does) that the same concept has relevance for the body politic. "Small closely knit communities have a very considerable measure of homeostasis; and this whether they are highly literate communities in a civilised country or villages of primitive savages." The key to this, says Wiener, is the amount of communally available information and he goes on to contrast the situation in the so-called advanced societies of large communities:

> "There is a belief, current in many countries, which has been elevated to the rank of an official article of faith in the United States, that free competition is itself a homeostatic process: that in a free market the individual selfishness of the bargainers, each seeking to sell as high and buy as low as possible, will result in the end in a stable dynamics of prices, and will redound to the greatest common good. This is associated with the very comforting view that the individual entrepreneur, in seeking to forward his own interest, is in some manner a public benefactor and has thus earned the great rewards with which society has showered him. Unfortunately, the evidence, such as it is, is against this simple-minded theory. The market is a game, which has indeed received a simulacrum in the family game of Monopoly. It is thus strictly subject to the general theory of games, developed by von Neumann and Morgenstern. This theory is based on the assumption that each player, at every stage, in view of the information then available to him, plays in accordance with a completely intelligent policy, which will in the end assure him of the greatest possible expectation of reward. It is thus the market game as played between perfectly intelligent, perfectly ruthless operators . . . The individual players are compelled by their own cupidity to form coalitions; but these coalitions do not generally

1. Quoted in Basil Davidson's *The African*, pp. 112-3.

establish themselves in any single, determinate way, and usually terminate in a welter of betrayal, turncoatism, and deception, which is only too true a picture of the higher business life, or the closely related lives of politics, diplomacy, and war. There is no homeostasis whatever. We are involved in the business cycles of boom and failure, in the successions of dictatorship and revolution, in the wars which everyone loses, which are so real a feature of modern times."[1]

New Models for Old

Social models are actual, that is they correspond to relations established by religion, law, economic practice, and in other ways. They are also in people's heads, concepts of society that guide behaviour. When actual social relations do not fit expectation, desire for change shows itself as discontent, criticism, and various forms of protest. What symptoms are there showing that the socio-economic model does not fit the people who live in it and by it? In what ways does the model not fit? How and where does discontent show? What kind of alternative models might be needed? What would better fit human aspirations? What alternatives could be realised starting from here and now, that is to say, within the socio-economic complex constituting the actual historical present? With a new model sketched against the old model we can look again in a more detailed way at possible functionings and interactions between technology and the socio-economic structure in the new model.

What is wrong now? What are protest movements about? What are the causes of disruption and explosion in social life? What chronic, more subterranean discontents are there? It would be a mistake to try to be too precise about diagnosing the world's ills. Where the world is out of joint it should be pretty obvious. There can be no logical or scientific settlement about the demerits of the old models or the merits of any possible new models. The only meaningful settlement will be the movement of human history – the resultants (though not necessarily the objectives) of men's thoughts and acts, their desire for change and their resistance to it.

We are trying to get some sense of what is to be required of a new model. We cannot, and need not, do much more than list, without weighting or ranking, various symptoms of social malaise. For example

Poverty amidst affluence

– despite man's new found powers over nature, for millions there is extreme poverty, lack of elementary food, clothing and shelter necessary to human existence,

– even in the wealthy countries there is much poverty, also much

1. *Cybernetics*, pp. 158-9.

uncertainty, anxiety and toil in earning a living,

- in many of the poorest areas of the world population growth threatens to outstrip production,
- expectations outstrip provisions (e.g. in housing),

Duller work, 'alienation', crime, drugs. (A note on the meaning of alienation follows this list.)

- many symptoms of frustration, such as vandalism and psychological disturbance,
- for the majority, work is distasteful with too much strain or too little interest;
- in the industrially advanced countries there are considerable trends towards opting out of society and also 'slow suicides', associated to some extent with taking of hard drugs; and
- on the one hand alienation, more 'strangers and afraid in a world they never made';
- on the other more crime.

Misuse of resources, production of wrong goods, technology made an end in itself.

- the plethora of consumer goods produced without enjoyment by those who must earn means with which to buy them, often cater for artificial needs; the consumer society is criticised as subordinating existence to material needs artificially created by those who sell the goods to meet these needs, in richer countries unemployment *and* rising prices and contrasting sectors of affluence;
- facilities for developing advanced technology are very unevenly distributed over the world and also within the technologically advanced countries, leading to a technical élite amongst nations and within nations;
- technology becomes an end in itself; bureaucratic administration equates technology with specialists and the ends to which technology is applied by-pass the quality of social life in favour of bureaucratically selected targets or a merely competitive realising of exchange values in the market;
- 'pollution' and squandering of scarce metals, fossil fuels, and so forth.

Authority in government, education, etc.; a growing gap between family and state.

- trends towards increasingly large, impersonal, authoritarian or oligarchically administered organisations on the one hand, and on the other hand a greater unwillingness to accept authoritarian structures, especially the rejection of authoritarian methods in teaching and the organisation of education;

- in an age when most people believe education to be of crucial social and individual importance, the educations and qualifications provided are regarded by many as being irrelevant and outmoded;

- concepts of democracy are extending beyond the right to vote, to challenge legal authority and customary bureaucracy in social and economic affairs;
- the tradition of authoritarian and property-based organisation is against handing out information; and the tradition of employees is against concerning themselves with what they are doing and why. The tradition is rather to inveigh against the blunders, the stupidity or wickedness of the 'they' who determine for 'us' our conditions of work.[1]
- there is a proliferation of legislative complexities in Britain and many other countries of the West; the social entities on which people are most dependent are family units, and these are too small to bear the burden of practical problems imposed on them, while national governments are too large, over-centralised in administration and burdened with historical traditions of intransigence to the outside world. The political power at the centre dominates all other social entities save only the large economic organisations. The social communities between the family and the nation lack life and power; and associations of ordinary people beyond national frontiers have so far failed to find political strength;
- in small communities and large, in rich countries and in poor, laws and procedures and property rights stifle initiative and hinder direct application of available resources to visible needs; ameliorative measures, bureaucratically administered, tend to become complicating obstructions while capabilities atrophy deprived of the stimulating and meaningful activity that natural inclination and initiative suggest;
- protest against male privilege and domination;

War

- in Vietnam, one of the richest nations of the world has been fighting

1. *Industrial Sociology* by Eugene V. Schneider, McGraw-Hill, 1957, for a good bibliography and summary of the nature of industrial democracy, for example, page 76: 'In each bureaucracy there is a distinction between the administrator or *hierarchy* of the bureaucracy on the one hand and the masses of people who are administered to or governed, the laity on the other.'

one of the poorest with appalling destruction of human life on both sides. The advance of technology in military applications has been rapid and weapons already created make self-destruction of the human race a possibility;

Protest, repression, violence.

Civil Rights movements erupt in many forms attacking class, race and sex privilege; discussions, arguments, criticisms, demonstrations, strikes, non-co-operation, guerilla actions, all clash in various parts of the world with various forms of repression by economic and military means, with dictatorship, in civil war, etc.

The above is a rag-bag of typical contemporary symptoms, complaints and grounds for attacking existing social systems. Dissatisfaction with the structure of society takes many forms and the weight of different factors in their power to cause change will vary; but by taking account of feelings of dissatisfaction, one has a starting point from which to consider feasible alternatives. If these are cries that voice what actual men and women feel, they have meaning, whether or not it is possible to count how few or many.

Many of the complaints and frustrations listed above are comprehended in the concept of alienation. It is quite crucial to the whole problem we are considering. It greatly influenced Marx's approach to politics and economics and in his early writings, *The Economic and Philosophic Manuscripts*, he roots the concept precisely in the commodity exchange system we have been criticising. In such a system man produces goods for the market – goods for exchange and not directly for use – and becomes himself a commodity for sale on the market. He is thus alienated both from his work and from his fellows. He sells himself for wages to another who uses his skills and energies in a manner over which he has little control. Work is done not for its own sake but to buy exchange values with which to live. Communities are broken up into atoms linked together by impersonal forces without social purpose.

Modern sociological studies (and in particular R. Blauner's *Alienation and Freedom*) have examined different occupations, industries and levels of technology to establish relative degrees ot alienation in terms of

a) process control (pace, pressure, rhythm, quantity control and choice of techniques),
b) meaning in work (standardisation, repetition, division of labour, fragmentation of processes),
c) isolation (work group, factory group, union, locality, whole society),
d) self-estrangement (lack of integration, of dull and interesting work, of social and individual life),

e) imposed standards (supervision in place of individual or work group, self-management),
f) insecurity of employment (redundancy, short time).

All these relate back to Marx's fundamental concept; but the variations in degree of meaningless and powerlessness that alienation implies are important for our purpose. This is because these studies show clearly that alienation is least severe for the traditional skilled craftsmen and worst for the assembly line worker or machine-minder. The craftsman is, however, less and less frequently found as automated machinery takes over his skills. But as a result a new worker is emerging with supervisory responsibilities over processes and machines in which work is once again more meaningful and interesting and the separation of management and men is reduced.

Intuitively it seems essential that we should find ways of using resources more directly and more simply, to serve the specific purposes of actual people, individually and as groups. If we are to bring control of the ultimate decisions closer to the many who are 'the people', what methods of allocating resources will take the place of the world market forces and of centralised governments? What part could the computer revolution, the information revolution, the scientific revolution play in the possible new socio-economic structures?

So far only a small step has been taken towards even formulating the problem of trying to see where the technological revolution, pivoted on the computer and associated electronics, could lead in terms of social change. Where we have got to may be summarised as follows. We need to make models of two very different kinds: (1) models that show the necessary constraints imposed by natural environment and human capacities and the legacies of man's social history and (2) models of feasible social change, how the socio-economic structures *might* be 'remoulded nearer to the heart's desire'. What this is may be hinted at by the various, and often conflicting, expressions of feeling and protest within the existing social structure. In what follows an attempt will be made to assess in barest essentials some constraints of technology and economic necessity, and then in the final sections of the book to sketch the elements of new socio-economic structures appropriate to the possible new directions of technology. Even to guess how human society may shape the collective intentions and ideas, that will guide the course it takes in making its future history, is hazardous in the extreme. But if there is to be a future, something of this kind must be attempted as part of the process of finding this future. And when the attempt is made it may surprise us to find that on some fundamentals of economic and social structure the range of likely choice is possibly narrower after all than we might have expected.

Technology and Size

We now enter a difficult area of study. We need to look at the interactions between technology and society in a somewhat deeper way. So far we have been looking mainly at the implications of important technical changes occurring within the commodity-producing market system. The difficulty of the area of study we are now entering is that we wish to see the interactions between technology and society in a two-fold way. We are asking what kind of society our technology can give us and at the same time what kind of technology we need to serve our social purposes. (And who, incidentally, in this context is 'we'? A partisan standpoint cannot be evaded; we put ourselves in the camp of those desiring social change, though the specifics of change may, indeed must, be left to those who make the change.)

There is a view of the relationship between technology and society that may briefly be described as 'technological determinism', like the economic determinism we considered and rejected earlier. Crudely this position is as follows: the motor of social change is technological change. Technological conditions determine all. Theories about change and views of society that tend in this direction are in fact very widely held. It is fairly commonly thought to be the Marxist view of historical development and not altogether inaccurately. Such views appear in the Stalinist version of Marxism but also in the writings of Marxists who opposed Stalin, for example Oskar Lange[1].

Oskar Lange in this work develops a Marxist model that is articulated with great logical clarity. He argues that, come what may, productive forces go on developing. This he calls the "Law of the progressive development of productive forces", which, he says, "undermines, sooner or later, the conformity between production relations and the character of the productive forces. The inner harmony of the mode of production is broken, it ceases to be an internally balanced whole, and a contradiction arises between production relations and the new productive forces"[1]. Such a model corresponds broadly to what happens in a capitalist society but does not throw light on the specific forms that technical change takes in particular forms of society and the way in which motivating forces within a particular social structure react on technology itself. That technical changes create contradictions in an economic system does not mean that they determine what the system will be.

In terms of economic policy, technological determinism leads to unqualified support for anything that may be described as technical progress. Those who oppose progress are described as Luddites. Technology is regarded as neutral and any development of technology

1. *Political Economy,* Vol. 1., p. 34., Pergamon, 1963.

is regarded as a step forward towards some social millenium. That such views are not those of Marx, nor of all who follow Marx (but only of some), is argued by Georg Lukacs, the Hungarian Marxist, who criticised the technological determinist approach to Marxism made by the Russian Communist, Bukharin.

> "Bukharin", says Lukacs, "attributes to technology a far too determinate position, which completely misses the *spirit* of dialectical materialism . . . technique is a part, a moment, naturally of great importance, of the social productive forces, but it is neither simply identical with them, nor . . . the final or absolute moment of the changes in these forces. This attempt to find the underlying determinants of society and its development in a principle other than that of the social relations between men in the process of production . . . – that is in the economic structure of society correctly conceived – leads to fetishism . . . "[1]

As an illustration of technologically deterministic views that are widely held by those who do not follow Marx, one might quote those of Professor J. K. Galbraith in, *The New Industrial State*, in which he argues that man deludes himself if he thinks he can decide what kind of economic system he can have.

> "His area of decision is, in fact, exceedingly small. He could, conceivably, decide whether or not he wishes to have a high level of industrialisation. Thereafter the imperatives of organisation, technology and planning operate similarly, and we have seen to a broadly similar result, on all societies. Given the decision to have modern industry, much of what happens is inevitable and the same."

Here the whole problem that we want to look at has been swept under the carpet by the apparently innocuous words 'modern industry'. If by 'modern industry' is meant a commodity producing economy, such as the economies to which the industrial revolution has given rise, then all that Galbraith is saying is that the technology of the commodity producing system is the technology of that system. However, to say that commodity production generates its particular technology and that this technology makes commodity production what it is both statically and in the way it develops, is to describe only what it is. This excludes from consideration the question that is our central concern, namely the possibilities of social change; that is to say, a change in the whole complex of human relations in society.

It is essential to recognise that the technologies that we have are

1. P. 29, Lukacs' review written in 1925, of Bukharin's *The Theory of Historical Materialism, A Popular Textbook of Marxist Sociology*, 1921. The review was translated in the *New Left Review*, No. 39, September/October, 1966.

technologies that have developed within the commodity producing capitalist economies and that these technologies have been shaped by the motivating forces of the economies in which they have developed. Essentially, as we have seen, they are technologies designed to increase productivity and productivity means increasing an economically homogeneous product, i.e. exhange values in excess of the exchange values used in the production process, or, in other words, stepping up the output/cost ratio measured in money terms. Of course technological progress is not just progress in serving capitalism, nor the advance in scientific knowledge that lies behind it no more than science serving the existing economic system. Within the particular historical system, the commodity-producing market system, that has given rise to the great explosion of industrial technology, mankind has established command of new knowledge and new skills that greatly extend his command over nature. A relationship between man and nature in production is common to all stages of human society but in different stages it takes very different forms and with very different results. There are two aspects to technology, the one specific to certain social structures, its particular form under particular circumstances, the other its more general underlying potential, as an advance in the sum total of knowledge and skill that human society has come to possess and may apply to the production process.

The essential point I want to make is that technology is shaped by forces within a certain social structure and is adapted to particular forms by the social structure as well as itself acting upon the social structure. If we take the commodity-producing market economy with some degree of centralised planning superimposed, we may argue about how much is or is not pre-determined by what Galbraith calls the 'technostructure'. (By 'technostructure' Galbraith means all the scientists, engineers, planning staff, accountants and other organisational personnel operating the complicated, increasingly specialised, science-based industrial complexes of today.) Galbraith nowhere goes to the root of the technical reasons that govern modern industrial organisation. It is beyond doubt that the controlling capital in economies such as those of the United States and Western Europe is concentrated into very large units. In 1962 the twenty largest manufacturing corporations in the USA held about one quarter of the total assets of U.S. manufacturing companies. Thirty-six per cent was held by fifty companies, 46 per cent by 100 and 56 per cent by 200 and 75 per cent by 1,000.[1] The reasons for which capital tends to be concentrated in a commodity-producing economy may be demonstrated; but such reasons do not relate only to technology as such but

1. See *In a Few Hands* by Senator Estes Kefauver, Pelican edition 1965, p. 206.

also to the specific forms in which technology tends to be developed in a commodity-producing economy. (We shall limit ourselves here to considering economic organisations but note in passing that there is a close connection between centralisation of economic power and centralisation of other forms of power – over government, the information media, etc. This will naturally tend to be so since no form of power can continue long to exist unless it has or is able to establish roots in economic power.)

In a market economy there are some natural reasons for large organisations. It has been pointed out above that technical advance often called for large-scale plants (e.g. steel plants) requiring a heavy capital investment. In this way requirements of new technologies have been an important stimulus to the concentration of capital; but, as I shall here argue further, there are quite other forces leading to the formation of very large organisations that go well beyond the requirements of technology alone. Competition between capitals dominated by the necessity of producing more capital must lead to greater and greater concentration. Furthermore, if luck, talent and opportunity are randomly distributed in their impact on the economic system the big firms tend to run away from the small firms.[1] There are many specific features that help the large firm in the market system to grow larger. Division of labour will facilitate a high degree of specialisation. The large firm will surmount the 'R & D' threshold – that is it will have a sufficiently large research and development department to get useful results. Fairly extensive studies have been made of innovation processes which suggest that whilst the threshold differs for different products, a research and development organisation below a certain size cannot keep abreast of advancing scientific knowledge, cannot compensate for time spent following false trails, cannot overcome the practical problems of putting good ideas into effect, and cannot devote enough time to keeping close liaison with producers and users. There are other technical advantages of size *within a market system.* It should be noted that the particular feature of the market system is competition between organisations. To increase competitive strength, organisations keep trade secrets, productive know-how, fruits of research, and suchlike to themselves and will, if the organisation is effectively run, encourage interchange of knowledge, experience and other forms of help in the production process within the organisation and discourage the passing on of advice, information and other forms of help to competitors.

The argument for the technical advantages of large scale then becomes in large part one that says that the economic advantages of

1. See J. Steindl *Random Processes and the Growth of the Firm,* 1965.

keeping the division of labour out of the market are so great that firms large enough to integrate many aspects of the production process, or of other economic processes, will make bigger profits per unit of output than others.

If one considers the advantages of competition, one also meets a number of perplexities. It is competition, it may be argued, that has made the large firm large. Efficiency has bred efficiency and the large firm is still kept on its toes because, however large it may become, it can never become a single world monopoly. There will always be other large firms competing with it. Even if it appears to have a complete monopoly in a particular product in a particular territory there is always a danger of another firm producing a substitute product or entering the territory of the monopolist and reintroducing competition. Even if there were only a hundred large firms responsible for all he economic activity of the capitalist world, there still would be competition between these hundred firms.

The weakness of this line of argument is exposed if one asks how are the constituents of these giant firms kept efficient? Statistics put the labour force in the United States, producing a Gross National Product of about $900,000 million (1969), at just under 80 million. In the UK we have a domestic product in the neighbourhood of £30,000 million[1] with about 23 million people in civil employment. If we were to settle for a policy of large-scale, but competitive, organisations this must mean a proliferation of giants such as our biggest giants today, for example Unilever or ICI. (ICI employs about 120,000 people.) This means thinking in terms of, say, 100 or 200 organisations in Britain and of 400 or 500 in the USA employing some hundreds of thousands of people each. We come back to the original question, how is effective division of labour to be achieved within such organisations? If the answer is by competition, what then is the advantage of large organisations? If the answer is that there is some 'pseudo-competition', then one is forced to ask, if this can work within large organisations, why should it not work throughout the economy as a whole?

We do not seem to be getting nearer to an answer to our problem. The problem itself seems elusive. We have been asking questions about 'effective' organisation, 'effective' division of labour, and so forth. Here, indeed, is the kernel of our difficulties. If by effectiveness we mean ability to make profits, that is to realise exchange values in excess of costs incurred within the structure of the commodity-producing economy, then we have a fairly definite meaning to attach to effectiveness; but we have by the very way that we have posed our problem ruled out consideration of alternative economic structures. If we ask

1. £33,000 million in 1971 at 1963 prices.

ourselves what size of unit, what size of production team, is appropriate in modern production then we see that we have a question of quite a different sort. It is a question we cannot answer in general terms because different processes are required to produce different things. All we can do at this stage is rather vaguely to say that work teams in modern industry are commonly of a fair size running often to several hundreds but, as a rule, only a small fraction of the total labour force controlled by a 'single capital'. (By 'single capital' I mean unified ownership as, for example, through the shareholdings of a company or complex of companies or state holding.)

The reasons for the continued existence of large economic organisations are that the large organisations are more powerful than the small. The large organisations are able to pursue strategies that work to their advantage against the small organisations. Furthermore the very structure of the market economy is such that once inequalities of size are established, the tendency will be for the share of economic activity in the hands of the large to get larger.

The gigantic organisations of the present-day are not in any absolute sense economically more efficient or technologically necessary. All we can say is that in the circumstances of the commodity exchange economy the pressures of competition, translated into pressures to increase productivity as a means of increasing profits, led to new techniques of mass production symbolised by Fordism and Taylorism. The workshop organisation underpinning mass production provided the pre-condition, the soil for the development of the automated plant, once the computer had been invented. In the automated plant the tightly disciplined and carefully drilled teams of workers adjoined to the machines are replaced by interlinked machines co-ordinated by computer control. The labour force required in such plants falls dramatically. An altogether new stage of production is in sight towards which, however, capitalist economy may for various reasons move less rapidly than the technological potential permits.

Big plants with costly machinery are not identical with large organisations. The large international company of today controls many complex, costly installations in different parts of the world. There is no technical reason for these many plants being in one organisation other than the exchange of information and experience. There is, however, the crucial economic reason related to a market economy, namely that the large worldwide organisation is best able to obtain and maintain worldwide outlets, the mass market that mass production requires. Key questions looking to the future are, therefore, what is the role of mass production, for what products is mass production desirable and advantageous, and how is it to be brought into harmony with consumer wants? What if automation is developed as rapidly as possible will be the typical size of the mass producing unit? In fact, looked at in this way, the problem of scale concerns not the technology of production but it may possibly arise in the sphere of distribution. Or to put the matter another way, if decentralisation in the management of production units is deemed desirable a comparatively small producing unit will often be supplying a very large community of users.

Summing up, it is possible to establish that large-scale organisation is not dictated by modern technology but by laws of economic development in a commodity economy. Since the predominant factor is the process of capital accumulation, it would be useful to ask why in the Soviet Union and other centrally planned economies with publicly owned means of production, large trusts nonetheless predominate in industrial organisation. The political/historical investigations necessary for this would, however, take us too far afield and for present purposes it must suffice to mention again the many similarities with those of the West in the economic methods adopted throughout the industrialisation of the Soviet economy. In China and elsewhere somewhat heated debates are proceeding questioning Soviet economic practice and raising the whole question of the extent to which techniques and methods of economic organisation from a capitalist economy remain suitable for transplantation into a socialist economy.

Alternatives to Large-scale Combines

In looking for alternatives to large-scale centralised organisation in a society based on advanced technology, there are no prototypes on which to draw. The alternatives must be constructed in imagination by studying what exists to find the germinating points from which new relations could emerge.

The problems we face are the problems also of other countries and in time there may be fruits of experience to help us; amongst these, for example, the theory and practice of decentralised economy in Yugoslavia and of new economic forms developing in China will deserve study. We, however, need to think in terms of an economy in which an advanced industrial sector already predominates.

Despite widely differing outlooks most social observers and, indeed, socially conscious participants in modern society agree that the gulf between ordinary people and the big organisations where the important political and economic decisions are taken, is very wide. Yet these centrally made decisions remote from the practicalities of each individual's daily life determine the framework and the texture in which these daily lives are lived. It is when one comes to the question of possible remedies that differences of opinion begin to emerge. I have argued that these problems arise from the basic socio-economic structure and that this can be changed without losing the benefits of modern science and technology. But it should be added that socio-economic structures have an inertia that can be overcome only by most powerful social forces. Continuance of social life necessitates constant reproduction of the material means of production and of social relations determining the division of labour and the distribution of the products. By what social processes, by what social forces can the cycle of social reproduction be changed?

There have been a number of thinkers in the socialist tradition who have, from its earliest days, looked for a society in which men and women shaped their own destinies, organised their own affairs, consciously, simply, purposefully, in their own way. We may cite William Morris in England and Michael Bakunin, the emigré Russian. Most socialists have shared the ideal of anarchy in the sense of a self-ruling community free from the domination of superimposed class or state power, but big differences have arisen over the route by which to attain such a society of free men and women. At the same time, many socialists have seen the main defect of the market system in its lack of planning in the sense of lack of purposeful co-ordination of economic activity. (Those who see this as the main point of socialism range from Stalinists to Fabians.) Syndicalists (Tom Mann), Guild Socialists (G. D. H. Cole) and others (see K. Coates and A. Topham *Industrial Democracy in Great Britain* for reference), have been strongly opposed to centralisation but have not given much attention to the problems of co-ordinating production when it is carried on by separate producer-controlled units.[1]

In relation to the technological revolution, we need to look at centralisation from two points of view. First, does the new potential of technology put more power into the hands of the centralisers? Second, to what extent is deliberate co-ordination inescapable and to what extent do the new techniques help human society to achieve this co-ordination? Does such necessary co-ordination of itself mean centralisation of power? If it does are there safeguards against its abuse?

The information revolution, as already mentioned, creates horrifying possibilities for central control. The computer enables a central bureaucracy to record in very small space a huge number of facts about individuals. Quite harmless information (for example payments for goods bought made by quoting a bank account number) may be combined and analysed to give information about individual movements and activities. Complicated decision making models may be used, as they already are to some extent, as a smokescreen to hide concentration of power in an administrative oligarchy. At the same time there is unceasingly rapid advance in the spate and speed of

1. G.D.H. Cole recognises this in his foreword to P. Pribicevic's *The Shop Stewards Movement and Workers' Control* 1910-22, Oxford, 1959.

communications and a good many people are aware of the danger they are in. The public unease about the 1971 Census revealed this. The sheer technical potential for centralised control of information does, and will increasingly, become engaged in battle with political and social feelings resistant to control by a central bureaucracy.

The technological feasibility of operating highly centralised organisations of increasing size is only one side of a many-sided situation. The new planning techniques already being used by large organisations, such as linear programming, mathematical programming generally, computer-aided simulation, computer-aided planning design and information retrieval, mathematical techniques for stock control and forecasting and much else, might also be adapted to serve as instruments of co-ordination in decentralised economic structures very different to large organisations within a market system or a bureaucratic plan. The technological potential for decentralised media and information dissemination (e.g. 'piped television') is tremendous, but the existing social structure has focussed development on nationwide T.V., papers, radio, etc. In short, the socio-economic structure dominates technology – not vice-versa.

The problem is to see what other forms of social structure might be realisable. One essential that seems to be indicated for any viable society of the future is that people must gain a simpler and more direct control over the way their energies and resources are expended and over the ends to which these are put. To say this is to say a lot. At the moment in Britain ultimate allocation of resources rests with international market forces plus intervention of public authority at a national level. In a country such as Britain a great deal of administrative work is done below national level, particularly by local authorities. Much money is spent by local authorities but national legislation and administration by national ministries to a very considerable extent decides what services they are to provide, to what standards, and so forth. It would therefore be misleading to over-stress the importance of decision-making at local authority levels. In reality financial stringency and regulations from Whitehall leave local authorities little power to shape the pattern of socio-economic life and the local bureaucracies which often cover populations well in excess of 100,000 are already far removed from day-to-day affairs. The important development here is the grass roots movement which is pressing decisions against a bureaucratic apparatus throttled by financial stringencies and traditions of administrative secrecy. (The campaign on the Loraine Estate, Islington in February 1972 for a children's adventure playground is a good example; the authority insisted that the demand was incompatible with their development plans; it took direct action by the mothers and children to force the issue open and reveal that this was not so.)

The 'devolution' of decision to privately-owned enterprises is real, but apart from the size of the dominating enterprise, already dealt with, this is limited by the fact that each enterprise is free only to make the best of the conditions imposed by the market and a highly centralised financial system. Focus of effort on increasing 'productivity' in practice means increasing marketable values, that is, values determined by the forces of the market and the commodity/money relations of which it is an expression.

Centralised administrative planning attempts to replace the market by assuming that someone knows broadly what is wanted and then concentrating attention on the co-ordination of effort to obtain the desired end. In a war economy, a general staff will stipulate required numbers of tanks, torpedoes, aircraft, shells, gunboats, and other military equipment. The subsistence needs of a population can be worked out. The desired end product is specified and the job of the central planners is to allocate resources so as best to meet the specified requirements. In an underdeveloped economy making a forced march towards industrialisation (such was the situation of the Soviet Union in the 1920s and 1930s) centralised administrative planning has also been effectively applied to the industrial sector. Under such circumstances a fairly straightforward statement of the products required can be made. Even so, there are very many problems about the most efficient allocation of resources that the intuition of an intelligent administrator cannot solve, and where implementation by simple directive is not adequate. There are also many problems of how to encourage initiative and produce a flexible plan capable of adjusting itself to unexpectedly favourable or unfavourable developments.

Once the most simple directives of industrialisation have been achieved and a more complex economy begins to emerge with increasing expectations of choice in consumer goods and services, new problems arise which a centralised administration cannot cope with. Such problems are already being felt in acute forms in the Soviet Union and Eastern Europe. New theories of economic organisation, such as those of Liberman in the Soviet Union, Ota Sik in Czechoslovakia and others, are exploring possible new forms of organisation in planned economies. Liberman wished to restore profitability as a major criterion of economic performance, thereby allowing managements to have a more unified and meaningful economic objective to replace the multiplicity of targets and directives, often contradictory, to which administrative planning had subjected them. Ota Sik, though violently attacked in the Soviet Union, pursued similar objectives and worked out more fully their implications. He looked to the central economic authorities to take only broad strategic decisions shaping the general direction of longer-term development. Individual enterprises, he suggested, might be left free to establish relations with others using the market to determine prices. The central administration would monitor the actual performance of the system and would hope to be able to steer any elements that threatened to go off course.[1]

The problem is to explore economic relationships of a new kind that make use of the technological potential and give people, that is groups of people and not only individuals and households, (a) the means of subsistence that they require and (b) suitable means for themselves undertaking the economic and social activities they want to undertake. Peoples' needs and conditions of life as producers as well as consumers have to be provided for. I do not think it is possible to conceive of such a society unless the main centres of energy, socially and economically, are to be found in comparatively small social and economic organisms, communities of people living and working together and associated in their work and their other activities in a natural way. At present the individual, plus dependants, is economically free in theory but in reality an isolated unit carried on the tides of a worldwide money/commodity economy. Freedom of the individual could only become reality for everyone within community groupings of a few hundred people in which each person's voice could be heard and carry weight. Such social organisms could indeed run a technologically advanced, science-based society, provided they could effectively communicate and co-ordinate their relations with similar social groupings. The problem is to discover the possibilities of such groupings becoming the centre of gravity in social and economic decision making.

At this point it may be useful to try to collect some first ideas on alternative socio-economic structures; we should not expect great clarity or precision; we can only indicate some essentials about the constraints within which any movements for change must operate. It is in this spirit that the following points are brought together:

1. Commodities are things produced for exchange. Their exchange is mediated by money. The means of continued social existence are reproduced insofar as the decision makers in the productive process have means in money terms of replacing or enlarging resources consumed. Socio-economic relations express themselves in money terms. What alternatives are there to a money-mediated economy? Is it possible to move towards an economy in which production is not essentially production of commodities, that is, exchange values, but production aimed *directly* at specific needs?
2. The only alternative to centralised control that could effectively devolve decision-making would be the one in which basic work

1. By way of supplement to these brief remarks the reader is referred to Chapter VIII of Michael Barratt Brown's *What Economics is About*, Weidenfeld and Nicolson, 1970.

teams themselves determine their own activities.

3. It would be a great waste of production time if large-scale production did not meet a considerable range of ordinary needs.
4. As has already been argued above, the large-scale element associated with advanced technology relates to (a) the large number of people who may be supplied from one productive unit and (b) the large costs and many-sided skills that may be embodied in productive equipment; the work-team in the productive unit will rarely exceed a few hundred and the tendency is for the effective work team in science-based production to become smaller. Effective co-ordination between productive groupings is evidently essential, but large-scale centralised organisation as it exists to-day is necessitated by money/power competition between capitalist groupings, and not from the standpoint of practical and technical feasibility. In short, *material* conditions do not determine the large-scale, centralised socio-economic organism; these are determined by the existing structure of *social* relations. The essential centralising factor is the social relations of capital, which in turn are an expression of commodity/money relations.
5. Central planning which involves central control of the interacting components of national or international economies, has in practice led to serious political and economic defects, and it is therefore necessary to ask whether and how the emphasis can pass to the *co-ordination* of useful activities each controlled by relatively small work teams or work units. Is the technically essential element in centralised planning different from co-ordination?
6. What forms of social relations between men and women in production are compatible with advanced science-based techniques?

In looking for alternatives to the present centralised, external control of economic activities, whether it be by distant administrative offices or by market forces, we are trying to give more tangible meaning to rather old ideas. These involve the desire for the conscious, explicit administration of things so that people who produce things may determine how they produce them and people who use things may specify what things they want.

The necessity of giving freedom, that is, self-determination to the basic groupings of people in the socio-economic system, does not imply the destruction of all bonds between the component parts of human society. On the contrary new bondings, stronger and wider, will need to take the place of impersonal market forces plus centralised power. A striking and penetrating commentary on this question of 'social bonding' is to be found in Christopher Caudwell's *The Concept of Freedom* (Lawrence & Wishart, 1965). (Christopher Caudwell died in the Spanish Civil War in 1937; his intense and brilliant theoretical work, published posthumously, was packed into two short years, 1935-36.)

> "If our definition of love," he writes (p.32) "is correct, it is true that love makes the world go round. But it would be rather truer to say that society going round as it does, makes love what it is. This is one of those relations like that of knowing and being, which can only be understood in a dialectical manner. Thought guides action, yet it is action which gives birth to consciousness, and so the two separate, struggle, and return on each other, and therefore perpetually develop. Just as human life is being mingled with knowing, society is economic production mingled with love." And to this he adds (pp. 49/50) "Today it is as if love and economic relations have gathered at two opposite poles. All the unused tenderness of man's instincts gather at one pole and at the other are economic relations, reduced to bare coercive rights to commodities. This polar segregation is the source of terrific tension, and will give rise to a vast transformation of bourgeois society. They must, in a revolutionary destruction and construction, return in on each other and fuse in a new synthesis. This is communism. Thus the forces that produce communism can be viewed from two aspects. From the quantitative aspect, productive forces, that have outgrown bourgeois social relations, burst their fetters. But the fight is fought to an issue in men's consciousness. Man, the individual, feels the out-moding of these relations, their sloughing by reality, as the death of all that is valuable to him. The demand to bring back to consciousness these vanished values appears as hate for the present and love for the new, the dynamic power of revolution."

The basis for the organisation of people as producers probably already exists in the work teams of a modern economy. In a pit, in a unit of a factory, in a hospital, in a school, on a railway, people are naturally combined together in a work team by the requirements of the job they are doing. From time to time they are given specific objects of work, determined by some outside authority or by a manager or owner. Such teams, even as they are today, provide in a certain sense the basic units in socially linked production processes and other economic activities that encompass the whole world. A form of more direct control over the economic apparatus could emerge if these work teams operated not merely as work teams but also as small-scale 'parliaments of the people' deliberating on the manner and the direction of their economic activity. And, in fact, the struggles that are proliferating in the name of 'workers' control' are evidence of people moving in this direction.

But whereas basic community groupings can be imagined as growing out of the existing economic structure, the basis for corresponding groupings of consumers is far less evident. Yet if there is to be a more simple and direct control, by which to shape the quality of social life, some basic groupings of consumers would seem to be essential. Increasingly, we object to remote organisations, whose purposes are not ours, deciding what we are to have; but if this objection is to mean anything we must be able to set up an alternative as an objective for which to fight, towards which to direct our struggles of protest against things present.

What we all require as consumers may perhaps be considered to fall into three broad groupings:–

(a) Social consumption, for example, water, housing, education, general amenities of the environment etc. There is no hard and fast line between those things that the community would like to have provided as a 'social service' and those things that must be so provided. One might expect roads necessarily to be provided as a social service (though there are still some toll gates) and bread to be an individually purchased commodity. But there is no reason why, should the community so desire, bread should not be laid on as a free or unmetered supply, like water. It may be a great convenience and save distribution costs if many of our needs are met by public supply. Some social consumption meets individual needs that are for convenience sake supplied socially; in other cases it meets more than individual needs. The water we drink or wash in is an individual need supplied socially; it is water to wash an individual's face or to quench an individual's thirst. But the water in a fountain in a square or in a lake meets community rather than individual needs. Life as an individual is one aspect of the whole of which another aspect is life as part of a community.

(b) There will be other needs that are for goods, economic products and services that we consume as individuals, but in the requiring and consuming of which we are very much like other human beings. Again, the dividing lines between one type of need and another are by no means hard and fast. Above I suggested that bread might be put on social supply. One would think of it as an individual requirement that with some variations is similar for most men and women. In a country such as Britain shirts are widely and generally required. But not identical shirts. Fairly simple statistical analysis would reveal the probable distribution of size requirements over the country as a whole, but as to style there will be wide and changing variations.

(c) Finally, there will be requirements that are unique to individuals or to small groups of individuals. Some may want a particular type of window in their houses. Someone who is interested in photography would require special types of equipment, an artist special facilities for painting.

This division of consumer needs into three groupings is not clear cut or precise; the groups overlap. But it is sensible broadly to say that human beings have needs (a) through and for the community of which they are a part, (b) as standard specimens of *homo sapiens* needing to be fed, clothed and sheltered from the elements, and, finally (c) as means of expressing and realising their own individuality. Or, one might say: type (a) needs are those of a social, political being; type (b) are those of man as a living creature requiring food and protection in much the same way as other men and women; and type (c) are those of men as individuals differing from others. Consumer groups in different localities are needed to express and explore social needs (type a) and to determine how they are to be met. For other types of need the group would be a wider social or political unit through which to formulate requirements and give force to criticism where provision was felt to be unsatisfactory.

The Concept of Basic Community Units

In all that has gone before we have been exploring the constraints and the potentials of modern society. In introducing the concept of basic community units we are broaching the problem of a new socio-economic structure. From what standpoint are we to approach this problem? Our task is not to engage in historical speculation; it is for men and women in society to make it what they will and what they can. Our task relates to the future only through the present. We are to reveal possibilities and constraints inherent in the present so that those who act to bring about social change may have some vision of feasible alternative socio-economic structures. The concept of such structures is, of course, an important element itself in the process of social change. The validity of such concepts turns on a number of things. They must in general express what people want. One must also find a sequence of steps in the process of political and social development linking the future aim to present actualities. Or, to put the same point another way, the credibility of an objective implies demonstration that forces already exist within society, albeit in embryo, capable of achieving the objective. We also need to demonstrate that a viable process of production of material goods and reproduction of means of production exists and that social relations appropriate to it can be effectively expressed and realised. This latter point comprises not only commonly shared concepts of social obligations and rights but also adequate means of communicating information in a human society now seen to be worldwide in its interactions.

Our concern in this book is with the problems of technology, production and information flows in the process of realising social relations. We are not, that is, dealing with the question of political forces and political power which, nonetheless, warrant examination at least as full as our present study. For present purposes it must suffice merely to indicate that a strong social and political consciousness and corresponding actions are developing amongst the people of Britain (as also in many other countries of the world) in favour of what is often described, for want of a better term, as 'grass root democracy'. The evidence for such movements is ample. In industry, sit-ins, work-ins and other new forms of struggle demonstrate unwillingness to accept remote decisions whether these be attributable to the person of a director or to the impersonal forces of finance and the market. Forms of organisation appropriate to these forms of struggle, as for example shop stewards' committees, assume in the process a greater social significance. In the community outside of industry and other forms of economic activity, forms of grass root action are varied and numerous – by tenants, by parents about education or play facilities, by children themselves, by claimants' unions, by objectors to traffic noise or danger, by various bodies against pollution and on many other issues. These various movements reflect people's feelings about what they have a right to expect from modern society and, as a rule, develop most actively 'where the shoe pinches'. As I have already said, I do not intend here to explore more deeply the exact nature of these political forces, important though such a task is. But it is necessary to establish at this stage that there is a basis in modern society from which to develop structural change in the direction of social devolution. It would be absurd to expect social change to emerge solely at the level of ideas or to think that whole peoples can be enticed by the rationality of blueprints. Having made this point clear, however, one should emphasise that the whole point of the kind of discussion on which we are engaged is to develop ideas which give a sense of understanding as to the feasibility of alternative possible courses of development arising from the actual movements and historical processes taking place in our society at the present time. It will be useful once again to summarise the stage reached in the development of our argument:–

1. Large-scale organisation is due not so much to technology as to competition and other economic processes in the market/commodity producing system tending to favour concentration of capital, finance and economic power.
2. Advancing technology may lead to very costly plant capable of supplying the needs of large numbers of people but not necessarily requiring a large labour force to operate.

3. Advancing technology almost invariably implies specialisation coupled with worldwide exchange of information and experience.
4. Advancing technology normally requires relatively high levels of expenditure and concentration of effort on Research and Development.
5. Basic work units in which humans naturally co-operate are relatively small, though these units need many close external links to other units.
6. The production unit, that is, the production process operating as a relatively self-contained system, tends with the development of automation to become smaller, typically a few hundred persons against the thousands working as a unified work team in the earlier stages of mass production.
7. If social control is taken to mean that those whose activities are most affected must also take the major decisions concerning such activities, then conscious control of economic activity, as opposed to market control, must imply devolution of decision-making to smaller basic units than at present.

The next stage in our argument is to explore what is to be meant by basic community units and to elucidate their role in the socio-economic structure. We have dealt at some length with existing structures and social change; that is, transition to new structural forms, however revolutionary we may wish it to be, must always be relative to existing socio-economic structures. That is change either modifies or replaces what there now is in respect of certain essential processes. The essentiality of these processes derives from the necessity of social production and reproduction continuing in some feasible and appropriate form. However vigorous moves away from market control may be, some market influences will certainly remain operative for a very long future. Similarly devolution of political decisions cannot entirely replace functions now performed by economic policies at the national or international levels. In talking therefore of new socio-economic structures one is, for the foreseeable future, talking of directions of change rather than total transformation, even though change may come about as a series of sharp breaks with the past and leaps expressing radical change in outlook, motivation and organisation of social and economic activity.

Focal points in the existing socio-economic structure are the nation and the family, the large-scale enterprise and the small-scale enterprise, all in their various ways subordinated to the exigencies of international market and monetary forces. Domestic economy is organised within the family, outside the market system but crucially dependent upon the market system. Members of the family or household must go to the market system to earn the means of buying the goods that maintain the existence of the household. The nation-state organises activities that go beyond the market, the apparatus of war, the welfare state, etc., but to maintain these activities must go to the market. Small-scale enterprises are in the main in a position of clients to the very large organisations. These, though their internal planning may be considerable, are governed by objectives determined by the market; their criteria of achievement are measures of profitability. So the argument comes to this. In the market system ultimate evaluation of possible ways of deploying resources is automatically handled by the market system. If there are grounds for seeking alternatives to this, what alternative structures are there? We are looking for an alternative to automatic market control. One cannot easily imagine any self-operating system, that is in essentials not another form of the market system. By an alternative, therefore, we mean a system in which deliberate, conscious human decision steers economic activity and development.

We have many starting points to build from. Already there exist new possibilities of large-scale organisations guided by a steering team – a cabinet, a council, a board of directors. The technological revolution as essentially an information revolution evidently puts powerful control instruments into the hands of the steersman of such large organisations. But in considering this as the relevant alternative to the market system, we are in fact evading the problem that we have posed. As already pointed out, the centrally planned commodity economy is in essential structure similar to the market-controlled system. Moreover, how does the steersman know what the component elements of his large organisation want as producers and how does he know what products are wanted by society at large? If the answer is that he only knows what he and his associates in a position of control want, then we are back where we started with the problem of the tensions between a powerful controlling minority and society at large.

Our argument has already established the necessity of developing some forms of basic community units – that is social organisms of a few hundred or at most a few thousand people having a considerable weight in the social and economic decision making process, that is becoming new focal elements in the socio-economic structure. It is only along some such lines that it can be possible for conscious human control to replace the control which the market at present exercises as a force external to human society, and at the same time to overcome the impotence of the isolated individual vis-à-vis the market and also vis-à-vis centralised planning operated at the level of the nation-state. Alienation in social life results from atomisation of individuals in relation to centralised capital. Control of social life consciously by man for himself/herself can only become real at the level of basic community groupings.

We need to consider basic community units of two kinds:–

(1)basic community units of consumers, and

(2)basic community units of 'producers'.

I have put the word 'producers' in inverted commas since I wish it to mean any economic or social activity to serve or to meet the needs of human society beyond the basic community unit itself. It might be a factory making bottles, a health centre, an orchestra. A community of consumers might coincide with a community of producers. For example, a hospital might be a complex of buildings in which people lived, worked and found their recreation. But at very least the conceptual separation seems to me essential at this stage. We are talking about possibilities submerged in present actualities. We should not alarm ourselves with artificial visions of parochial utopias. We are trying to envisage the minimal structural requirements for deliberate, conscious, democratic control of ends and means in a technologically advanced society.

In production and in other creative activities men and women belong, as I have already suggested, de facto, to basic community units – those with whom they co-operate every day in work. These units may be clearly defined (as an orchestra, for example, or a specialised workshop in a factory) or only rather vaguely delineated (for example delivery van drivers might under some circumstances be regarded as attached to the supply unit whose goods they handled and under other circumstances as a group in their own right). But, while these basic units exist, they rarely have any formal status, they rarely have recognised means of deciding upon or regulating their own activities, nor facilities to formulate and communicate views about their social functions. The formal structure of their activities is predominantly imposed from without.

Apart from productive activity (in the wider sense) other basic units of social life in a modern society are, for the most part, only faintly delineated. But at the present time in Britain and elsewhere there is considerable evidence, in widely differing quarters, of pressure to give more scope to basic social units. This is a question to which the investigations of sociologists are being addressed in many forms, as protest against bureaucratic administration in social services, in planning and elsewhere becomes more vocal and explicit. At official levels the need for consultation with local communities on planning matters is recognised, (see, for example, the report of the Skeffington Committee, *Planning and People).* The Maud Commission on the reform of local government was subjected to criticism for not giving more powers to local community units. The commission in its Research Study on Community Attitudes recognised that most people define the home area to which they belong as a small neighbourhood 'approximately the size of a group of streets or smaller'. Dr. W.A. Hampton's study of Sheffield, *Democracy and Community*, 1970, carried the Maud Commission enquiry much deeper through a sample survey of the Sheffield electorate. In a chapter on 'Perceptions of Community' he reveals how small the perceived home area generally was, for three quarters of the respondents smaller than the ward – a few streets only – and frequently named as an older village incorporated in the city or a new housing estate. Dr. Hampton found evidence to support the claim of the Community Attitudes Survey of the Maud Commission that "Community feelings are concerned with the interaction of the individual with other people – rather than with his relationship to his physical environment". *(Democracy and Community,* p.115). The home area was perceived as quite separate from the place of work. Civic consciousness, moreover, in terms of interest in, or knowledge of, local politics (less than half of the respondents knew the name of their Ward, Constituency or M.P.) did not appear to be related to neighbourhood attachment. This does not tell us that they would not be more interested and knowledgeable if civic affairs appeared to be more neighbourhood-based; indeed it is to such a development that Dr. Hampton looks forward. He is not alone.

A group of planners, scientists and sociologists, calling themselves the 'Open Group', in a recent pamphlet *Social Reform in the Centrifugal Society*[1] advocated "New neighbourhood councils . . . to represent the wishes of the local inhabitants, the right to be consulted by the higher level authorities on any proposals affecting their communities and the power to spend any money they raised locally on amenities such as open spaces, fair grounds, theatres, community centres and concert halls." They wanted the bottom tier of local government machinery to take responsibility "for the provision of services in housing, education and welfare" and they wanted "to break away from the traditional forms of representative local government and give a trial to direct democracy." (An Association for Neighbourhood Councils has been formed.)

It is desirable for a number of reasons to treat separately the fact of men and women coming together in small community groupings, (1) as consumers and (2) as producers. First of all both these activities are basic and real in the sense that they are not peripheral activities tucked in as an afterthought amongst many other calls on time and energy. We

1. Published by *New Society*, 11th September, 1969.

envisage basic activities in the sense that human beings regard them as basic to the practical arrangement of their lives. It would not be right to define this quality of being 'basic' in terms of time or of any other quantitative measure. The point is that we wish to regard the community of consumers and the community of producers as basic channels through which men and women and, no doubt, children too, arrange the practicalities of their lives. In the satisfaction of human wants men need association of a close and, in some sense, collaborative kind with other human beings. As consumers, in making use of the goods and services, they also need association with a grouping of other human beings, well known to them and close to them in a number of senses and not necessarily in terms of physical distance.

The circumstances that give life to basic community action are hard to define and hard to predict. Like anything else that involves a way of life what is implied here is a social and intellectual acceptance of the rightness, the properness, the appropriateness of acting in the new way. Human beings are very sensitive to the judgment of their fellows and it takes a long time, and, often, bitter experience to evolve new social outlooks. New forms of social behaviour by contrast may appear and disappear again fairly rapidly. Dr. John Morris[1] tells of a Residents Federation which in a new town in the early 1950s stopped plans for a motor road favoured by local developers, evoking wide support from many unexpected quarters, and then succeeded in tackling a number of other local problems such as immediate access to empty houses for use as youth clubs, sports centres, etc. This record of achievement and enterprise ended when those directly affected ceased to take part actively in deciding what was to be done.

The liveliest centres of activity by basic units are in industrial undertakings. Here over many years the outlook has formed that workers must act in unity in protection of their interests; the very nature of factory work has clearly defined communities of interest and communities of activity in the production process. Currently, there is a rapid growth reflecting a variety of philosophies in the interest of employees in questions outside of wages and conditions under such titles as workers' participation, industrial democracy, workers' control.[2]

The Institute for Workers' Control, for example, states in its aims, "A great movement is beginning to sweep through Europe and the whole world, evidencing a new determination of people to control their own destinies. This movement is concrete and specific, expressing a

1. *Direct Democracy*, published by Jane Prince, 106 Goldhurst Terrace, London N.W. 6.

2. See for example, *Can the Workers Run Industry?* ed. Ken Coates, Sphere Books, London, 1968, now published by The Institute For Workers' Control.

revolt against external authorities imposing their decisions on the content and context of everyday life. . . . . it is the aim of the Institute for Workers' Control to help any groups in factories, hospitals, schools, univerisites or elsewhere that are trying to frame policies for and influence the behaviour of the social organisms in which they work, or to which they belong."

It has been necessary to explore possible bases for new types of socio-economic structure, since it is not permissible to regard technological change as an independent variable determining (but not determined by) the structure of economic – and hence social – relationships. This is the mistake made by Galbraith when he suggests that we have no choice but to accept what he calls 'the technostructure', implying centralised administration of economic life by a specialist élite.

We need to turn the problem around and ask how can the computer help a new social structure? To answer this we must first ask what functions is the socio-economic system to perform? The types of question that need to be considered are:–

- How will social life be energised (in the sense that money as a means to life, status, power, etc., provides a driving incentive in the commodity economy)?
- How will needs and ends of economic activity come to be defined?
- How will the interlocking and interdependence of one activity upon another be accommodated and facilitated?
- How will exchanges between activities be measured and equated?
- How will technological potential be matched to requirements?
- What facilities of a technological or economic structural kind may be needed to safeguard against concentrations of power?
- How will choice and implementation of economic policies involving others be effected?

There are many other questions that could be framed but these should be more than sufficient to display functional areas in which technical change has particular relevance to social change.

Social Systems with Decision-Takers within the System

We have already discussed some of the differences between models, such as Newton's, of the physical world and socio-economic models. At times it is legitimate to treat a socio-economic system as a system external to its observers; but the point is that restriction to such an approach excludes the possibility of solving our problem. The problem is to use science well to create the kind of human society we desire; the elements of a socio-economic system are human beings or groups of human beings, the problem to be solved is to enable these elements within the system to control the system. The external approach – that is, looking at the system as if it were governed by laws outside human control – may be appropriate to a system in which automatic control through self-interest is effected by the market; but this approach may no longer be appropriate when we are looking for an alternative to this system. (Though the external approach may still be relevant perhaps for sub-systems that may be left to look after themselves, or to see what happens if control from within is not exercised.)

It has already been pointed out that computers and electronic information systems in the hands of an élite could provide a source of far-reaching and detailed information about the populace at large and could be used as a weapon of manipulatory control to serve the ends of an oligarchy. A restricted control of an information system could be very dangerous. Analysis of information which in isolation may seem innocuous, can, by the use of sufficiently sophisticated techniques, lead on to information that may be used damagingly. As a safeguard against such dangers it would seem necessary to aim at an information system that is equally available to every member of the community so that it cannot be used as an instrument of sectional advantage. It would also seem necessary to engage in the widest and fullest debate about the possible misuse of computer-based information processing, to discuss technical and other safeguards and to delay the introduction of any methods about which there is popular disquiet.

We have made in this book a certain use of the external approach following through some of the implications of techniques that greatly increase productivity, that replace labour and introduce automated production within a market system. One of the main deductions from this external analysis was that the impact of the technological revolution cannot be left to look after itself and that the market system was not an adequate instrument through which to determine major social and economic directions. In short, other means of socio-economic control are necessary. What means? – this is the question to be answered. The logic of the problem forces us to equate the decision-makers within the system with all men and not just some decision-making minority.

We are trying to find out how man might control his own social system. We are pointing the scientific revolution as much at this target as at the target of controlling the natural environment. We live in a world of extreme mutual interdependence. The things that any man or woman uses in daily life are products of chains of directed economic effort that circle the whole world. It is a simple exercise to consider at any moment of the day the origins of the goods by which one is surrounded. We have seen what energises this world economic system on which we depend. Mainly it is the desire for money as a means of buying goods. People go to work to get wages to buy the means of existence. Also money is sought after as a means to power and status. There are other motivations: fame and interest spur on inventors, scientists and others by whose efforts the quality of daily life is considerably influenced. But such motivations are not the driving force of the economic system. The driving force is very simply the pursuit of money as a means to life, power and freedom of action. This fact is very directly an expression of the market or commodity system. If we are to step away from the commodity system, how is economic life to be energised? When one first poses this question it sounds alarming. Dare we risk switching off the energising force of economic activity? Will we not sink immediately into a torpid stagnation?

Do we know what happens once the spur of economic compulsion is removed? What sort of evidence would support such views as there may be? It is probably true that you cannot get people to work for ends which are not their responsibility or concern, without the threat of poverty or starvation hanging over their heads. But we are, in fact, posing the problem in alarmist terms. In the sort of world we have about us at present, no group of men and women can possibly expect to receive from others the goods and services they require without themselves contributing some sort of equivalent. To think only in terms of what we see about us is to run the risk of unwittingly assuming that there can be no alternative to the system for which we have set out to seek an alternative. Motivation by poverty or the fear of poverty prevents anything but a limited, relative escape from poverty. The problem on hand is how to use the potential to create wealth for all, although this will not, of course, be the extravagant conspicuous consumption that we now associate with the very wealthy. To say that fear of poverty is the only effective motivation is to say that there must be poverty to fear, and that the alternative of a society wealthy for all cannot exist. Similarly to regard competitive greed as inescapably the basic motivation is merely to assert the impossibility of an alternative system in lieu of exploring the possibility of alternatives.

In fact it is one of the more striking results of sociological studies that the money motive for work appears quite low down in the ranking of incentives. "Except under conditions when wages are very low or during periods of inflation money is one of the least powerful incentives," writes J.A.C. Brown[1].

We are naturally afraid of what we do not know and cannot imagine what we have not experienced. We cling to a society disciplined by

1. The Social Psychology of Industry, 1954 quoted with the similar evidence in S.R. Parker, R.K. Brown, J. Child and M.A. Smith, *The Sociology of Industry.*

punishment and an economy disciplined by money. Such a society creates cruel, soulless institutions but does not succeed in destroying the spirit of man. For this is also motivated by the need to give and receive human warmth, the desire for activity and for recognition of usefulness and esteem from others. Social organisation in terms of the cash nexus has not eliminated these more fundamental human motivations; our fears arise simply because we are in the dark about how they are to come into play when organisation by the money principle is removed.

The problem in re-structuring the economy so as to be less dependent on the market mechanism will be to determine (1) whether it is unnecessary, and if so how to establish equivalents in exchange and (2) how to enable each community of producers to know what it had best produce. Can one ask people to do what is fairly required of them if there is no adequate measure of fairness nor adequate knowledge of what is required to be done? The problem is to find appropriate interconnections and relationships between a multiplicity of community units.

As we formulate the problem a few things begin to become clearer. In the first place, removing the market as the *basic arbiter* of economic values and objectives does not necessarily imply cutting out all use of money and market mechanisms in the exchange of goods. Secondly, an obvious pre-condition for deliberate control designed to improve deployment of resources is the fullest possible information about what goes on in the wider economic system of which any one unit is a part. Here, quite certainly, the new technologies can help. But before asking how, one needs to see what kind of information will be needed, in what forms, by whom, for what purposes.

In fact, social and political needs even at present compel governments to undertake activities not dictated by the market. Such activities include not only education and other social service expenditures by the state but also measures against unemployment and other failures of the market system to meet demands that people regard as their social right. Mounting claims by people becoming conscious of what a modern economic system should be able to provide as of right, for example, the right to work, will increasingly dictate economic undertakings against the indications of the market, for social and political reasons. Insofar as the market system is regarded as basically adequate these measures will be handled again and again as temporary expedients whilst economic policies continue to be governed as of old by the economic philosophy of the market system. By contrast those who aim to move towards social control as opposed to market control approach all such measures that operate against the criteria of the market as the beginnings of a new system, requiring new motivations and new economic and social philosophies, plan against market not only in the organisation of economic programmes and the use of resources but also as a philosophy of social behaviour. The raison d'etre for the socially conscious individual becomes quite simply his or her participation in socially controlled activities out of which he or she expects also to receive appropriate requirements for life seen as a whole. The motivation of active participation to achieve social and economic objectives is, quite simply, that this gives them a way of life alongside their fellow men and women, it is their insurance that they are integrated into a society that is concerned for their spiritual and material welfare. It is surely quite reasonable to suppose that such motivations are as valid or more valid than the interrelated negative/positive motivations of the self-regulating market economy, namely fear of poverty interacting with desire for money. Provided the new social values are seen as a new outlook on things fashioned only in constant struggle against an old outlook that has a strong basis in existing and past practice, provided social expectations are realistically presented and met then the possibility of transition to new motivations must seem quite feasible and reasonable.

Within large organisations a considerable amount of thought and study is given to what is called the management information system. Few organisations have produced successful management information systems. Everyone feels sure that the new computer and systems technologies should be able to give a much improved flow of information. It is possible that the difficulties are more than technical and may not be overcome until the nature of the management system, as a system of social relationships within a large organisation, is more clearly understood and defined. The relevance of this to our problem is that *in a technical sense* the large organisation is grappling with the same problem as faces us. A large organisation has no internal market unless it artificially creates one. It is a knitting together of a number of smaller organisms, which we may call unit communities or elementary organisms within the co-ordinating organisation.

The objectives of the large-scale commercial organisation are simple. They are to make money, to grow larger, to out-strip competitors. As ultimate values such objectives are empty, stupid and sordid. Their pursuit can be defended only on the ground that they are merely intermediary objectives, means to socially desirable ends. This, in effect, brings us back to the question: 'What energises the economic system?' One answer is that the pursuit of profit, plus hard competition, tightens up the sinews and leads to advance and progress. As a means of generating the impetus that enables the productive system to escape from the restrictions of guilds and feudal customs, and to generate industrial expansion, this claim was true. But today, in criticising the market system, we are questioning whether the now greatly increased productive powers are any longer being well directed by it. It is only natural to assume that if one does what everyone else is doing, one cannot go far wrong. If one man gazes up at the sky, many others will also copy him without knowing what he is gazing at. How much more do we, surrounded by elaborate purposeful organisations, naturally assume that someone knows where they are going and why. But sometimes the simple fundamental questions need to be asked. Even in academic research questions thrown out by previous research tend to be pursued with little reflection about the ultimate purpose of the original research. So it remains possible that objectives which were thought to be means are in fact ends. It is indeed certain that competitiveness easily becomes an end in itself.

In considering the internal relations of a large organisation there are, then, some rather important differences but also some analogies for our problems. The main difference is that the large organisation within the market system has a simple clearly defined objective. It also has a tradition of hierarchical organisation. The similarity is that it needs to structure the division of functions internally by deliberate conscious planning. If it uses the market it does so for convenience; the market does not provide the basic principle of internal organisation. The decision-makers are not the whole collective of workers within the system but those with authority delegated by the owners of the capital. (The formal right of owners to decide how resources are used is, in practice, modified by the impact of public opinion, by intervention of public authority and by workers' pressure on management.)

Despite important differences it is, I think, quite legitimate to conclude that the linking up of basic groupings of producers throughout a large society, say a nation or group of nations, may be able to adapt some techniques from the present co-ordination of the basic units out of which large commercial organisations are made up.

In this context we may equally well look at economic planning in the centralised economies in the Soviet Union and Eastern Europe. It has, on both sides, been recognised that there are many similarities in the organisation problems of the large privately-owned commercial companies of the west and the large state corporations of the planned economies of Eastern Europe. The objectives of the privately- and publicly-owned corporations differ, being, for example, profit for the former and planned production targets for the latter; and for the wider economy this difference is, of course, important. But here we are concerned with their *internal* structures. Much of the inadequacy, equally of the centrally-planned economies and of the large-scale privately-owned organisations, results primarily from centralisation of control involving the lack of control by the people generally over the end results of production. (Powerlessness to control the manner and purpose of producing things is reinforced by the division of labour traditions of a commodity economy.) But both types of organisation also face difficulties, due to centralisation, involving internal economic inefficiency looked at quite narrowly.

Information as the Chief Instrument of Organisation

The complexity of the economic connections generated in the market/commodity-producing system is very great, as we noted at the outset. To revert to village self-sufficiency and a homespun economy of craft products is impossible. But is the market the only possible instrument of economic intelligence and linkage? Consider, for example, the technological potentials that now exist from the following two standpoints. First, power to produce necessities of life has vastly increased and preoccupation with economic efficiency is becoming self-defeating. To seek a fine adjustment of economic exchanges through the market may be far less important than seeing that available resources are used freely and fully in such ways as those engaged in productive activity see fit to use them, subject to social rather than market sanctions. We can in other words afford to be less concerned about efficiency measured in terms of value in exchange. Secondly – and it is this aspect to which I now wish to turn – the potential of modern electronics and of the computer in particular makes it possible for anyone to have immediately retrievable information about sources of supply and about requirements of users and to communicate his responses to this information. Linkages which hitherto have been made through the market may now perfectly well be made through computer-based information systems. This is the crux of the matter.

Since already large-scale organisations need to effect linkages without reliance – or at least without complete reliance – on the market, our problem is one that is not altogether new. We need to establish means of communication between the small basic organisms out of which the wider socio-economic system is made up. In any economic organisation information needs to flow between producers and users and between producers and suppliers. Producers need to know what users want, they need to inform suppliers what productive equipment, materials and so forth they require. What is needed is a sequence of information flows so as to communicate awareness of the end use of products and the requirements of other people. The function of each organisation needs to be tested for ethical/social/aesthetic value; of this economic-exchange value is not an adequate criterion. Each organism requires greater power to shape the pattern of its own achievements and at the same time greater discrimination as to its function in the wider pattern of socio-economic organisation.

At present we have a whole number of levels of economic organisation – international, national, regional and local – with giant firms straddling the lot. The demand for decentralisation does not imply the elimination of the higher levels of organisation but *their subjection* to groups of people at quite low levels. This is, of course, the whole problem of democracy that has puzzled political scientists since the days of the Greek city state; and this is not the place to deal with all its aspects. What is being argued here is that the new techniques of information processing create totally new possibilities for organising and co-ordinating economic activity. Once the meaning of this potential is grasped, it is easy enough to see that arrangements worked out mutually by producer and consumer groups on such things as the phasing of non-recoverable mineral extraction, the planting of crops, the destinations for which goods are manufactured, the flow of international exchanges, shipping and much else are likely to be socially far more satisfactory than those that have resulted from market and capital flow criteria. And if the money criteria are eliminated, society can do far better than rely on the memories and intuitive judgments of top statesmen or captains of industry. At present information and means of communication tend to be centrally monopolised. This is due to political reasons or to the persistence of organisational traditions solely; there can be no technical justification for it. The memory and analytical capacity of the computer could be made available to all and universal electronic communications, linking anyone to anyone, are becoming technically and cost-wise feasible. (*The New Scientist,* 17th February 1972, quoting *The Economist,* speaks of "Almost costless telecommunications plus rapid and powerful computer-assisted training facilities".)

Of course, the power of states and of giant firms remains immense. At first sight indeed it appears greater than ever today; but the need to centralise information and control no longer has organisational or technical justification. Paradoxically, this is especially true of the firm when it is larger and more powerful than ever. But change implies seeing an alternative; it is to that our discussion is directed.

The firm is a creation of the market/commodity system; it was generated by capitalism for reasons that analysis of economic development, within the system of commodity relations, makes fully intelligible; as an organisational concept it has been taken over in the planned state-owned economies but, one may ask, what social or economic function does it serve? If one abstracts the commodity/market/money relations, one may regard the firm's productive organisation as a federation of work teams. The unifying factor in a commodity economy is the provision of finance and assets, the capital, ownership of which carries with it control and choice of objectives.

Industries have no formal or legal unity. An industry is, in mathematical terms, a set whose elements are firms engaged in making similar or related products. Similarity of products may vary widely in definition and individual firms may produce the products of more than one industry. Usually there is some form of trade association linking firms in the same industry for limited purposes. The question is what are they used for. Need the association be between firms?

On the side of consumption there is little or no analogous structuring. Here, in looking for basic organisational units, whose function it is to shape and execute socio-economic policies, we need to imagine the emergence of consumer communities of a kind that do not at present exist in a substantial form. But on the production side it is not difficult to imagine a structure in which *the basic work team* is the key unit in economic linkages. The rather arbitrary frontiers that at present demarcate firms within industries would become less significant once changes were made in the forms of ownership and control.

Imagine production no longer geared to production of commodities for exchange on the market. For practical, organisational and technical reasons some basic production units will still have particularly close associations with others. In some areas of production, groupings of much the same size as the firm today might prove to be necessary on other grounds than ownership and common financing. But what assemblages of work teams are most rational on technological/organisational grounds cannot be determined *a priori;* the rationality of producing things for use is not the same as that of producing commodities (exchange values) for the market. No group of producers on their own can complete all aspects of the production process from materials in nature to finished goods delivered to the consumer. All take something from someone else. The relations of interdependence take many forms, to which technical/organisation groupings need to adapt themselves in whatever ways are most suitable.

There are a number of different types of economic relationship that will need to be established. The problem is to see how this may be done in such a way as to give a diffused, consciously co-ordinated functioning of the system as a whole. The life-blood of effective relations is full, suitable and rapid information. Any work team or consumer group in doubt about what it should do can only resolve its doubts by asking questions and getting answers. It is just in this area of rapid understanding and interpretation of changing situations that the computer revolution makes altogether new facilities possible. To exploit these facilities implies both a clear vision of what is wanted socially and energetic development of the potential that is already there.

In Computer-Aided Design the designer sketches on a small cathode ray tube display screen (similar to that of a television set). He could be designing a house, a town, a piece of machinery or circuitry for electronics equipment. Stored in the computer system attached to the screen is a mass of information of a standard kind used in working out a new idea, testing it and evaluating it from a number of different standpoints; for example, cost, strength and performance. If an architect were designing a wall and he was interested in what the wall did rather than what it was made of, he would communicate to the computer some general indication of the performance required, and the computer would supply from its store of information details of materials, methods of construction, cost and so on. Having worked out a number of ideas and tested them from various points of view, the designer may then choose some of the designs that he regards as most attractive and begin studying them more closely. If he is interested in the shape and appearance of the object he may have a three-dimensional drawing of its exterior projected onto the screen and he can manipulate it so as to look at it from any desired angle. He may then ask the computer to give him an indication of any materials in short supply, or with long delivery dates, that he has used in his design. He may obtain estimates of construction time, cost, etc. Having decided on one or two choices, he may then obtain from the computer full details giving the exact specification of every component in the object he has designed, details of cost and any other information that he wants in written form. He can also get 'hard copy' of any diagrammatic or graphical representation of information or calculations.

Computer-Aided Design calls on a bank of information relative to the problem in hand and such routine calculations and techniques of manipulating data statistically or presenting it graphically that the designer requires. He simply presents the idea. The data and routine programs in the computer measure and test the practicality of this idea in relation to such things as (1) the internal consistency and co-ordination of the system being designed (for example making parts in the mechanical system fit into one another), (2) strength, (3) technical performance, (4) appearance, (5) cost and much else that varies with the nature of the design process being undertaken.

Facilities required to provide effective co-ordination of general economic activity are not greatly different in principle. As new plans for the organisation of production are being explored their implications will need to be worked out in relation to a mass of information about the rest of the economic system. Proposals will also need to be presented in brief, clear forms for communication to others. One may imagine each unit of the economic system having immediate access to a mass of information most likely to be needed in relation to its problems, with standard routines for processing information and displaying it. Where new or unusual types of information are required these will be met – possibly more slowly – by access to data banks storing much wider ranges of information than that currently required and used by each unit.

Clearly the tackling of economic and social problems will call for extensive collection of information relating to all aspects of life. Slowly new and easier methods of collecting information in computer-readable form are being developed; and one may imagine ultimately every relevant aspect of social and economic activity being 'photographed' in computer-readable form and so stored and made available for analysis by computer as required. So much information can now be stored in computer-readable form in very small physical spaces that no problem of finding where to put all the data will arise. In fact there will probably be a very substantial economy in the amount of space devoted to storage of data. At present much space goes to keeping data in paper form, the same information being repeated in different places over and over again.

Prototypes of total information systems already exist on a laboratory scale. Moreover there is every probability that the existing potential of such systems will extend by leaps and bounds. It may not be long before the digital computer in its present form and present information storage techniques and input/output techniques may seem antiquated things of the past. Holographic/laser methods are being investigated with some preliminary promise that input to computers may be able to take in whole situations as the eye takes in a complicated pattern of data at one instant, and may be able to supply output data as a film displays whole situations all at once. Moreover, the possibility exists of selecting, on the instant, groups of data conforming with any specified pattern or code. This would be a great advance on the present sequential input/output based on the search for individual items of information. It is possible that the building of new computers, internally organised more like the human brain, may greatly speed and extend the range of feasible computer operations.[1]

As mentioned above, input to a computer whether on paper tape or through the more rapidly handled media, such as discs and magnetic tape, is sequential, that is the information comes in or goes out 'bit by bit'. To receive complex patterns of information all at once would be a leap into a new situation. This is technically feasible. In the United States, for example, a new method for using lasers to read in and read out information has been developed. A thin film of manganese bismuth which is a magnetic material, is deposited onto a base of mica in a single

1. Work on altogether new structural concepts for computer design is proceeding, amongst other places, at the University of Kent (see *New Scientist*, 4th September 1969, p. 473).

crystal layer two-millionths of an inch thick. A very strong magnetic field makes the magnetic atoms line up with their North Poles in one direction and their South Poles in the other. Then light from a pulsed laser is split into two beams, one going directly to the film and the other going via the information pattern to be recorded. Where the two beams combine and thus add to their powers, the heat warms the magnetic material so as to cause the magnetic atoms to realign themselves. In this way a magnetic pattern is created on the film and a laser beam may again be used to read out the information. To quote from an article in the *New Scientist,* 24th July 1969, dealing with the potential of holography for information storage and retrieval: "The hologram can be likened to an electrical filter, tuned to pass only a narrow band of frequencies . . . the filter can be a normal amplitude hologram, which stores information and areas of transparent and opaque film, or a phase hologram, which stores information in a transparent film of varying thickness." Another note in the *New Scientist* (5th June 1969) recorded the discovery of a technique in Japan for fabricating very high density arrays of photodiodes needed to read out information stored in the form of holographic interference patterns. The technique packs photodiodes at more than 60,000 to the square centimetre.

A look at Computer-Aided Design helps to suggest, in a rough and ready way, what a first-rate information system could do. Equipment for Computer-Aided Design is still very costly because a tremendous amount of development work had to go into every aspect of the required equipment, programs and data preparation. To meet a general socially established demand it is quite certain that the cost of equipment can be brought down. Micro-electronics is surging ahead with new production techniques which have already very substantially reduced the costs of the hardware. Given a wide enough demand, what now exists only as laboratory equipment could be made cheaply available.

More serious problems arise about secrecy and confidentiality. If we are to be able to co-ordinate our activities with others and know anything we need to know about what is going on elsewhere, all relevant social and economic information must be generally available. This kind of situation implies an end once and for all to bureaucratic and company secrecy. To know what various social and economic organisations are doing and why they are doing it can no longer be the prerogative of a few officials only. But does this mean that anyone anywhere can find out anything about the private affairs of any other citizen? There are rightly very grave fears on this score. Currently there is too much secrecy about public affairs and too little privacy about personal. Already private detectives, insurance companies and others, as well no doubt as a number of public authorities, are collecting all sorts of information about other people's private lives, using the computer to store, sort and extract any particular details they are anxious to have. To deal with this problem extensive public discussion is needed on the twin problem of (a) making full information available to anyone who wishes to have it, on any topic of social concern and (b) making sure that no one can 'steal' private information. Public discussion of the principles involved is beginning; for example, the students' claim to have access to their own files. Full and continuing public debate is essential since fear of misuse of the computer to undermine personal freedom is well founded, and as yet the full potential of social information systems is not being developed. The wider the public discussion the more likely is it that the socio-economic information systems that emerge from it will be well-conceived and well-attuned to actual social needs.

The more alarming dangers of misuse of data banks and information systems can in fact be met. Access codes can hold information as securely in a data bank as the combination lock to a safe secures its contents. We are confronting a problem of socio-economic co-ordination to meet the impact of technological change and at the same time, to use the potential of technological change. We have suggested two elementary foundations, namely, (1) definition of basic units, elements of the system that is to be co-ordinated and (2) recognition, in very general terms, of the kind of information facilities that might be required and are technically available. We now need to look more sharply, and more concretely, at the content of relations between elements of the system; for example, how to link producers and users of products, how to regulate exchange of activities, how to determine social investment policies in which relationships embrace not only many elementary units at a particular point in time but step far away from the transactions and activities of the present into future activities and relationships.

To summarise the argument so far. The commodity market system *works by using the threat of poverty as its motive force.* In looking for a system designed to remove the threat of poverty and the inadequacies of the market we must look for a new motive force. To this we must return in a moment, assuming so far no more than that the desire to engage in activity and hence to exchange products, together with a simple sense of social obligation, will cause people severally to perform their socio-economic functions. However, a necessary, if not sufficient, condition for any economic system to work is knowledge by each unit of its place in the whole. The crude information conveyed by prices on the market can be greatly improved by using the new potentials of electronics to create social information systems such as no past human societies could have imagined, even in their wildest dreams.

Change Generated by Social Action Interacting with Social Theory

The possibility of a self-directing community of people implies a much greater and more general awareness of function and social relationship. This is not just a matter of facilities and techniques for information transmission and handling. It implies an interest and concern that is absent at present in Britain and most other countries. The percentage of people who care or know what is currently being done by national government, local administration or the management of whatever organisation they work for, is very small. If this is so, why should it be different in the future? There is a very good reason for lack of interest in public affairs; it is pointless to waste time on something you can't do anything about. That the man in the street can do nothing is not, of course, strictly true; but the impact on public affairs of anything he can do is so remote and intangible as to seem, if not nothing, then next to nothing. Social atomisation – a society of isolated individuals – is a natural corollary of social relations expressed as commodity relations.

One cannot usefully say very much, at least in the context of this present analysis, about how there might take place a transition from the present non-involvement to a future of public involvement. Nor would I suggest – bearing in mind the difficulties to which, for example, China's Cultural Revolution attests – that the process of transition is likely to be easy or rapid. In industry there are legal-economic grounds for non-involvement. Those who work in a firm do not own it, have sold their skills to those who do and, in a formal sense, have no responsibility for what is done with them. However, it is in this area where the legal-economic structure is loaded against involvement, that actual involvement is generally most real. Associations of employees in trade unions have long become involved in determining pay and conditions; but currently, through trade unions and in other ways, the general economic policies of firms are increasingly becoming matters of concern to those who work in them and are most immediately affected by their actions.

There is possibly here one of those ambivalent situations that commonly arise when a change is beginning. New processes, once they start, may easily gather momentum, but cannot easily start without receiving an initial impetus. Where is the initial impetus to come from? The determination to exercise control would no doubt increase wherever it was felt that this was a practical possibility, but the most convincing way of generalising such a conviction is some actual experience of exerting control. When we examined the basic community unit, we saw that in various ways and various areas of activity attempts are being made even now to take direct action at the base and to create pressure groups to obtain specific concrete ends, for example, tenants' action groups, movements to get housing space, Child Poverty Action, demands by trade unionists at workshop level, etc. In such situations the midwife to the birth of the new has to be theory and analysis. Comprehension of the possibilities, as much as of the need and the justifications, of new forms of social action cannot convert whole populations overnight, but such comprehension may well stimulate embryonic forms of social action which, if inspired by valid theory, may snowball and involve more adherents. The validity of theory in this context means:–

(a) taking into account the laws of operation of the socio-economic structure, and

(b) getting in tune with the aims, hopes and outlook of a wide enough range of people in society capable of making themselves effective as a political force.

Put in a slightly different way, (a) means a proper assessment of the hard facts of technical possibility and (b) means the development of sufficient active, intelligent protagonists of change.

The socio-economic structural changes we are considering imply involvement of people. One cannot assume that such changes will come about externally, by some outside authority redesigning socio-economic relations and then asking people within the community to align their behaviour accordingly. The absurdity of this position needs only to be stated to be seen. A society of involvement can only be the outcome of collectivities of people generated within the existing socio-economic structure. To begin with these may be only small groups expressing criticism of and attempting some form of action to change things.

At the same time external events will help or hinder, speed or delay social changes. Essential to the new is devolution of power to take decisions. Essential to the old, the status quo, is centralisation. The behaviour of central authority must have repercussions on the attitudes and behaviour of people in the socio-economic system at large. This interrelationship will not be simple. It is not simply that devolution will grow if central authority encourages it and not grow if it obstructs it. It will grow as an understanding of human needs and possibilities extends in the community at large and this understanding will in turn react on the behaviour of central authority – possibly in very complex forms. For example, I made reference above to the views of a number of people calling themselves the 'Open Group' on 'social reform in the centrifugal society'. They draw attention to the fact that most people regard the community to which they belong as being quite small, a few streets for example. They would like to see this bottom tier given responsibility for services in housing, education and welfare. Supposing this was done statutorily, it pretty certainly would give an impetus to democratic involvement. But it is most unlikely for anything of this kind to come about or for any considerable power of decision to pass to such basic units in society, unless there is a considerable campaign afoot backed by grass-roots movements. On such matters as housing, road safety, education, there are quite a number of people taking matters into their own hands. It is quite possible that campaigns on separated issues could merge into the demand for a more general control over the running of local affairs.

An example here is the rather unusual position of voluntary bodies in Britain which receive Government funds for their activities. Some, like the Workers' Educational Association, are described as 'responsible bodies' and receive grants for particular types of educational service, subject to inspection by Her Majesty's Inspectors. Unlike local government bodies, these are groups of citizens with a particular interest, not a particular location of residence, who elect their own committees and officers and tutors. What is more, they are made up of local branches which not only provide the lowest level of democratic organisation but choose their own subjects for study, their own tutors, and themselves control the manner of class activity. In practice much of their activities have been devoted to defence of the status quo but under certain circumstances they can be turned against bureaucracy into effective means of studying peoples' problems from their standpoint, that is from a working class standpoint. Such voluntary bodies at present only fill gaps in state services, but they may also be capable of stimulating alternative forms of social action.

In short, development of new, mass-based centres of social power may develop in many different ways and in unexpected forms. They will involve shifting the centres of gravity in existing centralised organisations of power as well the emerging of new centres of power. Devolution is in one sense the opposite of centralisation of political power; but it is not conceivable that the modern world could revert to social isolation of small separate groups like the villages of feudal society or tribal communities of the primitive world; devolution must go with co-ordination and communication. To consider what precise forms this might take would carry us too far away from our immediate theme and, moreover, it is reasonable to expect that the form of such co-ordination can only be decided in the social struggles that win the devolution of power. These struggles since they will be challenging centralised power must discover their own means of centralising their own opposed powers based though they be on the devolution of initiatives.

Use-Oriented Production

How will consumers discover the way their needs can be met and who can meet them? How will producers discover who wants the goods or services that they can provide? The same question may be put in a slightly different way. How will basic communities of consumers define and determine their realisable requirements and how will basic communities of producers determine the disposition of the resources at their disposal? Put this way the questions sound very complicated, since it is necessary to avoid, at this stage, the terminology of the commodity-market exchange system to which we are accustomed. In this terminology the questions would be – how most profitably can we sell the goods we can produce? How most profitably can we spend available funds? Now we have to assume that the decision is not to be left to the market or to any form of evaluation that ultimately depends upon exchange-value or money valuation. Let us remind ourselves why. One reason for rejecting this system is that we do not want to limit our choice as consumers to such goods as are imposed on us by a profit or exchange-value maximising machine. Another is that we do not want to be deprived of choice about what we spend our own productive energies on, and about what we get in return for them.

What we do want is simply that if we see to hand resources that can be put to some useful purpose, we shall be able to go straight ahead and put them to that purpose. We do not want a market and a money system to stand between us and the initiative that we as individuals or rather as groups want to take. We would like to settle directly anything that we can settle directly. We would like to regard (a) people with skill and time to spend in social economic activity and (b) plant, equipment, materials, etc., belonging to our community , as a fund or resources in the use of which we ourselves can freely take the initiative.

It is hard to conceive that the starting point of change could be anything else but exchanges of goods through existing markets. Buying and selling and the establishment of prices on a market is bound to persist for a long time yet in the economy of the world, but straight away a society may set itself the objective of ending the subordination of economic activity to market laws and monetary laws. This implies new ways of organising economic activity. This also implies new economic motivations and cultural values.

Given new attitudes of people towards one another in their economic activities, it may be that the solution to the organisational problems will come mainly from the establishment of manifold information flows between consumers and producers. For example, it is technically possible for individuals and groups of consumers to communicate their requirements through computerised information exchanges; to which producers would communicate their availabilities and from which they would receive suitably processed information about demands. This would not be barter, but a form of reaching understandings, a new model of social relations to replace the market.

How basic community units would federate or reach agreement on the structure of their relationships, again would be determined in the historical process of social change. The first step is the winning of economic, social and political power by the community groupings at the base. Such power could not be absolute. It would be power in the first instance within a framework of centralised government. The political power at the base, of course, will not be able to wash its hands of overall economic policies, but will have constantly to fight for policies favourable to development at the base. Forms of central planning at the outset will undoubtedly be essential; but it will be up to the peripheral grass-roots power to see that centralised activities are constantly controlled from below.

A socio-economic structure such as that of Britain today contains many intangible barriers. It is very difficult directly to apply ready-to-hand resources to immediate needs. In extreme emergency these intangible barriers are surmounted. Flood, fire, war create an atmosphere in which the restrictions and legalities of normal times are disregarded with, sooner or later, the sanction of authority. But in normal times initiatives calling available resources into creative use tend to be stifled for a number of reasons that include:

(a) non-availability of funds,

(b) property rights,

(c) a multiplicity of regulations, the understanding and observance of which make the setting up of a new enterprise difficult,

(d) disinclination bred out of experience of real difficulties as above reinforced often by the power of big organisations to crush local initiatives that are not, for some reason, pleasing to the power at the centre.

The forms of organisation that have prevailed and proved themselves most viable in the existing socio-economic structure tend to combine atomised property rights in the hands of individuals with a tendency towards a high degree of centralisation of regulation and control. In the earlier days of the emergence of the commodity market/private property model, men saw in private property the safeguard of initiative and in the market an invisible and light-reined co-ordinator. Today, the socio-economic structure has evolved into something very different from what Adam Smith was aiming to fashion some 200 years ago. The problem is to consider to what extent the barriers to initiative that have arisen are a necessary price to be paid for socio-economic order and to what extent they could be done away with.

The question of order is not an easy one. Every change threatens disorder. Society cannot afford the extravagance that appears to occur in biological change due to mutations. (A few favourable mutations enhance the power of survival, the majority are unfavourable and lead directly to the destruction of the organism.) Most social systems are 'ultra-stable'. They so adjust themselves as to be resistant to structural change. The established order is in a strong position to maintain itself provided it functions tolerably. Comparison with alternatives is more usually in imagination than in practice. Of the points above, (d) is secondary – the spirit of initiative can only be made to grow if actual opportunities for initiative grow. Again complexity of regulations may well be a symptom rather than a cause. The crucial questions (a) funds and (b) property rights concern the essentials of the economic structure – private property and the regulatory mechanism of the market. Where private property is required to be controlled for social purposes public authority can, and frequently has, in various ways, brought it under control or acquired it outright. Some measure of public ownership or control is pretty certainly a necessary condition to fuller use of social resources. (Only socially used resources, of course; personal possessions for personal enjoyment are not at issue.) But it would be meaningless to argue that the mere act of public acquisition of material resources would release new initiatives. Ownership itself does not allocate resources to effective use. (a) is the heart of the matter – how are funds to be made available or what can replace money as the permit to free access to resources?

The paradox of unused resources in the capitalist, market economy, has long troubled economic and social theorists. Since money in the commodity system is, inter alia, the instrument for allocating resources, money cranks have abounded. They have argued in various ways for manipulating the monetary system so that purchasing power may be generated and put into hands that, by using it, will activate unused resources. Schemes for social credit are an example. The underlying idea is, of course, sensible. But most of these monetary remedies look for solutions in the monetary system alone, as if it could be isolated from the whole commodity-exchange market. This is impossible since the system is energised solely by compulsion to earn and accumulate money. Technically there is no difficulty about printing money, creating credit and in other ways creating purchasing power. But whoever does this is handing out the prize to those who have not competed to attain it. To do so is to destroy the key mechanism of the commodity system. In theory at least this is so; but one must admit that the banks, and public authority too, insofar as it controls the banks, are able to pursue policies that enlarge or restrict credit (easy money policies or tight money policies). If the result of such policies is to be more than a general easing or a general tightening for those already actively engaged in the economic processes, some specific planning of how additional resources are to be allocated is implied. At once we are back again at the problem of control of economic activity by some criterion other than that of the market. (It should be added that control of banks and other large monetary institutions is a much sought-after prize within a private property, market system. It carries with it great advantages in the matter of fund raising. It is also worth observing that within the operation of a world market economy and a world monetary system, such as that within which Britain and countries of Western Europe and the United States operate, easy money policies at home generate acute balance of payments problems and are rarely compatible with allowing trade, currency exchanges and prices to be regulated by conditions prevailing in the world market system.)

Once again, we are up against the problem of how to regulate economic activity if not by the market. In the ideal competitive market system it is supposed that funds will be available for use whenever and wherever it is to the best advantage of the community that they should be used. If funds are not there, then that means that the community cannot afford the proposed expenditure however desirable on the face of things it may seem. Few today believe that perfect competition through the market does or could so operate. But if there is not rationing by the purse how then is expenditure to be rationed?

To fix our ideas, consider an imaginary situation. In a country town it is desired to build a hall of local stone. Suppose that all the labour required and 90 per cent of the materials are locally available. We will assume that all problems of property and regulations are overcome and that everyone in the community wants the hall built. The men who work on the job will have to be paid weekly, say; they will have to buy some materials outside the region and they will have to buy tools and machinery outside the region. This enterprise cannot be fairly undertaken unless the community sells to the outside world goods and services equivalent to the food, machines and materials that it needs to acquire from the outside world. Despite the fact that the project is essentially using local resources for local needs, its undertaking has repercussions on the economic system external to the locality. Thus funds as the wherewithal for laying claim to supplies from outside the locality are indispensable. If, instead of a hall, this building were a factory the problem would be different in that, in due course, the factory would be producing goods which might serve as supplies from this community to the external economy to offset against supplies received from outside by the local community.

The meaning of 'fair and equivalent exchanges' has still be defined, but, leaving this problem aside for the moment, our whole line of analysis points to the conclusion that once the *ultimate decisions* about allocation of economic resources can no longer be left to the market and once we rule out centralised bureaucratic planning, exchange of economic activities must be regulated instead by explicit, conscious understandings entered into by those that have economic relations with others. This implies that we have some means of measuring what is a fair transaction; but it also implies that the demands by one party on another party cannot at any time become unreasonable or inequitable, that is outside the terms of some agreed or understood relationship. There is no possible way of establishing equitable relationships and at the same time allowing a maximum devolution of decision-making and initiative, unless 'budgetary' control as far as possible is taken over by the lowest-tier groupings of the units of the economy.

To get some idea of what may or may not be possible in the devolution of budgetary control one must look at the technological and organisation constraints, remembering that existing structures have been shaped by constraints in the market system rather than in its technological conditions.

Each community grouping wants to be able freely to use the resources at its own command, but these are not in general available in kind. Much must be exchanged fairly with others. This necessitates accounting and 'fund-providing' facilities that permit each community grouping to bring into activity whatsoever resources are at its own disposition whilst not making calls on the resources of others which it is not able to make good by supplying products or other resources in return. Such a centralised banking or accountancy system – which might, with interest, be studied in some detail – will not be examined further here beyond noting that once again the wealth of information and the speed of analysis that the computer revolution makes feasible guarantees the technical possibility of such a system, given the social will to establish it. In the sections that follow the discussion will focus on the two corner-stones of devolution – information and measurement of values in exchange; but already one should note that methods of measuring needs and requirements directly, that is, otherwise than by demand on the market, are being fairly widely applied. There is, for example the government Social Survey in Britain already investigating a wide range of consumer needs. Government departments, local authorities and other official bodies are constantly doing more and more to collect information about social behaviour and social requirements. Similar aids to planned production (e.g. various forms of market survey) are being more and more widely adopted by the big commercial organisations. However, while all these measures clearly point towards the need for new methods of economic and social organisation, they cannot, in any sense, be regarded as the same thing as, or a substitute for, the information flows that decentralised social organisations and decision-making would imply.

Whilst the social and economic information now being collected in Britain and elsewhere on a wide scale, and more thoroughly than ever before, can help us understand our society more fully, it could also become the instrument of a form of social control that obstructs democratisation. Democracy, if it is to have meaningful content, implies that people settle for themselves what they do with their own lives and how they do it. Incorporation into some vast social organisation, surveyed and managed, though it be with the wisest paternalism, is in no sense democracy (i.e. power in the hands of the people). It is necessary to make this point somewhat forcibly, since the tendency for centralised bureaucratic planning to take over from the market system is real. Moreover some of the measures used in such anti-democratic planning may appear to resemble aims for which the pioneers of social progress have campaigned. But whilst liberty for the mass of people implies planning, it also implies diversity of power. The problem before us is to consider what forms of co-ordinated diversity may be feasible.

Some Principles underlying Computerised Information Systems

An indispensable concomitant, if not precursor, of devolution is information. This was the conclusion of the last few paragraphs. Any collective unit within a wider socio-economic structure must understand its relations with other elements in the structure if it is independently to decide its own path of development. It is a real danger that the importance of this understanding may be underrated. For example, suppose that a foundry in a large engineering works began to consider itself as an independent unit. Irked by what it regarded as a bureaucratic or pig-headed management, it might well turn eagerly to supply new users. Whilst the capacity might be adaptable to general-purpose use, the requirements of the engineering firm might be peculiar and specific, not easily replaced from any other source immediately. The freedom of the foundry could disrupt and dislocate an elaborate complex. It is clearly desirable that the foundry should not make any change until all the facts about its relationships to others have been fully explored. This exploration is, in itself, a preparation for change. The mere statement of this situation will necessitate an examination of alternatives by other parties.

This line of thought suggests a very important conclusion. Devolution is, in the first place, a matter of information. First steps towards devolution in a social/political sense can be made immediately if constituent members of a large centralised organisation begin to consider what is the function of the basic unit to which they belong and what alternative functions suggest themselves. *The attempt to understand function generates a demand for information. This in turn indicates concretely the required performance of an information system.* This may be simply described in the circuit diagram III.

DIAGRAM III
Function and Information Analysis

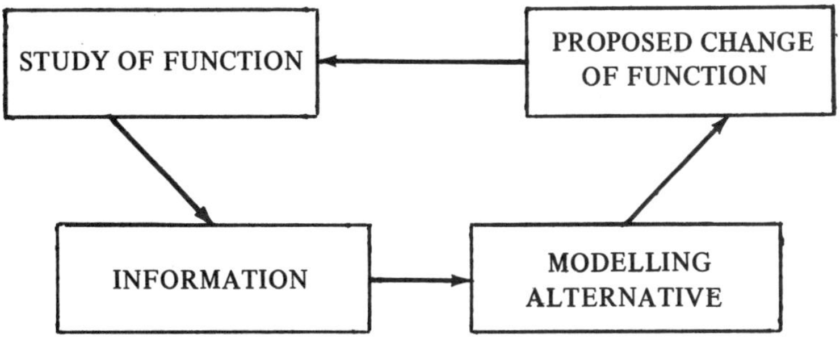

The demand for information might, one hopes, give an appropriate form to the information system. But here again things may not be simple. People do not know what kind of information they want until they know what kind of information they can get. The appetite grows with feeding, not only for the amount of information but for the kind of information. The extensive information that a computer system could provide must be tailored properly to the user's needs. It is quite possible that the provision of an appropriate widely diffused information system might become a major issue of political dispute. It implies a particular kind of social and economic policy; it could not become a reality without considerable expenditure of time and money. Also as some sociological work is helping to demonstrate, the asking of questions and the expression of needs is a social activity that is not simple. Consciousness of the community unit through which an individual's social relations are defined may be a necessary pre-condition of meaningful communication by individuals with society at large.

It may be useful at this point again to sketch out what might be involved. The main components of an information system are:–

1. Definition of purpose.
2. Collection of information.
3. Storage.

4. Retrieval.
5. Manipulation and analysis.

The definition of purpose in an information system is crucial. The notion that information is a good in itself is absurd. There is an infinity of scraps of potentially usable data. An information system implies the provision of a particular kind of information for particular kinds of people for specific purposes. Huge centralised collections of information, not available or even not readily available for anyone to use who cares to, must be regarded with the gravest suspicion. Who is going to use this information for what? The computer, as we have shown earlier, makes the management of vast information stores by a handful of people for a handful of people a feasible proposition as never before. Where not generally accessible, one cannot but suspect such systems as being instruments to be used against some people by other people. We concluded that in relation to all computer information systems the fullest and widest discussion of what should and should not be kept secret is an essential safeguard that cannot be dropped for considerations of administrative expediency. But the dangers of misuse of *some* information systems cannot be interpreted as meaning that *all* computer information systems are socially harmful or dangerous. With properly defined purposes computer information systems can be designed to strengthen greatly the articulation of a society of free individuals and free groups of individuals.

Collection of information must certainly involve some form-filling. For example, an organisation of producers will itself wish to choose the description of its present and probable future production and must state this in writing or some other communicable form. But an effective information system must rely primarily on the use of information that arises naturally from the functioning of the economic system. If, for example, wages are to be paid this implies knowledge of hours worked on particular jobs by men with particular skills. If such information can be collected in computer-readable form with the minimum of extra effort, as the operation to which it relates proceeds, it can then be passed into a data bank, that is into a centre where the information can be held and drawn upon as may be needed. (The Department of Employment and Productivity at present uses computerised wage information from firms using computers, for occupational wage surveys in industry.)

Once the value and the raison d'être of a comprehensive information system is generally recognised, more effort and ingenuity will be put into solving the problems of quickly and easily capturing data in computer-readable forms. There is every reason to believe that electronic techniques and, in particular, various types of remote-sensing devices will result in a great simplification of present practices, which involve excessive form-filling and transcribing.

The problems presented by *storage* of data will become increasingly less with the further improvement of techniques, already advanced, for recording and reading information into a computer. Already, as we have seen, massive quantities of information can be held in very small physical spaces, on discs or magnetic tape, and many new possibilities. e.g. using magnetic bubbles,[1] lasers and holographic techniques, are within sight.

The major problems to be solved are in data *retrieval.* Much work remains to be done on the identification of information types. This is in effect a coding problem to aid users of information to know where to look for information required. The way the information is coded and stored needs to be related to the uses to which it is to be put. The logic of the information storage system is in fact the abstract model of the system to which the information relates. For example, to say that a set of figures indicates wages paid for a particular kind of labour expended on a particular kind of product is to say that these figures are meaningful as giving specific values to relationships in the model which is being used to interpret and communicate information about the economic system.

It has taken surprisingly long for the computer world to realise that problems of information retrieval are not technical problems of computer programming, coding or design of peripherals. The problems are in fact much deeper and more intractable. A perceptive article by Mrs. Karen Jones[2] draws attention, at long last, to the essence of the matter.

> " . . . Using a computer to manipulate information", she writes "in anything more than totally trivial cases (like seeing whether the digit 7 occurs in a stored expansion of π to 10,000 places) involves us in the characteristic and very intractable problems of what language is like and how it is used. Note that this is not simply a matter of coding. . . . The fact that we may make a given procedure work more easily mechanically by providing it with data in some smartly coded form does not remove the problem of what to code; it is essential to avoid the trap of thinking that because information may be fed to the machine in a simple code, the information itself is simple. We have to decide what features of it are to be coded, and this is exactly where our problem lies . . . . We are concerned, since we have a computer store of information, with automatic techniques, but the central problem is that of linguistic analysis and not computation."

To be able to extract the information that we want, we must understand its *meaning,* that is we must have a structure in terms of

1. *New Scientist,* 12th April, 1973.
2. *Bulletin of the Institute of Mathematics and Its Applications,* Vol. XI, No. 1, April, 1970.

which to interpret the data that we extract from the stores of information. The work of Noam Chomsky, already mentioned, is very important in this connection. He is exploring the general characteristics of the deep structures underlying all human language. The principles he is getting at enable us also to understand better what kind of problems underlie the organisation of computer-based information systems.

Any information system must be infused with a structure defined by the purpose that it is to serve. If this is so we cannot expect to take over computer technologies lock, stock and barrel to serve new social purposes; it is the *potential* of computers and of the electronics industry rather than existing, fully developed systems that will serve the purposes of new social organisations. However, despite the problems of devising a good retrieval system, the speed and accuracy of the computer will make it possible at least to exploit some existing systems more effectively.

Again there will be much to learn about analysis and manipulation of data. The point is to get *relevant, significant* information. Isolated facts acquire meaning only when their relations with other facts are revealed. As better techniques are found for the analysis of data, computer programs for carrying out these techniques may be developed. A big problem for the user will be that of understanding the significance of particular techniques. To take a trivial example, the average of the four numbers 4, 40, 100 and 256 is 100, so also is the average of 99, 100, 100 and 101. But the sets of numbers are very different. If they represented the scores of marksmen out of a possible 260, the first would represent a set that included one very brilliant marksman and two very poor shots, whereas the second set would be remarkable for the similarity of somewhat indifferent achievements. The information-analysis facilities must be such as will help the users to explore the meaning of the available data and also help them to understand the significance of analytical techniques, as well as executing the routines needed to use them. The information system must inform, in the sense of educate, as well as manipulate. Blind use of recommended statistical processes may be quite dangerous; a good information system would need to help users to understand the meaning of the analytical methods for which routine programs are available.

Above all, statistical treatment given to figures needs always to be adapted to the questions asked of them. A really effective information service for the purposes we are considering would require many expert statisticians and mathematicians precisely to help users to ask the right questions and understand the meaning of the answers. The statistician and the mathematician would need, to a far greater extent than at present, to communicate with the layman, and the layman would need a much better understanding than at present of the principles guiding the work of the numerical specialists. It should be possible also to apply, on a much wider scale, the mathematical and model-building procedures at present used by some of the more advanced organisations. But the fact that complex techniques may be involved in information systems no more debars their universal use than the complexities of water supply or electricity generation debar universal use of water and electricity. In fact, however, some rather deeper understanding of information systems that most people have of electricity will be needed to solve the problems raised in this book and it is precisely to open up the discussion that will lead to such understanding that this book has been written.

The Co-ordination of 'Decentralised' Activities

What degree of integration and co-ordination is technically and organisationally best? What forms might co-ordination take? Is there conflict between what is best socially and politically and what is best technically and organisationally? The common assumption that economic efficiency increases with scale has already been challenged. I have suggested that the advantage of big firms is the advantage of big resources of capital in a market economy. In the planned economies where means of production are state-owned, I have suggested that a tendency to favour large-scale centralised organisations results from the concentration of political power. For the contrary case, that a decentralised, less closely-knit organisation would be more efficient, there is no direct evidence. Naturally enough, opportunities for testing in practice have not existed. The evidence, such as it is, is indirect – and, indeed, the same criteria of efficiency might well not apply. Those who work in the constituent parts of large organisations frequently feel that the people at the centre of things, who take the crucial decisions, do not understand the real issues and stifle intelligent use of initiative. An extremely experienced T.V. writer and producer, Stuart Hood, has frequently criticised the B.B.C. on just these grounds. The contrary argument is that what appears to be good for one part of the organisation may not be good for the organisation as a whole; the people at the centre can balance overall advantages against overall disadvantages and choose the course which, on balance, gives the greatest sum of advantages over disadvantages.

There is a weakness in the argument of the centralisers. If the advantages they claim for an organisation of size X are true, would they not be still truer for an organisation of size 2X? This leads to the conclusion that the best thing is complete centralisation of all economic activity under one single central control. This is absurd in the sense that it is impossible for one man to control everything. It was always accepted by economists that there would be an optimum size for firms where diseconomies of scale began to operate; but it is often now said that the computer has greatly increased the span of one man's control or that of one small group of men. The assertion that co-ordination between all economic activity is needed is, of course, true but irrelevant to the question of centralised *control*. One of the arguments for the unified market was exactly that it effected such co-ordination. The suitability of this self-operating mechanism is what we are now challenging. To accept authoritarian centralised planning would be to jump out of the frying pan into the fire. What we are looking for is a consciously controlled mechanism in which control is diffused, 'multi-central'. The desirability of co-ordination is unquestioned. The problem is how to co-ordinate.

I have argued earlier that large centralised organisations are not necessary on technological grounds. One must go further and recognise that there are technological dangers in excessive centralisation; in particular, total dependence on centrally controlled, technically sophisticated means of communication and power, for example, can cause very serious disruption in the event of a breakdown. By contrast, if the small community groupings look after their own requirements where reasonably possible without great loss of efficiency, resources can be used more flexibly and in an emergency are more easily adapted.

Carried to an absurdity centralisation means no more than making the judgment of one man or one central committee the final and absolute authority. This is certainly simple and clear cut, well tried and long rejected in the political sphere, whether it goes under the name of absolute monarchy, dictatorship or oligarchy. In the economic sphere property rights have given an absolute, or near absolute, authority to the owner of the business. This served well enough, for reasons already considered, in the emergence of modern industrial societies. Moreover the newness of the organisation principles we are trying to evolve is greater than it may seem. Bureaucracy, or organisation via an administrative élite, is (as many authors have noted – cf. Eugene V. Schneider's bibliography referred to above) a very old and widely adopted method of organisation. It is more than a simple division of labour allocating the job of co-ordination to a specialist profession. It has its roots in class structure. The élite administrators have traditionally either been members of the class holding power or their close and trusted associates. They were at all events quite distinct from the excluded mass who were not to know, not to interfere, not to ask the reason why. The very word hierarchy stems from the priestcraft that became the instrument of rule in the earliest class societies to emerge in human history.

To move, therefore, to forms of organisation in which to be

responsible, to be informed, to know and to decide are rights and duties of all participants in social activity, is to take a much bigger step than is apparent. It is to move out of an order of things that has prevailed over the practice, the psychological orientation and the legal forms of human societies through some four or five millenia. Attempts, in any practical sense, to recast society democratically are barely two centuries old and experience of the practical organisation of activities on any but hierarchical principles is very meagre. (Athenian democracy for example, was on a small scale and limited in effect to a slave-owning class.) In the earliest tribal societies men lived as animals in herds and shared a common poverty. The first escapes from poverty could touch only a small minority whose relative wealth also meant power. The new economic and technological situation is that most of what we call 'wealth' is now feasible for all, without the appropriation by some of other men's produce.

These facts help to explain why quite simple methods of co-operation, dispensing with the principle of hierarchical authority may be practical, although hitherto not adopted. Consider the argument put above that people at the centre know best how to balance overall advantage against disadvantage. Looked at non-hierarchically, the issue would be put quite differently. To be sure overall evaluation of alternatives is necessary and specialists in so doing are needed. But why should they serve 'the centre'? Their findings need to be available to all and to guide the decisions of each basic unit in the several areas of their competence. Decisions that concern a wide community must be taken by representatives of all elements in that community if they are to be well taken. This, of course, does not exclude allocating to particular people tasks of co-ordination. As for some types of musical performance, conductors are required, so for various types of economic activity, various types of co-ordinators are required – but there is a definite distinction to be drawn between *centralisation of power* and *co-ordination of activities*.

We have a starting point here in the social cost and social benefit studies that are made today before a major public investment is embarked upon, for instance in a motorway or new tube line. These are as yet very inadequate and the value judgments built into them can hardly be reliable until there are better means of canvassing the views of people whose lives are most affected; however, they represent a step in a new direction, though still a very small step.

In looking for better types of organisational relationship there is no need to regard existing firm sizes as in any way sacrosanct. The main argument for firms as they are is that history has given them a certain cohesion as organisms which it may be desirable to retain in some measure. Even so, it is perfectly possible to consider new relationships within the firm which dispense with centralised authority as a principle of organisation and replace this with something more like federation with control by the producers themselves at different levels.[1]

Here and now information about possibilities, pressure on specific issues, argument and new understanding interact in a process of shaping a new outlook as a basis for social change. The problem we face is how to harness the potential of the technological revolution. Before we can define how and where our science and technical powers are wanted we must understand ourselves as a community of producers and as a community of inhabitants who want to live, spend our time and occupy ourselves in particular ways and particular places. That is, we need to take stock of ourselves and the resources we command. It is for these reasons that intermediary objectives towards control over technological powers include essentially (1) activisation of basic social units, that is collectives of people as consumers and producers, (2) clear and conscious definition of functions and formulation of policies desired by them and (3) provision of social information systems to serve the needs of these basic groups.

The computer and the electronics industry provide the technological basis for information handling. We have already discussed at length the importance of information in the production and distribution processes. We should recognise also that it is fundamental to all the processes of social life. Class societies have always elaborately structured the forms in which information is transmitted in such a way as to protect their power.[2] The key question is symmetry or reciprocity of communications both as regards access to information and transmission and its obverse, exposure to information and transmission. Murray and Wengraf make their point clear by referring to George Orwell's *1984*. In this horribly predictive novel Winston Smith the hero "is involved in a technology with a high level of generated asymmetry; he has a television set in his room that cannot be turned off (compulsory reception); the screen also transmits an image of his behaviour back to agencies of social control (compulsory transmission)." But, of course, he has no choice over what he receives and from whom or over what he transmits and to whom. We are not in 1984 yet, but it is a point of great importance that private transmitters are illegal and channels of transmission are monopolised in Britain at the present time.

The issue confronting modern democracy is how to structure the use

1. Some first thoughts on this possibility will be found in K. Coates (ed.) *Can the Workers Run Industry?* and especially the chapter on 'Nationalised Steel' prepared by a group of Sheffield Steel Workers.

2. See *The Political Economy of Communications* by Robin Murray and Tom Wengraf, *The Spokesman*, Summer 1970, No. 5.

of modern technology so as to advance democratisation and to destroy class power. The latest developments in television make it possible to have simultaneously available to households and other groups a very wide range of programmes transmitted from many parts of the country and indeed of the world. Important discussions of interest to many different groups of individuals can be made available while they are going on. Problems of co-ordinating and planning the new social economy could be discussed in such an open forum – and what is more crucially important – groups of viewers with a point of view could be brought into the discussion; for the multi-channel systems can, of course, be two-way. There is no need for television and radio to be a one-way line of communication as it has been heretofore – with the most dangerous results in terms of imposing a consensus view, not to say a kind of thought control.

In Place of Money

The information processing potential of the computer is immense and in the last few sections we have been looking at the possible significance of this for new types of social relation. We have, in particular, mentioned that the means today exist for men and women to be fully aware of the circumstances of others with whom they have social and economic relations. In production and economic activities these must include relationships of interdependence. On what principles will these relationships be shaped? One might imagine a technically advanced wealthy community being able to distribute all or most of its products free of payment by users. Under such circumstances the management of the economy might become a specialist occupation based on scientific principles with which the public at large no longer need greatly concern themselves – as today in Britain few of us concern ourselves about the technicalities of water, gas or electricity supplies, vital though water, heat and light are to human existence. (Control of services vital to life, should it pass into the hands of an isolated group, would give an immense and dangerous power – cf. control of irrigation in early Egypt and Asia – and at all times means of ensuring social integration and popular control would be essential.)

Economic interest has, through the ages, roused in man the most violent, sordid passions. To live man must get money. Money is status and power; lack of it poverty, humiliation and degradation. To have money is to have freedom, to have ease; not to have it constraint and anxiety. Money is a universal entitlement to material goods. It is the bowl with which one dips into the national product. It is the measure of economic value, value in exchange. If the matter at issue is money, men in their relations with one another tend to become suspicious, intractable, stubborn. But as well as arousing the vilest passions, money serves also a very practical function as co-ordinator of economic activity. The problem that we are now approaching is what, if anything, is needed to perform the function that money performs in the market economy.

Money has in the economist's thinking three quite different, although related, functions. It is a unit of account that we are suggesting here can in many areas be replaced by other means of reckoning. It is a store of value – accumulated in private hands as capital or by taxation as state funds. This accumulation of claims on resources we shall suggest in the next section can be made into a more consciously social act through the new means of information collection and dispersal. Money is also a means of exchange. Money we likened earlier to an electric charge that individuals and corporations and governments put into the market system thereby generating the flow of the whole current. But we have been led to question the distribution of these charges between individuals, rich and poor, between corporations, large and small, and the limitation of the flows generated in relation to the enormous potential of the new scientific revolution. The market commodity-exchange system works through the determination in the market of a money price for goods and services and also for labour, land and capital considered as factors of production and it is the possessors of these factors who receive the price according to their endowment.

However fair or unfair, price is determined in the market. (Price is the money expression of value in exchange.) The idealised concept of the market system sees it as determining through competition the level of prices at which the seller gives and the buyer receives equal economic values. Even to the most cynical it has the virtue of tossing a coin to settle a dispute; however arbitrary and unfair, the market at least appears as an arbiter independent of the parties to the exchange. If a measure of economic worth is needed to replace the market, then what should it be? From a theoretical standpoint the answer may not be difficult. The main difficulties may be social. Whatever measure of economic worth is decided upon it must be (a) generally understood, (b) generally acceptable.

A well-defined measure of economic value may be necessary for a number of reasons. If economic decision-making is to be dispersed, limits of authority would need to be defined. If a community, or a group within a community, is to decide for itself, in part at least, what it is to spend and what it is to produce, its power to call on resources not directly at its command would need to be defined in some way. In the case of a community of producers available resources for future use will presumably bear a relationship to the amount of products which that community has produced. In the case of a community of consumers its spending rights will also presumably relate to wealth produced by members of that community and even if this were not so spending rights would still have to be defined in one way or another.

It is natural to think of general economic measures as money, though as we are envisaging a somewhat different situation we should be cautious in the use of such words as value, money, etc., which may imply relations from which it is desired to escape. Many economic activities will certainly continue to be centrally undertaken and, however effective control from below, those who undertake them must be given some principles to guide their actions. Possibly the finding and allocating of supplies and suppliers will itself be one of the centrally undertaken activities; but the tensions that today such jobs involve should disappear provided there is no scarcity of basic necessities and the main economic motivation is no longer pursuit of wealth, that is of exchange value for its own sake.

The economic measure or principles of exchange must not only be fair, they must also be economically appropriate. That is, they must be such as to ensure that what individuals and social groupings do in pursuit of their several aims, advances, so far as possible, the general aims of human societies. It was one of the major defects of the centralised administrative planning of the Soviet Union and other Eastern European economies that administrators were exhorted to follow socially desired policies that did not coincide with what gave them the greatest gains in terms of money. Pricing policy was seriously out of gear with economic and social aims. The theory of money, pricing, etc., in a centralised planning economy has hardly been developed at all. The work of Ota Sik in Czechoslovakia[1] is an important attempt to develop this theory. He suggests that the use of money and the market should be retained within a firm overall plan, as a means of passing control out from the central bureaucracy to the individual enterprises. It may be argued that this implies a return to capitalist economic relations, or that this is only viable as a temporary, transitional step towards some new forms of decentralised co-ordination still to be discovered but likely to emerge from a more active stage of workers' control such as that which began to develop in Czechoslovakia when Sik's policies were being implemented. This was in 1968 and before the political superstructure was radically changed by the Russian intervention. Similarly, it is argued that the economy of Soviet Russia is socialist only in the limited sense of having public ownership while the persistence of a money economy and structural features taken over from capitalist society combined with authoritarian organisation, to some extent assimilate it to a capitalist economy. This

1. See for example his *Plan and Market under Socialism,* IASP, New York, 1967.

is the line of argument for example of the French Marxist Charles Bettelheim of the Ecole Pratique des Hautes Etudes in Paris.

There are many reasons (including those mentioned above) for favouring a very wide discussion of the problems of pricing and economic measurement with a view to getting at the deeper questions about how best to effect exchange between economic activities. It is not sufficient that principles adopted should be theoretically sound; they need also to be understood and accepted widely. It is probable that the determination of specific principles will be greatly aided by the information techniques, analysis techniques and simulation and modelling techniques that the new technology makes possible. But these techniques cannot be applied in this area until a number of deeper questions have been thrashed out about the new economic relationships that people want. Some of the topics that seem to me important are as follows:–

(i) *Making effective use of resources.*
We are talking about the possibility of everyone's energies, ideas, knowledge and skills being used creatively to provide what our human society needs and wants. We assume we have the means to provide more of what we want and to provide it more effectively in a way that we find congenial both as producers and as consumers. But what some people and some communities have to contribute will be of greater social value than others. Sometimes social effort will be misdirected. Innovation involves failures as well as successes. How is a creative dynamism to be maintained? To what extent is this necessary?

(ii) *Economic 'fairness'.*
Some people and some regions will have great advantages in terms of capital resources held as a legacy from the past, in terms of natural resources and in other ways. Economic processes increasingly involve contributions calling for research, imaginative planning and scientific enquiry. How are the efforts of those who develop new methods to be assessed in comparison with those who use the new methods in production?

(iii) *Security of basic income.*
Some of the questions listed above may sound more perplexing than they really are since we are conditioned to thinking in terms of exchange values and scarcity. Will it become a basic principle of social life to ensure that everyone has an assured basic income and whatever minimum of supplies is necessary to continue at least their customary forms of economic activity? If it is right to assume that modern technology can assure supplies of minimum consumption and production needs, can the problems of exchanging economic

activities be seen as essentially problems of social decision about innovations? If certain minimum necessities for consumption and production are defined and each community grouping is entitled to these as of right, then for such products no problem of exchange arises. Or rather, the problem is settled by people as a whole defining what goods they are entitled to as of right and then ensuring co-ordination of economic activity to see that such goods are provided.

(iv) *Problems of transition, from market to non-market economy.* We can only start from where we are now. How would transitions be effected? It could be that more and more needs would be met socially, without individual payment, and consequently, with savings in distribution costs. If so, would the problem of pricing relate only to a sector of scarcity goods? To what extent would pricing be necessary and what principles would govern it, to ensure economic efficiency? Could pricing be used to encourage improved organisation, better use of resources and more productive methods generally? To what extent would measurement of output against input in general economic terms, in order to assure effective performance, still be of technical importance?

The general direction of economic effort and the broad lines and aims of economic policy can be determined by public discussion. Implementation of particular programmes within a transitional, that is, still largely market economy, would obviously be focussed on essentials. The main economic instruments for determining broad lines of economic policy would be the direction of investment funds and social economic policy. But since we are talking about hypothetical situations we cannot go into any great detail where the detail can only be shaped by the political actions of men and women in the future circumstances confronting them.

We are trying to weigh up the implications of a socio-economic structure that is not hierarchically organised and in which the main decision power is no longer at the centre but in the component units. We must imagine socio-economic organisations and groups of organisations settling as much for themselves, in their own ways, as they possibly can. But they still have need of (a) interchanges between one another, (b) collaboration in investment whether at a regional, national or international level and (c) collaboration in provision of certain requirements – (what above I have called 'social economic policy', which could mean water supplies, social services as today, and under changed circumstances, perhaps, free supply of basic foods, clothes, and the like). The problem we confront is how to organise these things. Rigour in measurement of exchange values might become quite unnecessary. We are already aware that economic competition may be uneconomic. If a money system and commodity production leaves potential activities or resources unused or if the costs of competition or exchange are high, it could well be that overall wealth and well-being would be increased by making free distribution of some goods and using only rough and ready measurements in some exchange arrangements. However, some methods for making these arrangements must be provided and agreed to by all involved in their operation. As regards (a) in exchanges between groups and organisations 'a free market' with prices and money as media of exchange might still provide a natural and convenient apparatus without undermining in any material way the principle of direct control over economic activities and production for use rather than to accumulate money or exchange values. However, except as an expedient in early transitional stages, this possibility needs to be scrutinised very critically; and a great deal turns on the manner in which exchange-prices are determined.

The problems of investment and social production involve, however, numerous groupings of men and women, numerous constituent organisations of the wider society reaching agreement about allocating part of their time and resources to purposes of wider social interest. Clearly quantitative measures of resources so involved will be required and also clear agreement about how the needs of those who contribute to the social projects are to be met. In all this it is natural, indeed to some extent inescapable, that measures used in the past and methods of negotiating exchange already tested by experience, should provide a starting point for changes that may be introduced in the future. The conscious direction of resources to planned uses will have to struggle against market forces in determining the pattern of economic reproduction. Reproduction in the market economy is the reproduction of capital, meaning by this not the machines and the buildings but the socio-economic relations whereby exchange values are used to produce more exchange values. The criteria of success are the magnitudes of the exchange values produced. Pursuit of profit is pursuit of exchangeable values in the abstract, money convertible into undefined commodities. The struggle for conscious direction of resources to planned uses is a struggle for new criteria in decision-making; instead of exchange values in the abstract, money, the objective will be to concretise exchange relations, to specify requirements and production capabilities *concretely*. Production of and trade in products of unspecified destination will require critical examination to ensure that it aids, or at least is not seriously damaging to concrete planning of the production of use values. To achieve the planning of production to serve concretely defined uses will require constant analysis of complex patterns of interrelated productive systems, massive up-to-date data, detailed modelling and much else that before the electronic information revolution it would have been possible to do only crudely and slowly. But to-day it is technically quite feasible to use computerised communications to assess the repercussions of interrelated plans.

The problem of economic measurement seems formidable, largely because of uncertainty about what it is we want to measure. We have already pointed out that the technological and scientific revolution is rendering meaningless the notion of cost attributable to individual products – and in the absence of this notion the market system loses rationality. Having in imagination done away with the market system we seem to find ourselves back at a point we thought we had left, requiring a measure of economic value little different from that of the market economy. In fact this is not so and there are great differences about the measure that we are now looking for. We now need not an overall measure, but principles to regulate exchanges and to assess economic effectiveness. In the regulation of exchanges we need aim only at seeing that these exchanges are reasonably fair. In detail, and from day to day, these exchanges would usually be negotiated freely between the parties concerned. But they would need some guiding principles and it would be important to check and correct unequal arrangements, especially if these were likely to persist. The possibility of satisfactorily, and with practical simplicity, laying down principles for these exchanges is greatly facilitated if there is increasing social provision of goods, such things as guaranteed basic incomes and generally plentiful supplies of essential goods. We have already suggested that supplies would as of right be made to each community pro rata simply to its population.

For the purpose of measuring efficiency in production and economic management, it will be necessary constantly to analyse processes to discover what factors might be in short supply and where the major social costs lay. Such technical measures of economic input/output ratios, need, of course, be applied only to inputs that are in some sense scarce – scarce, for example, because they called for activities that people did not like undertaking or only wished to undertake to a limited extent, or because they used up limited natural resources. In a more plentiful science-based economy the factors of production, which it was thought desirable to economise, might be conceived of very differently from the factors of production in current economic thinking.

One of the main factors which will have to be economised will be the non-renewable minerals in the earth's crust including the hydrocarbon fuels – coal, oil and natural gas. The chief glory of the market price mechanism is supposed to be that it reflects scarcity. But it reflects only today's scarcity not the exhaustion in ten or fifteen or twenty years' time of vital minerals. No speculator will buy up reserves and so push up the price by cornering stocks over that period of years. Yet there is no doubt that we are using up some essential minerals and other resources at a rate that means their exhaustion by the end of the century at the latest. In the interests of mankind constraints that reflect real scarcities need to be universally agreed and imposed even when productive capacity for many products is almost unlimited. This means that we have to face real problems of inequality of access and only emphasises the fact that inequality of resource distribution will remain a major problem on the international scale.

All we can say here is that inequalities in the past were made more unmanageable by two factors that it is possible to eliminate: first, the absolute poverty of most of the human race, and second the ignorance of men that made them easy objects of exploitation and repression. The major change in future in this respect can be the wide circulation of information and this will include the use of computers, CRT, telecommunication, and other means to transmit scientific and productive training and 'know-how'.

Money in the market economy serves as an abstract universal measure of exchange value, but has production planned for concrete uses need of such an overall economic measure? Principles to govern exchange of productive activities are needed and specific measures (as quality of wheat is measured differently from quality of steel) are needed also for specific purposes; but the functions of a universal economic measure when production is regulated to meet concrete needs, are not evident. We have emphasised that plan regulated production must for some considerable period of time exist alongside, though in conflict with, market production. The development of planned production will require thorough theoretical exploration but as the problems it meets are widely debated and analysed in the light of practical experience, a body of practical know-how will be built up.

The principles that guide accountants or quantity surveyors are even now shot through with many difficulties similar to those that we are here discussing. (Anyone who doubts this should look at the two different estimates, each made by reputable city accountants, of the Pergamon Press profit expectations in the 1969 take-over battle for this company.) However, guiding lines for practice that work after a fashion have been evolved. It should, therefore, be possible to develop economic arbitration committees to examine such questions as might be referred to them. In the course of time a considerable body of case history would be built up and whilst measures used might remain far from perfect, they should be adequate to ensure the functioning of what one might call a pluralistically planned economy. Social arbitration or effective negotiation when difficulties arise between economic organisms is hardly conceivable unless intelligent and flexible use is made of computers so as to display and study the relationships between the various parts of the wider community. Computer modelling, backed by extensive reserves of computer-readable information, could display quickly and clearly the inner logic of problems confronting people. If one group thought that unreasonable demands were being made by another, it should be possible to calculate immediately some of the consequences that would result if these demands were not met. Social needs and social relations would then be far more clearly and sharply defined and conflict due to misunderstanding lessened. Computer-backed deliberations would make it possible to explore the meaning of a wide range of alternatives and so discover more acceptable solutions.

In a commodity producing economy the competition for exchange-values, for money, is furious and desperate. Even so, negotiation and arbitration is possible. In an economy so structured that money is no longer the only passport to survival it is reasonable to expect that agreements between recipients and suppliers of the means of productive and social activity and of the requirements for human well being, would as a rule be easily reached without friction, provided adequate information and facilities for its interpretation were available to all. In the final analysis, therefore, the problems of economic measurement are subordinate to the struggle through which social change comes about and in particular the contending outlooks on economic criteria and the organisation of production and reproduction of material goods.

Investment: Co-ordination and Decision-Taking

The problem of investment is the problem of how much of present resources to allocate to improving or changing for the future the methods of producing material goods, the environment in which we live, or, more generally, the facilities that support our activities as human beings. Man lives both in the present and the future. He cares about how he behaves, what he does in the present, but he also cares about the kind of future his present activities are creating and will create, beyond his own lifetime as well as in the future he may live to see. He is part of a living process that goes beyond himself. He cares about the society that fashioned him. He cares also about the way he himself is fashioning the society to which he belongs.

So man's choices about the future are not in kind different from his choices about the present. Again, we need not concern ourselves so much with what a man does simply as an individual on his own. The problems to solve are those of man as a member both of basic social organisms in themselves and as constituents of wider complexes. What new possibilities does the information revolution create for attacking these problems? To plan for the future is to create a model simulating a future course of development. The plan must show the sequence of actions that will create some future situation. The point of planning is not to fix future situations but rather to open up a wider range of possibilities, more alternatives not fewer alternatives in the future. The point of planning is to remove the constraints of external events. To substitute situations in which conscious human decisions have a wider scope and in which the compulsions of chance external events are less imperative. But removal of constraints takes time; and investment is concerned with actions which must be taken now to remove constraints in the future. As well as what is done, it is the way things are done that matters. For example, protection from the elements is necessary but the building providing this must also delight us.

The new potential that the information revolution opens up is that of modelling aspects of the future so that the implications and costs of various lines of action may be quickly grasped. We shall be able more precisely and more rapidly to measure the social, economic and technical implications and the feasibility of several alternative plans for the future. We shall be able more easily to translate models from numerical to graphical forms. For example, suppose the question was whether it was desirable to move a steel works from an inland site to a coastal site. One would have a model of the social and economic system into which the proposed change would be introduced. That is, one might have a means of showing where the existing economic activities were located, where people dwelt, what the traffic flows were, and other key factors. One might then calculate the resources needed to effect the move and the ease of operation in the new site. One could prepare a general display, including a graphical display of how life might be for the various people involved if the changes were effected. The great advantage of such an information system would be the facility of interrogating, that is quickly getting calculations made, diagrams drawn and so forth, to see the meaning of alternative courses of action. Each in his own way could evaluate the alternatives. With use and experience the potential for developing such modelling/information systems is huge. There is room for going far beyond the clumsy processes by which our investment decisions are taken today. Even in the planned economies with state ownership alternative mixes of investment are not presented to the people for discussion and choice.

The importance of these facilities for investment is that investment is about choosing alternatives, and if a community is to choose – and not just one person or a handful of people – precise communication and clear understanding of alternatives and their implications are vital. Quantitative evaluation of alternatives (particularly when the objective of an investment is simply to increase productivity) is often possible, and clearly such evaluations are sets of facts and figures that need to be calculated and disseminated. In the last analysis, however, investment decisions are qualitative. They are choices about the kind of future that a community wants and how much of present resources the community is prepared to allocate to obtain the future state that seems to its members to be the most desirable. (Of course, an element of probability enters into choice of future states and one of the facts to be brought into the reckoning is the probability of sought-after aims actually being achieved.) The wider the understanding of what investment choices are about, the more likely are decisions to be effective.

Investment decisions differ especially in that the number of people and the number of groupings of social organisms affected by them differ. Investment decisions by individuals will again be omitted from consideration. We need only to make reasonable estimates about the implications of such decisions for demand and supply of resources and as such they are not different from other problems of market research.

How might disagreements about investment of resources be resolved? One can only presume that in the future they will be settled as now, by struggle between contending views. But one might well expect that a society structured so that decisions tended to be taken by those to whom they were of most direct concern, would deal with conflicting views very differently. At present effective decision rests with the party that spends the money. In a very general way investment may be publicly controlled; for example in Britain the industrial development certificate may permit a manufacturer to build a new factory in one place and not in another. Other regulations may control the form of the building; in essentials, however, the investment will be shaped by a management accountable to those who own the capital behind the undertaking. In the case of investment from public funds in capitalist and in state-planned economies its form and character will be shaped by the administrative bureaucracy along general policy lines laid down by the political body to which it is responsible. Conflict takes the form of public debate, and involves such methods as lobbying and demonstrations, which may bring a general form of pressure on the administration and may ultimately influence elections to the bodies that exercise political authority. In short, conflicts express themselves as ill-defined tensions in which the real points of conflict are rarely specific.

One would assume in a society in which there was more devolution of decision-making and in which the techniques of information analysis and exchange were highly perfected that many causes of conflict would be removed and the disagreements would be much more finely focussed. Certainly conflicts due to ignorance of particular circumstances and due to poor appreciation of matters of fact should be considerably lessened. Where, as in contemporary Britain, one cause underlying many forms of disagreement is difference of standpoint of differently placed classes in relation to the economic system, the conflict will necessarily have a blunt elemental character.

In what has gone before we have envisaged the possibility of the firm, the enterprise, ceasing to have the importance it has at present as the basic unit in the economic structure viewed from the side of production. However things may turn out, it is quite reasonable to assume that social groups of consumers, and, more particularly, social groups of producers, will associate for various purposes, as practice and experience dictates, into federations on the basis of geographical proximity, similarity of activities in the technical field, because they supply the same body of users and for many other reasons. Such federations may in turn group with other federations. One may envisage a number of overlapping sets of groups, each constituting a sort of council, or parliament, addressed to a particular range of problems. In some such way as this the content of investment problems that concern society at large could come to be adequately understood.

This may be recognised by some readers as reminiscent of the Guild Socialists' concept of a man having as many forms of representation as he has functions in life – as producer, consumer, householder, sportsman, and so on[1]. The concept seemed to have lost validity with the huge scale of modern plants and modern economic organisation, as G.D.H. Cole himself recognised in 1955 in his foreword to B. Pribićević's book on *The Shop Stewards Movement and Workers' Control* already referred to. What we are suggesting here is that the computer creates new possibilities for this kind of decentralisation.

The political mechanism by which investment policies come to be determined must depend on a course of historical development that cannot at this stage be seen. But certain general points may be made. The co-ordination of economic life implies some contribution of resources by the smaller social bodies for use on wider social purposes (e.g. by taxation in a money economy). For present purposes the form this takes is not important beyond insisting that if the devolution of decision-taking is to be effective every social organism must have resources at its disposal for investment. In the case of organisms of consumers this reflects simply the fact that provision made is both for the present and for the future; since, if people are to determine for themselves the texture of their lives, they must interest themselves in the future as well as in the immediate present. In the case of social organisms concerned with production, or with the creation of economic values, in whatever form, investment funds, that is resources over and

1. See *Guild Socialism Restated,* G.D.H. Cole, 1920.

above normal running needs, are essential if changes are to be made in techniques of production and organisation.

But just as it is necessary for some investment funds to be in the hands of the basic social groupings, it is equally essential to provide means for investment on a much wider social scale. Investment may be looked at as falling into two broad types (a) investment in hardware, that is material goods such as machinery, building and civil engineering works, and (b) investment in people and ideas, as for example in research, in building up information systems, in education and in dissemination of scientific understanding. Generally it will be possible, in a rough and ready way, to define who is likely to use and benefit from (a), the hardware. But we are moving into times in which the most important investment, with the biggest impact on production and the quality of life, is in science and education.

If the routines of providing basic materials and social needs come to be automated to any considerable degree, proportionately more human activity will be concerned with new purposes. In the past there have been a number of well-defined trades and occupations in constant demand in much the same form. In all probability a man once trained for one of these occupations could well, should he so wish, spend his whole life in it. The future is likely to be one in which continuous change will be both desired and, over a wider area, also necessary. So education may cease to be a preliminary stage before entering working life and become rather a part of working life throughout its full extent. In the same way research and experiment and the communication of results from scientific enquiry may become increasingly important. These activities may be demanded as means to social and economic developments and also for themselves. At all events a great part of investment will amount to diverting resources in these directions. In these areas, as is already the case with scientific research, it may be quite impossible to see who is most likely to benefit.

Many decisions may need to be taken by society as, in one form or another, a widely unified collectivity. The point is, however that the active elements in the socio-economic system become the basic units; and these units then co-ordinate and act jointly where they have common problems, retaining their own separateness and individuality in those areas where no one else may take a decision for them. Such a relationship is not in fact complicated. Having defined what one requires in principle from, say, a railway system, an electricity supply system, a computer utility, or a water supply system, the detailed working out as to how to meet the users' defined needs will be the task of the workers on the job. The user must also, of course, have means of criticising and controlling defects on the supplier's part.

But by leaving decisions about how water is to be supplied to the producing unit, one is not losing but gaining freedom. As already suggested, there need to be effective channels of appeal open to anyone who feels that things are going wrong. Of course one could not leave those who run the water system, lay out the road system, the electricity supply or railway system, to get on with the provision of what we want if general principles have not been decided, for example about what rivers should be dammed and where, about where roads should run and the best mix of road and rail transport and sources of energy supply. Questions such as this would call for the widest discussion and participation by others outside the specialised utility service.

We are living in an economically interdependent society. In the future our interdependence is likely to be at least as great as it is at present. This is true not only at the national level but well beyond that, at the international or world level. Where we are interdependent we need to find effective methods of acting socially that express this interdependence. Once these have been found there remain clear areas in which community units or small groupings of such units can perfectly well look after their own affairs. However, the fact that some decisions need to be co-ordinated centrally is a quite different matter from the bureaucratic vice of centralised decision-taking used as an instrument of political power. Hierarchical or authoritarian principles of organisation that go with centralisation of political power, inevitably generate fear of allowing ordinary people to take their own decisions. Hence the absurdities of the many petty decisions centrally taken when they would have been far better left to others.

In an economically interdependent community, everyone in some measure has power over everyone else. Each person is a link in a chain which he may threaten to break. But in fact this interdependence of one another already exists in social life. Law and custom can establish adequate frameworks within which to provide the balance between freedom and interdependence that people want.

The possibility that we are envisaging is a new socio-economic structure appropriate to our technological potential. It is hard to imagine what forms an appropriate structure might take that are not in *general outline* of the types here discussed. The essential changes envisaged are:–

1. *Ultimate* recourse in allocation of resources, not to the market, but to conscious deliberate planning for use, not by the few but by the many.
2. Explicit decisions by men and women in their role as consumers on the purposes that productive powers are to serve.
3. Coupling with this a greater control by the producers themselves over the texture of their lives in the activity of producing.

4. Authority as a principle of productive organisation (that is, co-ordination by one person or a small élite making all the decisions) being replaced by responsibility to a collectivity of producers. (This does not mean that individual managers would not be appointed but, if so, they would take their authority from the collectivity of people for whom they work and not as in industry today from the power of appointment residing in the owners or controllers of capital.)
5. Information as a new technical factor, to effect the cohesion needed to replace the market; the computer/electronics revolution making possible the requisite speed, extent and richness of information flows and analysis.

If in fact some such socio-economic structure is necessary to make effective use of the technological potential and to make the quality of life what people want, how can a way to it be found? To effect social change means to exert political power. The argument developed in this book is omitting all discussion of the interplay of political forces and the conditions under which politically the changes discussed might come about; but clearly an important part of getting anywhere is to see where one is going. Argument and analysis contributes to building the way. Already there are many people who are no longer ready just to watch things happening to them. For 'no taxation without representation' one might substitute 'no decisions without the involvement of those whom the decisions concern'. If in every social organism of significance for social life groups of people begin to ask what is being done and why, to insist on getting all the facts relevant to the questions they ask and to insist on answers to the questions that they put, then embryos may be formed from which new structures may grow. Already trade unions and shop stewards' committees are beginning to take up a stance that shows concern not merely for conditions of employment but for the whole management policy of their employers, since it is upon the latter that they see their own future and that of the community in which they work as depending. In many other areas, in relation to housing, town planning, education, health services and so forth, the germs of analogous activities are apparent. The absolute relevance of the technological revolution to these trends seems, however, to have been less generally noticed.

To make ourselves What?

As yet, we understand but poorly the consequences of our actions in society. This is not surprising. Such understanding is perhaps the exact equivalent of mastery by man over the full potential of scientific knowledge – the problem that was our starting point. But to say that there are good excuses for our failures should not lead us to minimise the appalling consequences that they may entail. The more powerful the instruments of science become, the more horrific the spiritual and material devastation they may cause. Uncontrolled by us, by the people, the multitudinous individuals that make up society, social change follows trends that can be all too easily sketched. Men and women become cogs in vast organisations, giant companies, huge pyramids of state power, controlled by the decisions of a few at the centre. The new instruments of the computer revolution facilitate such control. The technological potential becomes actual in the context of the social structure it serves.

History moves slowly and men learn by bitter experience. The practicalities of daily life make it hard not to accept routines imposed by the social machine of which we find ourselves a part. Attempts at non-acceptance may become a contracting out, a non-involvement, as with the Hippies, to which the social machine itself is more or less impervious. In striving after change man is constantly learning and refashioning himself and the reality of actual experience is never totally lost; but the generations of successive failure have been running on. Struggle with ideas, struggle in the arena of social change, alone can find those forms of social action and that recasting of the structure of social behaviour that brings success in place of failure and makes man master of himself.

I come back to a quotation from Marx. Over 100 years ago in a speech delivered on 14th April 1856 Marx spoke of problems that sound very much like the problems now before us.

> "The new-fangled sources of wealth, by some strange, weird spell are turned into sources of want. The victories of art seem bought by the loss of character. At the same pace that mankind masters nature, man seems to become enslaved to other men or to his own infamy. Even the pure life of science seems unable to shine but on the dark background of ignorance. All our invention and progress seem to result in endowing material forces with intellectual life, and in stultifying human life into material force. This antagonism between modern industry and science on the one hand, and modern misery and dissolution, on the other; this antagonism between the productive forces and the social relations of our epoch is a fact, palpable, overwhelming and not to be controverted."[1]

The logic inherent in existing social structures that tends more and more towards the centralisation of political power and control over resources obviously has as its limiting term the most extreme form of dictatorship. This is the internal logic of leaving things be. But human

1. From *Karl Marx, Man, Thinker and Revolutionist.* A symposium edited by P. Ryazonoff, London, 1927.

society is in fact more than the structure and social forms of the day, of the immediate present; it is also thinking, struggling individuals embodying both an older inheritance of passions, thought and culture and also an intellectual vision that strives forward and looks far ahead into a new future. Modern capitalist society has made men as individuals more alive to their own individuality than was ever possible in the poorer life of earlier social formations. But at the same time it has made men cogs in a machine, alienated from their potential of all-round human creativity and feeling. It may seem that modern society has made men and women into slaves of external forces, but it has also made men and women into beings that are conscious of their slavery, of their sub-humanity. In this they have stepped out far in advance of those earlier phases of history in which the possibility of human individuality could only be recognised in the most limited, restricted forms. Man has always felt himself constrained by external necessity. He has expressed his sense of this constraint in many forms, religious and philosophical, and in the language of science. It is important that we should look down the other end of the telescope – that is, that we should be more sharply aware of the scope for freedom and human creativity within such bounds as are set by external necessity.

First, consider the doctrine of economic determinism that in open or disguised form runs through a great deal of pseudo-scientific writing at the present time. Economic determinism is a form of materialism that asserts that men and women are inevitably what their circumstances and upbringing make them. There is a tendency to adopt this position for a number of reasons. For example, we see such changing circumstances as the agricultural revolution long ago, or more recently the industrial revolution, utterly transforming the lives of people on this earth and the kind of people they are. We recognise that there are determinable laws governing these changes and we deduce that an external factor, which we call economic change, determines the whole situation. From another point of view it seems to accord with the experience of those who feel themselves to be helpless, powerless digits in a system they cannot control; for them economic determinism may paradoxically have a moral and political meaning in that it gives them courage to endure in the belief that the laws of history are working towards the millenium, which they themselves feel unable to advance but from which at least they draw the consolation and steadfastness of hope. At a quite different level this doctrine has a certain relationship to the conduct of the impartial expert; scientists, economists or historians are asked to express opinions that touch the future; a reply about how *they* would like to shape the future is not what is expected of them – such a reply would seem inappropriate, egotistical or be harmful to their professional interests; they are expected to eliminate their own political or moral motivations; and as a result their analysis will tend to be restricted to deterministic situations. What we do is not pre-determined; we act, however, within restraints, and if we are able to understand the laws of the necessity by which we are constrained, then we thereby become the more free to attain the ends we will. The freedom of our social existence is, in particular, constrained by the conditions of social labour and by the technologies available to the production process and, more widely, to all economic activity and social organisation.

Incidentally, the accusation of economic determinism is one of the more common misrepresentations of Karl Marx's views, perpetrated by his supporters as well as by his opponents. Marx himself said (Thesis II on Feuerbach):

> "The materialist doctrine that men are products of circumstances and upbringing, and that, therefore, changed men are products of other circumstances and changed upbringing, forgets that it is men who change circumstances and that it is essential to educate the educator himself. Hence, this doctrine necessarily arrives at dividing society into two parts, one of which is superior to society (in Robert Owen, for example). The coincidence of the changing of circumstances and of human activity can be conceived and rationally understood only as revolutionising practice."

We may also turn again to Marx for a particularly illuminating formulation of the problem from which we started. Our problem is to understand the framework of possibilities for the development of new types of socio-economic organisation. Marx gave much thought to structures of socio-economic organisation prior to the epoch of capitalist society when, as we have seen, man's economic activity came to be subsumed within one worldwide market system. Marx's thinking about earlier structures is very relevant to our understanding. This is to be found in the notes that he wrote, largely to clarify his own ideas, in 1857/1858 on 'Forms Which Preceded Capitalist Production'. I will attempt to paraphrase some points from these notes.[1]

Property is the form in which socially man's relations to his conditions of production find their expression. Each specific model of production "appears equally as the relationship of the individuals to one another and as their specific daily behaviour towards inorganic nature, their specific mode of labour." So according to the conditions of production, property will take different forms. In capitalism – the market system with which we have been dealing – the relationship of

1. The notes have been published in English under the title *Precapitalist Economic Formations* with an excellent introduction by E.J. Hobsbawm, Lawrence and Wishart, 1964.

labour to capital presupposes an historic process which has dissolved the forms of property and production "in which the labourer is an owner and the owner labours." Communal property in land "the laboratory of man's forces and the domain of his will" is dissolved; the craftsman's property in the tools of his craft is dissolved; his attachment to the house of his master craftsman and likewise the serf's attachment to the landlord's estate are dissolved. "These, then, on the one hand, are historic pre-requisites without which the labourer cannot occur as free labourer, as objectiveless, purely subjective capacity for labouring, confronting the objective conditions of production as his *non-property,* as *someone else's property,* as *value* existing for itself, as capital. On the other hand, we must ask what conditions are necessary if he is to confront capital?" (Marx's emphasis).

Our problem is to overcome man's 'non-property' – his 'objectiveless' separation from the production process, to discover a new relation for man to the new conditions of production, a new property form appropriate to man's aspirations as also to his technologies.

"Man", says Marx "is only individualised through the process of history. He originally appears as a *generic being,* a *tribal being,* a herd animal – though by no means as a "political animal" in the political sense. Exchange itself is a major agent of this individualisation."[1] We have become 'individualised' but in the process we have become separated from the production process, alienated. Our problem is exactly this – to recover property over the powers of modern science and technology. But the crucial question is what form of property? Whose property? Is science and technology to be the property of individuals? Of nations? Or of the worldwide commonwealth of mankind in such community units as men may wish to form?

The system to which we belong is one single system, one world, in which exchange links each to each. In more and more senses the natural environment in which we operate can only be regarded as the common property of mankind. Scientific knowledge also, as the increasingly predominant instrument with which we operate on this natural environment, can similarly be regarded only as common property, a common heritage of all mankind from the past into the future. 'Man's laboratory' is no longer a plot of earth from which his productive efforts win him a livelihood. It is the sea and the sky as well as the land. It is atoms and electrons and molecules, assuming and being caused to assume many different forms, moving into and away from the earth's surface, through electro-magnetic radiation linking man's activity with the depth of space.

Mankind in relation to the new productive forces that are coming

1. *Precapitalist Economic Formations,* p. 96.

into being is one vast single community. But at the same time man has become individual. Moreover, as such, he is a distinct member of small teams of men and women who work together or are grouped together by one or other of the active forms in which social existence finds its expression. The problem is to establish new forms of social relation and exchange such that we individual men and women in groups that seem relevant to us can control between us the common heritage of technologies and scientific knowledge in a natural universe which is much more than the land, or what man makes on or from the land. The boundary stones that marked private property as plots of earth or areas of the land's surface cease to be appropriate terms in which to define the infinitely small and infinitely vast environment on which the operations of modern science and technology act.

In the previous chapters we explored whether measures are needed to govern our exchanges with others, how decisions might be devolved and consciousness restored to the smallest component parts of the vast organisations in and under which humanity today lives and by which it fears to be destroyed. We have seen an almost limitless potentiality for increasing man's control over production even to the point where little human labour will be needed and automated means of production supply almost all the necessities of human existence.

In the electronic digital computer man has provided himself with a general-purpose programmed automaton. It is the development of this idea that will eventually make possible the almost limitless extension of automation; since any well-defined routine or procedure can, in principal, be made computer controlled. Furthermore we have seen how the computer makes possible the co-ordination of interlocking social and economic processes – and this may result in economic and productive activities being cast into quite new patterns and moulds with performance potentials of a new order. The digital computer itself – which has indicated the actuality of this potential – may prove to be no more than a primitive example of techniques in kind as different from the machine as the machine was different from the craftsman's tool.

But the computer, and the electronics industry from which it springs, mean much more than a new means of production. The computer revolution is more significantly an information revolution. The word information has such insipid connotations that one might well miss the immensity of the revolution that will spring from these new technologies. (Will spring, that is, if we can ensure that the new science bottled up in old political and moral systems does not first blow the whole world to pieces.) The life of mankind has become in kind quite different from that of all other animals, thanks to man's power to use language, to communicate experience and ideas, to transmit information to other men, to share a sense of social morality. "The human essence is the ensemble of social relations." (Marx *Theses on Feuerbach.*) It will become possible, thanks to electronic media, to establish these relations with a richness of articulated precision, in new visual, new aural forms, hitherto undreamed of. The impact of these media of communications – within a social framework not adapted to them – already causes alarm about their power. But these same media suggest the possibility of relations between man and man across the world knitting and harmonising the lives of communities, each freely shaping their own manner of existence. One may envisage new forms of social consciousness emerging, mediated by man's command over the atom and electron as a means of communication. What art and buildings were as forms of social communication in the middle ages, so electronically communicated constructs may become in the twentyfirst century.

I have tried to sketch the possibilities and the constraints of the economic and technological situation as I see them. It is the action of men and women in knowledge of these constraints and possibilities that will determine the future. They will act in the light of what they know and want from those viewpoints and positions in which they have been placed by the evolution of history to date. Of course, in considering these positions one needs also to take account of the constraints and possibilities of the political scene. This book has dealt only with the constraints and possibilities of technology in relation to economic practice and organisation. Those who want to change the world must also generate sufficient political and social power to effect the change. Such power must be power in the hands of the many not the few, or the change will be no more than the replacing of an old élite by a new one. Indeed, as we have seen, the very techniques of the information revolution make even more sinister the threat of vast social machines dominated by a few at the centre of power.

Power of political and social action to become more than an occasional intervention, as in a protest demonstration, a strike or an election, implies continuous exercise of control at key points of social life. It is hard to conceive any other basis for this but joint action by those who work together in basic units of production and economic life, and associate with one another in the basic activities of social existence. New techniques of communication and the course of economic development has made the world one world and at the same time enriched the understanding and activity of the individual in that world, the individual always acting in and with a social grouping to which he or she is immediately attached. In the extension and the individual articulation of this one world of interlinked groups of men and women, the rapidly advancing techniques of information-processing and transmission offer not only dangers but also a vast new potential of which only a small fraction has, as yet, been used.

The most crucial circumstance in changing human society and in 'making man what he can become' is the structure of relationships in economic activity. These have changed again and again, and through the experience of life man has learned to make mistakes and learn from his mistakes, and to find new forms of activity and association. It was man himself who made the society from which he now seeks to escape.

> "It is childish", says Professor Gordon Childe, "to ask why man did not progress straight from the squalor of a 'pre-class' society to the glories of a classless paradise, nowhere fully realised as yet. Perhaps the conflicts and contradictions, above revealed, themselves constitute the dialectics of progress. In any case, they are facts of history. If we dislike them that does not mean that progress is a delusion, but merely that we have understood neither the facts nor progress nor man. Man made the superstitions and the institutions of oppression as much as he made the sciences and the instruments of production. In both alike he was expressing himself, finding himself, making himself."[1]

Our world becomes 'one world'. We know more. We see more. We communicate more. We feel more. But to feel is to act, to know is to do. The life of man, of woman is 'practical, human-sensuous activity'. And knowing what we know, we shall make ourselves what?

1. V. Gordon Childe in *Man Makes Himself,* Watts & Co., 1941, pp. 236-7.

BIBLIOGRAPHICAL NOTE

There is a great number of books dealing with the rather wide range of topics touched on in this text. The purpose of this note is to provide a *short* list of suggestions for parallel reading.

A most valuable summary of contemporary economic ideas and facts is to be found in *What Economics Is About* by Michael Barratt Brown, Weidenfeld & Nicolson, 1970. The reader will get from this one book all that he needs as a basis and many suggestions for additional reading.

There are a number of useful introductions to the computer. For the more mathematically minded I would suggest *Introduction to Computer Science* by M. Levison and W.R. Sentance, Oldbourne Mathematical Series, 1968. For the less mathematically minded *Electronic Computers* by F.L. Westwater, English University Press, 1962 – a brief and clear volume in the "Teach Yourself" series.

For the historical background to computers I recommend the fascinating selection of writings by Charles Babbage and others titled *Charles Babbage and his Calculating Engines* edited by Philip Morrison and Emily Morrison, Dover Publications, 1961.

For straightforward accounts of how computers are being used in contemporary life and how they affect it the reader may go to *Automation: Its Uses and Consequences* by J. Rose, Oliver and Boyd, 1967, and *Computers, Managers and Society* by Michael Rose, Penguin Books, 1969. On cybernetics the mathematically minded reader cannot do better than read the *Introduction to Cybernetics* by Viktor M. Glushkov, Academic Press, 1966. Also to be recommended are Norbert Wiener's original essays *Cybernetics or Control and Communication in the Animal and the Machine,* M.I.T. Press, 1948 and 1961. (The greater part of these are non-mathematical and the highly mathematical sections may be skipped.) *Great Ideas in Information Theory, Language and Cybernetics,* Constable, 1966, and *Great Ideas of Operations Research,* Dover, 1968, by Jagjit Singh are both exceptionally clear, sound and wide in their coverage. A number of brief, clear and authoritative articles have been published in *Scientific American* on relevant mathematical topics. These are conveniently collected in *Information,* W.H. Freeman & Co., 1966, and *Mathematics in the Modern World* with an introduction by Morris Kline, W.H. Freeman & Co., 1968.

For the philosophical background I recommend *A Model of the Brain* (1964) and *An Introduction to the Study of Man* (1971) by J.Z. Young, both Oxford University Press, *Language and Mind* by Noam Chomsky, Massachusetts Institute of Technology, 1968, *The Structure of Scientific Revolutions* by Thomas S. Kuhn, University of Chicago Press, 1962, *Anti-Duhring* by Frederick Engels, (originally written in 1878 in collaboration with Karl Marx; this work summarises the social and philosophical outlook of Marxism and provides a good introduction to *Capital* and other Marxist classics; Part III on socialism, also published as *Socialism, Utopian and Scientific,* is particularly relevant to the concept of social change; English translations are published by Lawrence & Wishart), *La Pensée Sauvage* by Claude Lévi-Strauss, Plon, 1962, of which an English translation has been published under the title *The Savage Mind.*

MATHEMATICAL APPENDIX

NOTE 1

Concentric 'nesting' circles (such as a pebble makes when dropped into a pool) serve as an example of a general mathematical concept; a calculable representation of a similar idea is given by the formula

$$A = \pi (K \log_e t)^2$$

These are circles whose radii increase over time at a diminishing rate. Carrying out the operations implied by this formula – that is the process of mathematical calculation – gives it a specific interpretation; for example, with K = 10 and t = 5, A = area in square feet (of the outside circle), A would be about 800 square feet after 5 seconds.

The scope for such calculable representations is very greatly increased by the new electronic techniques of information processing. This is only one aspect among many in the complex process of human understanding but it would be a great mistake to underrate its significance and to fail to see the vast extension into new territories that the instruments now available to mankind make possible.

MATHEMATICAL APPENDIX

NOTE 2

A projectile launched at speed u and angle A will continue, the Newtonian Model tells us, to move in the same direction at the same speed except insofar as it is acted upon by a force. We neglect air resistance, the spinning of earth through space, etc., and that leaves us with only the force of gravity to be reckoned with.

Mathematicians using the instruments of mathematical analysis developed by Newton, Leibniz and many others since, easily deduce the following equations giving the position of the projectile at any time (t) –

$$(1)\quad x = (u \cos A)\, t$$

$$(2)\quad y = -gt^2/2 + (u \sin A)\, t$$

Note: (u is the speed and A the angle of projection from some point P, say; then x gives distance travelled over the surface and y the height above the surface after t seconds.)

Here in fact we have the model of the flight of a projectile. It is a convenient and yet quite powerful model. It is convenient in that it gives a simple rule or algorithm with which to calculate where the projectile is at any particular moment in time. We can ask questions of this model and get useful answers. For example, where will the projectile land? Assuming that it is being projected over a flat surface it will touch earth when y, that is the distance vertically above the earth, is zero. From these two equations we can work out that it is zero on two occasions, first at the start when x also equals zero and secondly when x or the range = $\dfrac{u^2 \sin 2A}{g}$.

This formula checks with commonsense. The greater the speed at which the projectile is shot off the farther it will go. In the formula the range varies as the square of the speed of projection. The trignometrical function *sin* is at its greatest for an angle of 90°, so sin 2A will be a maximum when the angle of projection is 45°. This again is sensible. If the angle is too steep the projectile just goes up and down without going very far; if too shallow, it will be pulled back to earth before it has covered much distance. The force of gravity, given here as 32 ft. per second, in fact varies slightly at different heights and in different parts of the world. So g is, therefore, a parameter, a number that is adjusted and fixed in the model to suit the circumstances that the model is required to represent. Similarly, u and A are parameters. If we want to see what happens, if the speed of projection is increased, we change u. If we want to see how the range, for example, is affected by changing the angle of projection, we run our model for a changed value of A. These mathematical formulae constitute a model that may run for a number of different situations by changing the parameters u and A. It is worth noting also that the parameters and variables in the model are of somewhat different kinds. The parameters in the sense of variables under the immediate control of the human agent are the angle (a) and the speed of projection (u); g is a parameter of a different sort – it is an element in the model that differs when circumstances differ in the sense that the projectile is being launched at a different place or on a different planet. Time (t) is again different; it represents a continuum of change underlying all models of events in the real world.

MATHEMATICAL APPENDIX

NOTE 3

The elementary logical processes performed by the computer; simple as they are, are more complex than the very simple manipulations of the normal algorithm. But the normal algorithm is worth examining as being one of the most elementary forms that the manipulations of an information processing machine can assume, bearing in mind that such a machine can, nonetheless, carry out even the most complex routines of calculations and modelling. What then is its essence?

The routine of the normal algorithm starts with an input of data (a string of numbers, string of letters, etc.); this leads to a string of processes in a set order which we can number 1 to N. N is the last process and is followed by an output – the procedure of handing over a string of numbers or letters as the output data.

Each process consists of following instructions (as in a game of snakes and ladders):–

a) looking at the string of figures to see if a particular grouping can be found,
b) if it can, substituting for it another specified grouping of figures,
c) either (1) going back to the beginning again if this is a 'normal substitution' or (2) going straightaway to the end, to output, if this is a 'concluding substitution',
d) if the grouping looked for cannot be found, going on to the next process.

Note, there are only two types of processes: (1) a normal substitution and (2) a concluding substitution. In all cases after doing what one is told to do one goes back to instruction No. 1 and starts working through the set of instructions all over again, unless one hits on a concluding substitution, after which one goes straightaway to output at the end. When one cannot do what one is told to do one always goes on and tries the next instruction and after the last instruction one goes to output. The procedure may be represented graphically as follows (at each stage the question being asked is 'Can the specified string of numbers be found?'):–

Diagram II.C **Flow-chart of the Normal Algorithm**

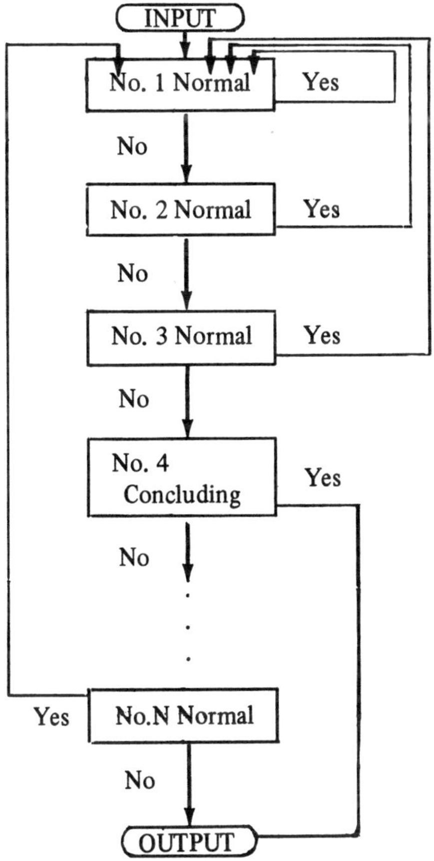

As an example consider the sort of addition process that is carried out by the very simple instruction illustrated below:–

Program of Instructions

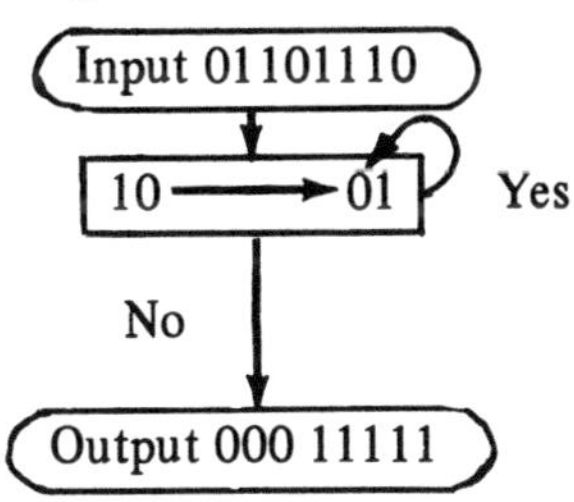

The process to be performed is simply to look for the grouping 10 and to substitute for it the grouping 01. It is a standing rule in the instructions that the operation is to be performed on the first occurrence of the grouping looked for, and after that has been done, one then goes back to start the string of processes all over again. In this particular case there is only one process to be performed. In the table of figures the grouping looked for at each stage is shown in brackets, then on the line below the substitution has been made and on the line below that the grouping is again looked for and after that the substitution made, and so forth until the whole process is concluded by the fact that the group of figures 10 nowhere occurs in the string of figures under examination.

Steps in Processing the Input Data to Obtain the Output Data	
	01101110
	01(10)1110
	01011110
	0(10)11110
	00111110
	001111(10)
	00111101
	00111(10)1
	00111011
	0011(10)11
	00110111
	001(10)111
	00101111
	00(10)1111
	00011111

MATHEMATICAL APPENDIX

NOTE 4

To illustrate what the computer does let us consider one fairly simple operation, namely addition of binary numbers. The basic principle that makes the functioning of an electronic digital computer possible is that it comprises a large number of logic units – that is electronic gates simulating logical operations – which suitably combined can carry out, in effect, any mathematical calculations or any algorithms. The circuits given below simply illustrate the correspondence between hardware and logic; the actual circuits which the designer chooses will vary and he will adapt his design in pursuit of technical advantages.

In this model I use three electronic gates simulating the logical processes:–

and, equivalent to 'intersection', $\cap$, in set theory,

or, equivalent to 'union', $\cup$, in set theory,

negation, equivalent to 'complementation', $-$, in set theory.

Set theory, of which the seeds are to be seen in the work of George Boole, provides the theoretical foundation of modern mathematics. Set theory is concerned with the surprisingly many properties of sets of things and sub-sets, that is sets contained in other sets, and combinations of sets. ('A pack of wolves, a bunch of grapes, or a flock of pigeons are examples of sets of things. The mathematical concept of a set can be used as the foundation of all known mathematics . . . . The principal concept of set theory . . . is that of *belonging.*' [Paul Halmos, *Naive Set Theory,* pp. 1/2, D. Van Nostrand 1960.]). A union ($\cup$) of two sets means pooling all the elements of these sets, for example $\{a, b, c\} \cup \{b, c, d\} = \{a, b, c, d\}$. Intersection ($\cap$) means selecting the elements common to the two sets. For example – $\{a, b, c\} \cup \{b, c, d\} = \{b, c\}$. The empty set is a set with no members, for which the symbol $\overline{\emptyset}$ is often used. For example – $\{a, b\} \cup \{c, d\} = \emptyset$ meaning that there are no common members to the two sets. Sets are thought of as being 'sub-sets' of a 'universal set'

– that is, a set containing all elements of the system under consideration. For example we might regard X = $\{a, b, c, d\}$ as the universal set. The complement of a set (indicated by a line, e.g. $\bar{A}$ means the complement of set A) is the set of all elements that are not in it; for example, if A = $\{a, b, c\}$ and B = $\{b, c, d\}$, then $\bar{A} = \{d\}$ and $\bar{B} = \{a\}$. $\bar{X} = \emptyset$, since there are no elements not in the universal set X; on the other hand the complement of $\emptyset$ = X since there are no elements in the empty set, the elements not in it are all the other elements.

Set theory may be applied to the binary alphabet with 1 corresponding to a signal or a set containing the element 1, and 0 corresponding to no signal or to the empty set; $1 \cup 1 = 1$, $1 \cup 0 = 1$, $0 \cup 1 = 1$, $0 \cup 0 = 0$; and $1 \cap 1 = 1$, $1 \cap 0 = 0$, $0 \cap 1 = 0$, $0 \cap 0 = 0$.

These processes can be illustrated by their use in ordinary language:

AND : The 'and' process requires two conditions to be fulfilled in order that some specified result may follow. For example, I might say 'If you have a degree from a British university and are over 21, then you are eligible for this job'. If you have a degree but are under 21, you are not eligible. If you are over 21 but have not got a degree, then again you are not eligible; both conditions must be fulfilled. Diagrammatically this may be represented as in Diagram B.(a).

OR The operation 'or' is illustrated by the sentence 'If you live in London or have a motor car, you may apply for this job'. The consequence follows given either one or both of the precedent conditions. Diagrammatically this may be expressed as in Diagram B.(c).

NEGATION: The operation of 'negation' is in language represented by insertion of the word 'not'; for example 'black' and 'not-black' as in Diagram B.(b).

Diagram C. gives pictorially the corresponding operations in set-theory, using what are commonly known as Venn diagrams.

In the example that follows we assume that the machine is operating in binary. The operation is simply the addition of 2 digits. Call these digits x and y and set up an addition table to cover all possible values for x and y. Since we are working in binary there are only two possible values for each of x and y, namely 0 and 1. The left side of the table

DIAGRAM IIE.

Diagrammatic Representation of Basic Logical Processes

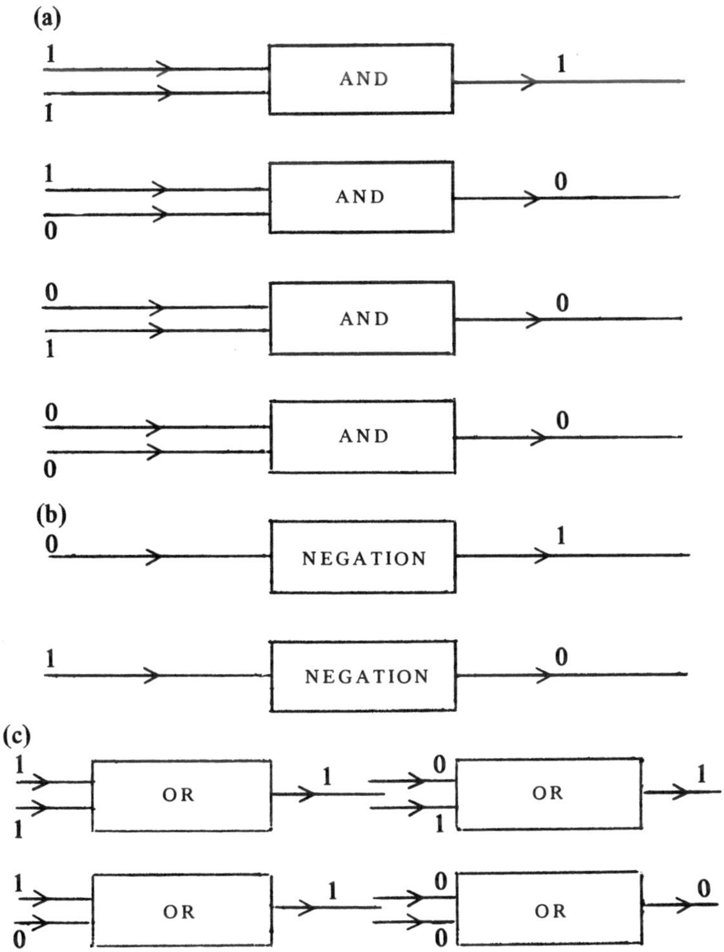

shows the four possible inputs. The output side must show i) the number to be written down and ii) the number to be carried forward and taken into account when adding the figures in the next door position on the left.

DIAGRAM IIF.

Venn Diagrams Illustrating Basic Logical Operations

(a)

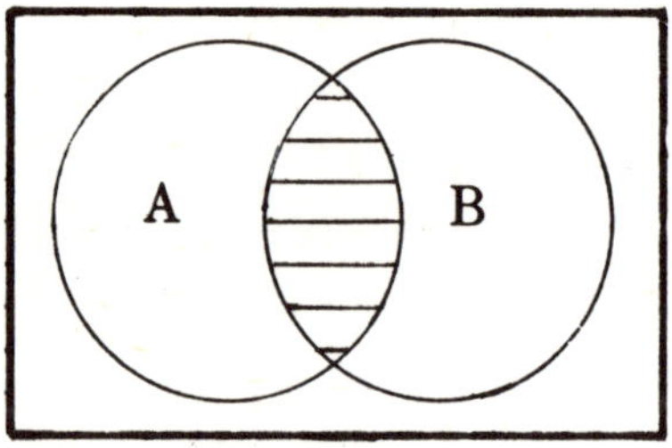

A ∩ B – the **intersection** of set A and B

(b)

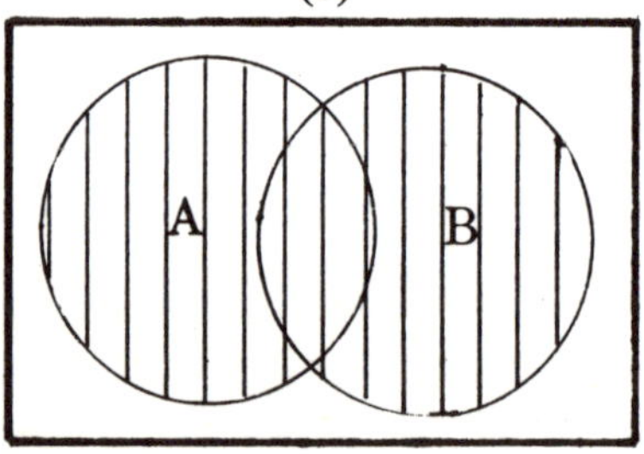

A ∪ B – the **union** of sets A and B

(c)

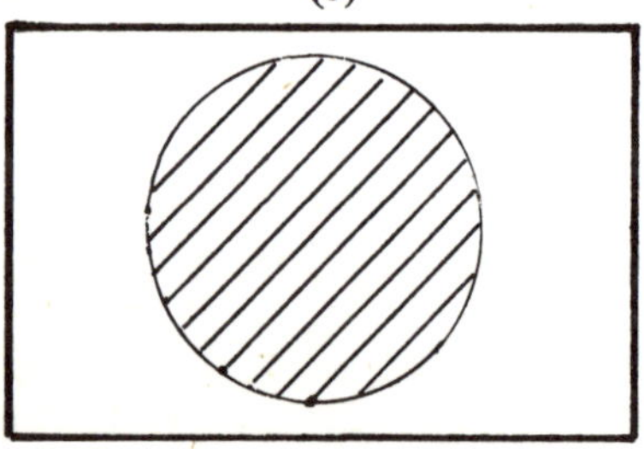

(d)

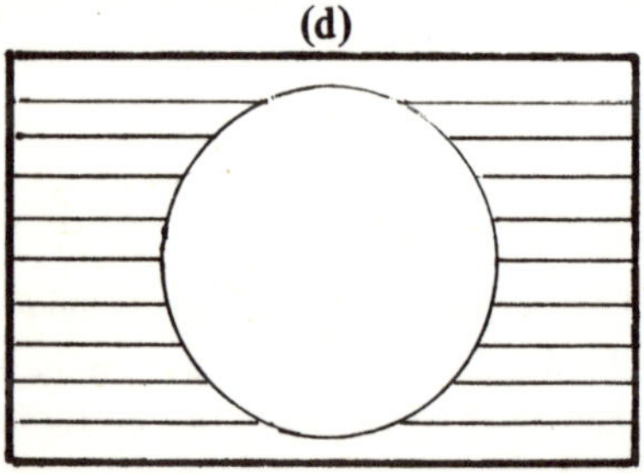

A – the **complement** of A

Addition of Two Binary Digits

Input		Output	
x	y	Sum	'Carry'
1	1	0	1
1	0·	1	0
0	1	1	0
0	0	0	0

This table defines the function that the machine must perform. The problem is to design circuits that will do this. Expressed algebraically using set theory or Boolean symbols:

$$\text{Sum} = (x \cap \bar{y}) \cup (\bar{x} \cap y)$$
$$\text{Carry} = x \cap y$$

(The bar over the letter indicates negation or complementation.) The circuitry to do the job is shown in Diagram D. A combination of gates to perform this operation is known as a 'half-adder'. It contains six separate gates.

Consider now what circuitry is required to add, not merely two digits, but two binary numbers. For purposes of illustration take two 3-digit numbers adding to a 4-digit number.

The circuit to add two digits can now be treated as a single unit; it is called a 'half-adder'. Symbolically we will represent it by the one letter H. Next, how are we to group these half-adders in order to execute the operation of adding binary numbers? In the example we are taking two 3-digit binary numbers which we will call x_3, x_2, x_1, and y_3, y_2, y_1. When the first two digits come in, representing units to be added, the 'sum' output by the half-adder will give the first digit (reading from right to left) of the result. The 'carry' will have to be combined with the sum of the next two digits. That is, the carry output of the half-adder which is handling the first two digits will have to be fed, together with the 'sum' output of the half-adder handling the second two digits, into another half-adder. (See Diagram E, numbered H.4 on the diagram.) The sum output of H.4 gives the second digit of the result, the carry from H.4 will become an input together with the carry from H.2 to an OR gate whose output will be one of the inputs to H.5 from which the third digit of the result will be output as sum.

So the process could be continued for any number of input digits to give any required number of output digits. These circuits are in fact imitating in binary the routine, the algorithm, that one learns at school

DIAGRAM D
Diagram of Circuit for "Half-Adder"

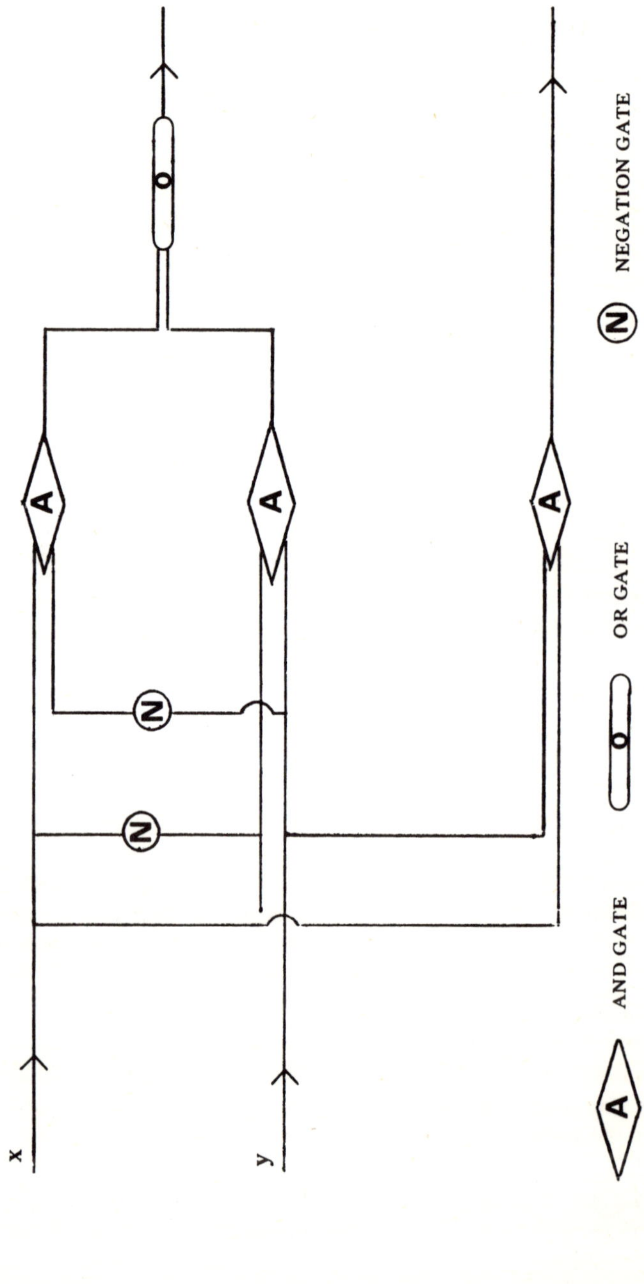

DIAGRAM E.

Diagram of Circuit for Adding Two Binary Numbers of Three Digits

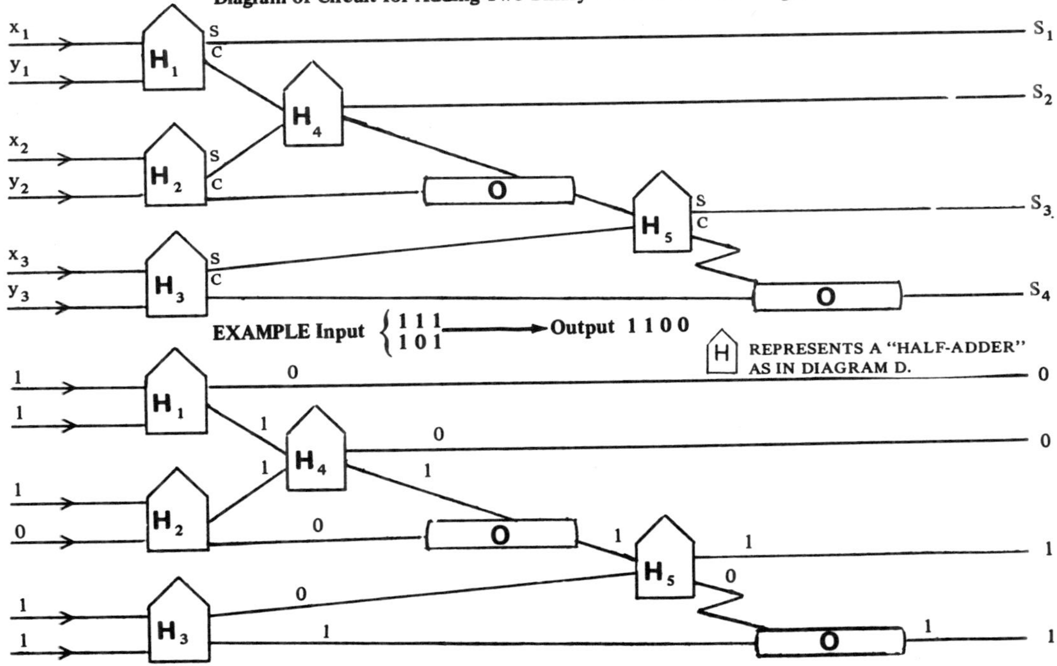

in the decimal language. We say, for example, 7 and 7 make 14 put down 4 and carry 1. We are expected to remember the amount carried, so as to combine it with the next addition sum, write one of the digits into the result and remember the next as the carry when we move on to the addition of the next two digits. Diagram E shows a circuitry for the addition of two 3-digit binary numbers. As a check choose any 3-digit binary numbers that come into your head and trace through to see what happens to them as they pass through the circuitry. An example is given at the bottom of Diagram E. Here 101 (5 in decimal) is added to 111 (7 in decimal) giving the result 1100 (12 in decimal). This circuit only adds numbers between 0 and 7.

The Elliott 803 machine normally handles numbers of 39 binary digits, that is, it is capable of adding, multiplying, etc., numbers between, in round figures, 0 and 5,000,000 million. (In fact, it scales numbers into rational fractions x in the interval $-1 \leqslant x < 1$, the smallest fractional step between two numbers being 1/549,755,813,888.) To do this it requires 13 times as many input channels. The 3-digit circuit requires five half-adders and two OR gates. Each half-adder has six logical gates; so addition of two 3-digit binary numbers uses 32 logical gates. To add numbers of the size that a computer needs to handle, e.g. 40 binary digits, would require, using the circuit sketched in Diagram E, over 400 logical gates.

MATHEMATICAL APPENDIX

NOTE 5

Mathematical Expression of the *Production Function* used in Economic Analysis

For the purposes of illustration, take, say, cultivation of land assuming three factors of production only, (1) the area of land, (2) capital goods employed represented by tractors and (3) labour. Suppose there are x acres of land, y tractors and z agricultural workers; then output (w) is a function of these three factors of production, i.e. $W = f(x, y, z)$. Suppose that one man working on one acre with one tractor gives an output of one ton of wheat and the production function is $W = xyz$. If the land in use were doubled whilst the number of tractors and men were kept the same, the output would be 2 tons and the additional output attributable to the factor land would be 1 ton. That is, bringing into use an additional acre, according to this formula gives an additional product of 1 ton of wheat. Mathematically the relationship between changes in factors and changes in output would be the partial derivatives –

$$\frac{\partial W}{\partial x} = yz, \qquad \frac{\partial W}{\partial y} = xz, \qquad \frac{\partial W}{\partial z} = xy.$$

($\frac{\partial W}{\partial x}$ is the partial derivative; it stands for rate of change and is called 'partial' because it gives the rate at which W changes when only x changes, on the assumption that all the other variables – in this case tractors and workers – are kept the same.) This means that if the amount of labour and the amount of capital is kept fixed then the increase in output as the amount of land is changed will be at the rate yz. Similarly if the land and capital are kept fixed the rate of increase in output resulting from the employment of additional labour will be xy. In general, if $x_1, x_2, \ldots . x_y$ are factors of production and $W(x_1, x_2, \ldots . x_y)$ gives output as a function of factors of production, $\frac{\partial W}{\partial x_i}$ expresses the productivity of factor x_i. This model is inappropriate for representation of typical production situations (despite its constant use by theorists) since continuous increase or decrease of factors of production is practically never feasible and does not correspond to the structural interdependence between specific means of production and specific skills in specific processes of production available under given historical circumstances.

MATHEMATICAL APPENDIX

NOTE 6

The Transportation Problem

To see what is involved in the problem consider it in its simplest possible form. Suppose there are two vessels at one port – P1 – and three vessels at another port – P2 – and three vessels are required at port Q1 and two vessels at port Q2. This problem may be set out in a very simple form, thus:–

Table IV.1. *Matrix for Movements of Vessels between Ports*

Ports	Q1	Q2	Total of rows (vessels)
P_1	x_{11}	x_{12}	2
P_2	x_{21}	x_{22}	3
Total of columns (vessels)	3	2	

In this table x_{11} represents the number of ships going from P1 to Q1, x_{12} the number of ships going from P1 to Q2, x_{21} number of ships going from P2 to Q1, x_{22} the number of ships going from P2 to Q2. (In general we may use x_{ij} to represent the number of ships going from origin i to destination j; similarly d_{ij} may be used to represent the distance from origin i to destination j, and these may be set out in tabular or matrix form as above.) The constraints of the situation are that the total number of ships sailing from port P1 must equal the number of ships in that port; that is if we total the first row of the table, $x_{11} + x_{12}$ must equal 2, similarly the number of ships sailing from port 2 can only be three, so $x_{21} + x_{22}$ must equal 3. On the other hand, wherever they come from, three ships are required at port Q1, so totalling this column, $x_{11} + x_{21}$ must equal 3 and similarly, as two ships are required at port Q2, $x_{12} + x_{22}$ must equal 2. For the very small matrix and the very small numbers of ships that we have taken there are three possible solutions as set out below:–

Alternative Vessel Movements

	(a) Q1	(a) Q2	(b) Q1	(b) Q2	(c) Q1	(c) Q2
P1	0	2	1	1	2	0
P2	3	0	2	1	1	2

Constraints

Row P1 must total 2
Row P2 must total 3
Column Q1 must total 3
Column Q2 must total 2

That is, no ships may go from P1 to Q1 with both the ships from P1 going to Q2. If this happens then all three ships at P2 must go to Q1 and no ships from P2 are required to go to Q2. If one ship from P1 goes to Q1 and one to Q2, then two must go from P2 to Q1 to make up its requirement of 3 and the other one from P2 will go to Q2. The third and last possibility is shown in the third matrix (c), that is both the ships from P1 go to Q1, no ships from P1 go to Q2, one ship from P2 goes to Q1 to make up its requirement of three and the other 2 go to meet the requirement of Q2 for two ships.

In order to choose between these three alternatives we need to know the cost of making the journey from one port to another. We will assume that cost varies directly with distance and consult a table of distances from port to port as in, for example:–

Distances Between Ports

	Q1	Q2
P1	200	500
P2	400	600

This says that the distance from P1 to Q1 is 200 miles, from P1 to Q2, 500 miles and so forth. The object of the exercise is to minimise the total sailing distance. Mathematically this may be expressed as follows – total sailing distance = $d_{11} x_{11} + d_{12} x_{12} + d_{21} x_{21} + d_{22} x_{22}$. In the very restricted example I have given there are three possibilities only. If we take the values for x_{ij} in the tables given and for d_{ij} from

Table IV.3, the results will be as follows:–

Possibility	(a)	0 x 200 + 2 x 500 + 3 x 400 + 0 x 600 = 2,200
”	(b)	1 x 200 + 1 x 500 + 2 x 400 + 1 x 600 = 2,100
”	(c)	2 x 200 + 0 x 500 + 1 x 400 + 2 x 600 = 2,000

It turns out that possibility (c) is the best since the total ship miles required is 2,000, whereas possibility (b) gives a total of 2,100 ship miles and possibility (a) requires 2,200 miles to be sailed. This extremely simplified example begins to get complicated as soon as we begin to consider all its aspects; from this one begins to see the complexities of the choices we need to make in real-life situations.

The problem may be generalised and expressed algebraically, without restricting ourselves to any particular number of ports or ships. For example, there are a_i ships in Port$_i$ and b_j ships are required in port Q_j. The number of ships sailing from P_i to Q_j is x_{ij}; the distance from P_i to Q_j is d_{ij} –

$$\sum_j x_{ij} = a_i \quad ; \quad \sum_i x_{ij} = b_j \quad ; \quad \sum_i a_i = \sum_j b_j$$

The object is to minimise the ‘objective’ function (in this case the distance sailed) – $\sum_i \sum_j d_{ij} x_{ij}$.

Note: The symbol $\sum_{i=1}^{N} x_{ij}$ means ‘Add the numbers’ x_{ij}, first putting i = 1 and going on until i = N; for example, if $x_{ij} = 2$, $x_{2j} = 3$, $x_{3j} = 4$, and N = 3, $\sum_{i=1} x_{ij} = x_{1j} + x_{2j} + x_{3j} = 2 + 3 + 4 = 9$. The rule is let the ‘counting digit’ – i here – shown below the symbol Σ run through the integral values, 1, 2, 3, etc., until it reaches the number shown above the Σ; if no starting or finishing numbers are shown, one should be able to assume them from the context here – $\sum_j x_{ij} = x_{i1} + x_{i2} + \ldots x_{iM}$, where M is the total number of Q ports requiring ships, and

$\sum_i x_{ij} = x_{1j} + x_{2j} + \ldots . x_{Nj}$ where N is the total number of P ports supplying ships. A double Σ Σ applies the same rule twice; for example

$$\sum_{i}^{2}\sum_{j}^{3}(i+j) = \sum_{i}^{2}\left[(i+1) + (i+2) + (i+3)\right] = [(1+1) + (1+2) + (1+3)$$

$$[(2+1) + (2+2) + (2+3)] = 21$$

MATHEMATICAL APPENDIX

NOTE 7

Linear Programming – A Simple Example

Linear programming is so called because the relationships between the variables are linear, that is they are of the form –

$$y = a_0 + a_1\,x_1 + a_2\,x_2 + \ldots\ldots\ldots\ldots a_n\,x_n$$

When relationship is only between two variables, say x and y, it can be represented graphically as a straight line, whose equation is $y = a\,x + b$, where a gives the slope of the line and b the intercept between the origin and the point where the line cuts the y axis.

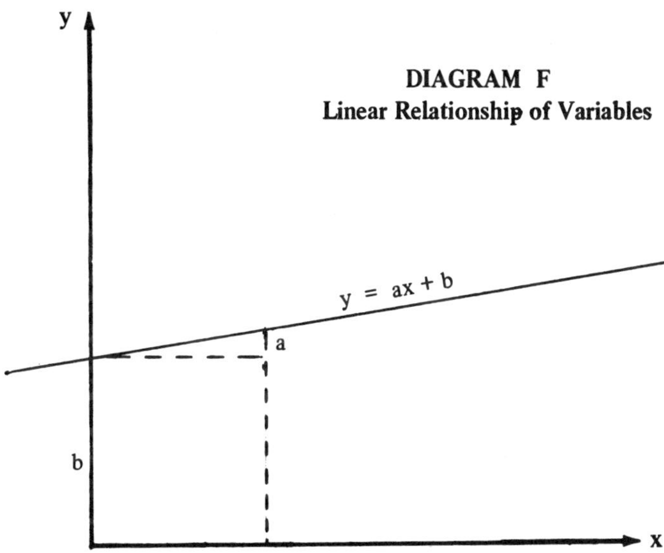

DIAGRAM F
Linear Relationship of Variables

Here, for example, the equation might be $y = \frac{1}{4}x + 9$, representing, say, the cost of a drilling machine which varied according to the number of spare drills (x) taken with it; e.g. cost with no spares £9 (b in Diagram F being 9), with 6 spares £10.50, with twelve spares £12 and so on.

A simple example will give some rough idea of the wider applications. Suppose a firm is making two products A and B. Product A requires two hours' machine time on one machine and one hour's machine time on a second machine, whereas product B requires one hour's machine time on the first machine and two hours' machine time on the second machine. Suppose that six hours' machine time is available on each machine and that the profit to be made on product A is £1 per unit and on product B £1.50 per unit. The problem is to find what combination of products will give the greatest profit. If a is the quantity of Product A produced and b is the quantity of Product B produced, then the constraints are $2a + b \leqslant 6$ and $a + 2b \leqslant 6$ and the function to be maximised $a + \frac{3}{2}b$. The meaning of these functions is as follows. The amount of time required on the first machine for each unit of product A, that is 2a, plus the amount of time required on the first machine for each unit of product B, that is b, must be less than or equal to ($\leqslant$) the time available, i.e. six hours. Similarly, the amount of time required for each product on the second machine must be less than the time available, and the purpose of the operation is to maximise the sum of the profit per unit of product A plus the profit per unit of product B. The situation may be expressed diagrammatically as in Diagram IV.B. The line L1 represents the con-

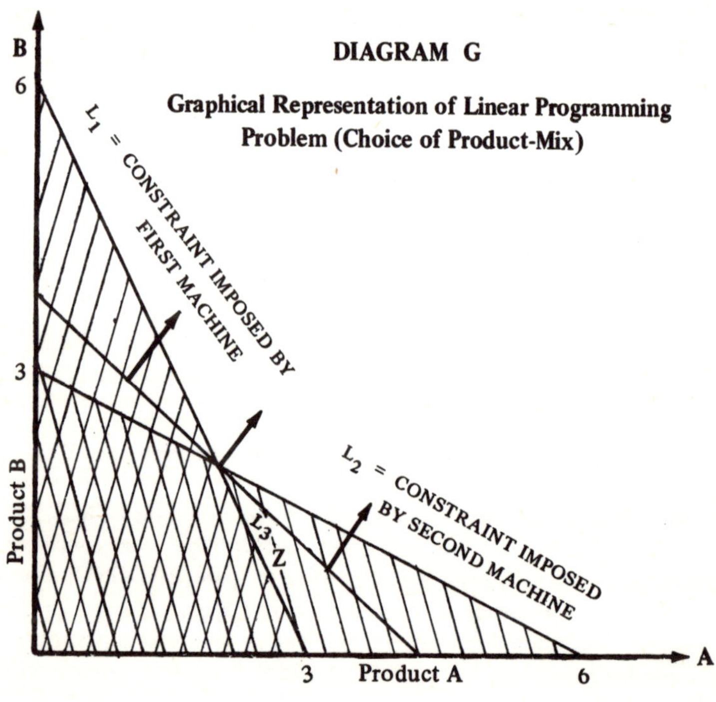

DIAGRAM G

Graphical Representation of Linear Programming Problem (Choice of Product-Mix)

straint imposed by the first machine, which may either be used to produce six units of product B or three units of product A or a mixture of products in proportions represented by this line. Similarly the line L2 represents the constraints imposed by the second machine. The objective function is represented by a whole series of lines parallel to the line L3. The farther this line can be pushed in the direction of the arrows the bigger will be the profit. The line shown is at the limit of possibilities, since if it is pushed further up it will exceed the constraints imposed by the machines. So the solution to this problem is to produce two units of product A and two units of product B giving a profit of £5. The point marked Z on the diagram represents a less profitable alternative. In this case 2½ units of A are produced and one unit of B. This would give only a profit of £4. The first machine would be fully utilised but the second machine would be used only for threequarters of the available time.

MATHEMATICAL APPENDIX

NOTE 7(a)

Linear Programming: Mathematical Generalisation

In generalised form the problem in linear programming is to solve a number of linear equations. Once problems have been formulated mathematically, the constraints are generally expressed in the form of inequalities, e.g. $ax + by \leqslant n$, but such inequalities can always be expressed as equalities with an added variable that may take a range of values. For example if a given constraint required that $x + y \leqslant 10$ and that x and y must not be negative, then the inequality $x + y \leqslant 10$ could be replaced by the equality $x + y + z = 10$ where z could take any value from 0 to 10; for example if x was 0 and y was 0, z could be equal to 10 and if x was 5 and y was 5, z would have to be equal to 0. Expressed in its most general terms, therefore, the problem of linear programming amounts to formulating a set of linear equations determining whether these equations have no solution, one solution (that is only one set of possible values for the unknowns) or a number of solutions. If there is no solution to the equations, there is no answer to the problem formulated. If there is one solution and one only, then there is one and only one answer and no question of choice between feasible courses of action arises. But if there are many feasible solutions the problem then arises of choosing the best solution.

This is the real problem of linear programming and to solve it an objective function must be formulated. This objective function represents some quantity that is to be maximised or minimised. (By what is known as the 'principle of duality' it is possible to translate any problem of maximisation to one of minimisation or vice-versa; and this is sometimes convenient in that the mathematics may be more easy to handle in one form than in the other). For firms within the market system the objective function normally can be expressed in terms of costs to be minimised or profits to be maximised. In wider social applications there may be difficulties in adequately formulating an acceptable objective function. So in mathematical terms the problem of linear programming is to solve the linear equations.

$$\sum_{i=1}^{n} a_{ij} x_i + x_{n+j} = c_j \quad \{\text{for } j = 1, \ldots\ldots m.\}$$

so as to maximise B in the following formula:–

$$\sum_{i=1}^{n} b_i x_i = B,$$

when $x_i \geqslant 0, x_{n+j} \geqslant 0$ for all i, j.

The mathematical formula given here is a generalisation from situations such as that of the machine utilisation examples considered above. The generalisation consists in applying the same general idea to other situations in which we might have any number of variables and different relations between them. Taking n = 3 and m = 2 the formula above written out in full would be –

$$a_{11}x_1 + a_{21}x_2 + a_{31}x_3 + x_4 = c_1$$
$$a_{12}x_1 + a_{22}x_2 + a_{32}x_3 + x_5 = c_2$$
$$b_1 x_1 + b_2 x_2 + b_3 x_3 = B$$

Here x_4, x_5, are 'slack variables' – which may take a range of values to turn 'inequalities' such as $a_{11} x_1 + a_{21}x_2 + a_{31}x_3 \leqslant c$, into the 'equality' shown above. Typically if there are, say, two variables and two equations, there will be only one solution or none at all. But if there are more variables than equations there will, if there are any solutions, be a number of possible solutions and the aim of the programming exercise is to find that which will be most favourable, the solution, that is, that maximises or minimises the 'objective function' B.

MATHEMATICAL APPENDIX – NOTE 8

A Very Simple Example of Network Analysis.

Diagram H represents the operation of servicing a machine. The average time for each of the operations is as shown by the numbers in the diagram. In this case, if the numbers represent days, the minimum time for the whole job would be 9 days and the path determining the time taken for the work as a whole – known as the 'critical path' – is A, B, C, F, I, J. It is evident from this diagram that the thing that takes the time is repair of foundations. Suppose this could be cut from five days to two days, then the critical path would be either A-B-C-D-G-I-J or A-B-E-H-I-J and the time for the job as a whole would then become seven days. Such a diagram also shows how much slack time there is for the operations not on the critical path.

DIAGRAM H

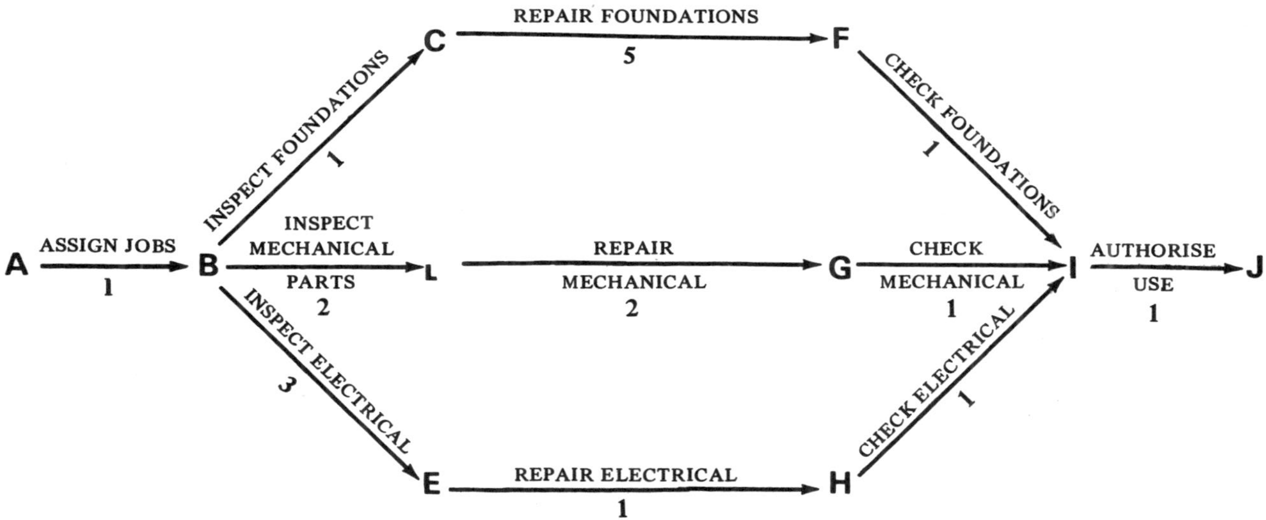

Servicing a Machine – Network Diagram to Show the Sequence of Operations

Numbers represent days required for each operation

MATHEMATICAL APPENDIX – NOTE 9
Input Output Analysis . The Leontief Model

To simplify the model, imports and exports are excluded. If X_i is the total product of industry i, part of this product will serve (a) as final consumption and part (b) as means of production for other industries, e.g. coal is used (a) for domestic heating and also (b) as a means of production in the steel industry heating furnaces, etc., in the gas industry making gas etc.

So if b_i represents output from industry i entering into final consumption (e.g. if i is the coal industry, b_i is domestic coal) and x_{ij} represents output from industry i supplied to industry j (e.g. if j is the steel industry, x_{ij} is coal for heating furnaces), *then* $X_i = b_i + x_{i1} + x_{i2} + x_{i3} +$ etc. This equation simply describes the output of an industry in terms of the destination of its products.

Next, in the short-run one may assume that if steel production, for example, increases by, say 30%, then requirements for coal will also increase by 30%. That is, there is a technical relationship that enables one to express one industry's requirements from another as a fraction of its own output. For example, if purchases of coal for steel production equalled one-tenth of the total steel output, x_{ij} would be $\frac{1}{10}X_j$. In this way one may build up a matrix of technical co-efficients (numbers a_{ij} such that $0 \leqslant a_{ij} \leqslant 1$) expressing the technical dependence of each industry on inputs received from other industries, e.g.

	Receiving Industries	X_1	X_2	X_3	etc.	
Supplying Industries X_1		a_{11}	a_{12}	a_{13}	etc.	
X_2		a_{21}	a_{22}	a_{23}	etc.	etc
X_3		a_{31}	a_{32}	a_{33}	etc.	
Etc.		etc.	etc.	etc.	etc.	

Using technical coefficients the following set of equations can be built from equations expressing the distribution of output (such as the equation above).

$$X_1 = b_1 + a_{11} x_1 + a_{12} x_2 + \ldots\ldots\ldots\ldots + a_{1n} x_n$$
$$X_2 = b_1 + a_{21} x_1 + a_{22} x_2 + \ldots\ldots\ldots\ldots + a_{2n} x_n$$
$$\vdots$$
$$X_n = b_n + a_{n1} x_1 + a_{2n} x_2 + \ldots\ldots\ldots\ldots \quad a_{nn} x_n$$

This may be more briefly expressed in matrix form as follows–

$$X = B + AX$$

Where

$$X = \begin{bmatrix} X_1 \\ X_2 \\ \cdot \\ \cdot \\ \cdot \\ X_n \end{bmatrix}$$ represents total output

$$B = \begin{bmatrix} b_1 \\ b_1 \\ \cdot \\ \cdot \\ \cdot \\ b_n \end{bmatrix}$$ represents total (non-productive) consumption

and A is the n X n matrix of technical coefficients referred to above. Thus the INPUT/OUTPUT model expresses relationships between total output (X), output used in the production process (AX) and final consumption (B). The 'parameter' determining the structure of this model is the matrix A, which specifies the technical coefficients (also described as input/output coefficients).

INDEX